ON THE STUMP

SEAN SCALMER

ON THE STUMP

*Campaign Oratory and Democracy
in the United States, Britain, and Australia*

TEMPLE UNIVERSITY PRESS
Philadelphia • Rome • Tokyo

TEMPLE UNIVERSITY PRESS
Philadelphia, Pennsylvania 19122
www.temple.edu/tempress

Copyright © 2017 by Temple University—Of The Commonwealth System
of Higher Education
All rights reserved
Published 2017

Library of Congress Cataloging-in-Publication Data

Names: Scalmer, Sean, author.
Title: On the stump : campaign oratory and democracy in
the United States, Britain, and Australia / Sean Scalmer.
Description: Philadelphia : Temple University Press, [2017] | Includes
bibliographical references and index.
Identifiers: LCCN 2017010533 | ISBN 9781439915035 (cloth) |
ISBN 9781439915042 (paper) | ISBN 9781439915059 (e-book) Subjects: LCSH:
Political campaigns—United States. | Political
campaigns—Great Britain. | Political campaigns—Australia. | Campaign
speeches—United States. | Campaign speeches—Great Britain. | Campaign
speeches—Australia. | Democracy—Cross-cultural studies. | Political
culture—Cross-cultural studies.
Classification: LCC JF1001 .S248 2017 | DDC 324.7—dc23
LC record available at https://lccn.loc.gov/2017010533

To my parents, Kevin and Joan

CONTENTS

PREFACE

To "stump" is to "go about making political speeches" in support of "candidate" or "cause," to "campaign or canvass," to "speak informally" as part of a political campaign. The verb is dated from 1838 in one notable dictionary, and the earlier noun, "stump speech," from 1820. But the precise origins of the practice remain somewhat unclear. *The Oxford English Dictionary* includes a use of "stump oratory" from 1811 and records John Quincy Adams's distaste for the delivery of "party insinuation" from "the top of a stump" in 1808. Other texts reference speech making from the base of a tree nearly one hundred years before.[1]

At first strongly associated with the frontier states of the American Republic—especially Kentucky and Tennessee—the practice was eventually accepted across the continent. By the middle years of the nineteenth century, stump speaking was widely considered to be "peculiarly" or "essentially" a kind of "American institution." The *Charleston Patriot* dubbed it a "power in the Republic," to rank alongside Pulpit, Bar, and Senate. Popular lecturers appraised the stump as "one of the institutions of the land."[2]

But the stump did not remain "peculiarly" American. As a symbol of rough and ambitious frontier eloquence, often exaggerated versions of "stump oratory" crossed the Atlantic in newspapers and comic fiction. Agitators and minstrel players—apparent embodiments of the American way—made the journey, too. In the rude and demotic vigor of these performances, democracy's opponents in Britain perceived the outlines of a bustling, tempestuous, and turbulent future. Scottish essayist Thomas Carlyle even composed a pamphlet dedicated to *The Stump Orator*, 1850, which identified this species of "public haranguer" with "universal suffrage," "tavern dinners" and "Kentucky stumps," mourning its "ugly" and "perilous" influence on a society threatened with "crisis" and "annihilation."[3]

From the 1850s, "the stump" was increasingly linked with the agitators of the British world—what had earlier been called "waggon-oratory" or demagoguery. There, however, the practice of "stumping" for elective office developed more slowly than in the United States. Hustings speeches by candidates were generalized into more dispersed oratory tours only from the 1870s; given the radical associations of "the stump," this was at first considered a highly controversial course. The stumping candidate was thought to threaten the customs of British politics and the culture of aristocratic service, redolent of the beer and peanuts of Tammany Hall or the bloody excesses of Jacobin France. Only at the very end of the nineteenth century did British candidates of all kinds unashamedly take to the stump. Even today, Samuel Johnson's dictionary records that this "now common" word is still felt to be "somewhat undignified" to the British ear.[4]

But whatever the linguistic traces of earlier controversies, it is the extent and completeness of change that impresses most fully: the space of one hundred years witnessed a profound alteration in the practice and meaning of democratic speech. In the first decades of the nineteenth century, "stump speaking" was identified on the fringes of the American frontier; by the beginning of the twentieth century, it was applied and mostly accepted across the North American continent and the British world, too. Like its more famous cousins—the mass political party and the social movement—the "stump oration" was eventually installed as a defining feature of Anglo-American political life.

The rise of stump speaking forms a fascinating and important episode in the history of nineteenth-century politics. In the diffusion of campaign oratory, the battle for elective office was reshaped: more aggressive and direct, less restrained and opaque. In repeated arguments over the meaning and significance of "stump oratory," the culture of public life became the object of recurrent contemplation: the dangers of demagoguery, the possibilities of contentious debate. As Americans and Britons took to the stump, so the contours of politics took on a more familiar, recognizably modern form.

And yet, despite the apparent importance of "the stump," no previous historian has sought to tell the story of its rise. This book is the first to systematically examine the career of "stump oratory." It aims to trace its origins, diffusion, remaking, and acceptance; to excavate its radical meaning; to establish its historical significance. The book is an act of rediscovery. It is also a historical argument for the importance of "the stump."

A history of this kind might have been written in many ways. To fully capture the transformations and the significance of stump speaking, I have adopted a particular approach to the past: a performative, culturalist, transnational, and biographical perspective. This combination of methods may be unfamiliar to some readers, but it underpins my argument for the import of "stumping," and it therefore merits a brief explanation and a defense.

A "performative" approach to stump oratory rests on the notion that political behavior works in ways akin to drama and that the concepts used to analyze drama might also be applied to the political domain. The method was notably ventured in the scholarship of sociologist Erving Goffman and anthropologist Victor Turner some five decades ago. It has been extended and refined in recent studies of gender, terrorism, liberalism, and nonviolence. Indeed, a large number of historians have begun to adopt the dramaturgical method, and one writer has even identified a "performative turn" within the discipline. Historians of nineteenth-century politics number among those who have experimented with the approach, including in recent studies of the hustings.[5]

Understanding "stump oratory" from this perspective, the historian is concerned not simply with what politicians say but also with the ways in which they say it: the modulation of voice, the animation of gestures, the choice of language, the exchanges with auditors and with rivals. Attending to these issues, the performance of a public speech can be understood as a dramatic episode: the assertion of claims and identities, the interaction of players, the conventional resolution in dominance or concord, the less frequent refusal to accept defeat. Studying the stump oration in these terms, the delivery of campaign speeches offers a privileged vantage for scrutinizing the relationships between electors and candidates, the subaltern and the elite. Challenges to power sometimes appear more starkly. In this way, the contribution of stump oratory to democratic change can be more fully understood.

A culturalist approach to the topic directs attention to the ways in which stump oratory became the object of representation: poetry, paintings, satirical fiction, minstrelsy. It also invites the historian to examine the changing ways in which stump oratory was defined or imagined and the sometimes impassioned commentary that it provoked.

Pursuing a cultural history, I give close attention to the meanings ascribed to public action, and I do not seek to fix or define the essential boundaries of stump oratory in advance. Across this volume, I attempt to rediscover the places where the performance of stump oratory was first discerned, to track its migration, to identify moments of metamorphosis, and to trace the different ways in which the action of stumping was apprehended and understood. This means that the book is not simply a study of electioneering speech. It is also an examination of the meanings attributed to the stump and of the cultural conflicts that they could produce.

It is also a history that spans regions, nations, and transnational exchanges. "Stump oratory" was named on the American frontier and was at first very strongly associated with the states of the Republic's Southwest. Its status as a frontier practice shaped the reception and meaning of the performance; it took several decades before stump speaking was accepted in America's Northeast. Once it had been confirmed as a national habit, however, the "American" identity of "the stump" in turn influenced political developments in other parts of the world. The passage of stories and orators outward from the United States helped establish the outlines of stump speaking within the British Empire; the vicissitudes of the Republic conveyed the method's possibilities as well as its dangers. As a result, when British subjects took to the stump, this move was quite explicitly understood as the adoption of "American" methods. The rise of campaign oratory was also an example of the Americanization of political techniques.

The apparent strangeness and radicalism of the performance outside the United States—and its strongly national association—reflected divergent political contexts. Britain was a constitutional monarchy, in which the power of the sovereign had been constrained by the rise of Parliament. In a bicameral system, governments rested on their capacity to command a majority on the floor of the lower house. Parliament rather than the people lay at the center of politics, and the right to elect representatives remained highly restricted. Voting was at first the sole preserve of a landed elite, and the Reform Act of 1832 shared the privilege of the suffrage with only the most prosperous members of a rising middle class. Even after a subsequent Reform Act in 1867, Britain was far from a mass democracy: only one-third of adult males were eligible to vote, and no woman possessed that right.

Australia was colonized by Great Britain from 1788 and at first administered by officials and appointments made from London. However, the major colonies in the southeast of the continent were granted "responsible government" from the 1850s, and local parliaments on the British model henceforth made laws on principal matters. The new colonial constitutions or reforms soon afterward extended greater rights of participation: property qualifications were abolished for voting and representation, and Australia pioneered the secret ballot. But although some British observers thought the people of the antipodes were rather more "American" than "English," political structures and assumptions remained highly attuned to British traditions. Those who flirted with apparently "American" principles or methods risked opprobrium.

The United States was a republic. Forged in a revolution that declared the self-evident truth of human equality, its political order gave greater scope for self-rule. Elections in the United States were frequent for local, state, and national offices. There was no king, but rather a president. Race and gender were confirmed as principles of exclusion, but over the first half of the nineteenth century, nearly all white men were free to participate. Mass parties commanded popular affection and organized the struggle for power. For observers as much as citizens, "nation" and "democracy" seemed increasingly intertwined.

As a transnational investigation, this book examines the export of stump speaking across these three very different contexts. Refusing the once customary "national" framework for political history, and aiming to enhance understanding of those relationships and movements that crossed national boundaries, I contemplate the circulation of a political performance from the United States to the British world. As its most distinguished practitioners have emphasized, such a transnational approach does not necessarily imply a neglect of the "nation," and neither does it reject the possibility of comparisons between nations. Rather, it attempts to "denaturalize" the nation, foregrounding the ways in which its boundaries, institutions, and traditions have been shaped by external as well as internal forces.[6] Across this volume, I blend attention to "transnational" and "national," reconstructing a previously undocumented traffic between nations, while also exploring how local circumstances could influence how, when, and why stump oratory might be adopted. In the book's Conclusion, I systematically exploit the possibilities of such comparisons: examining the United States, Britain, and Australia alongside one another so as to better understand the historical processes that drove oratorical and political change.

Finally, this book is also organized around the careers of a handful of important individuals. Such a narrative arrangement does not, of course, imply that the history of stump speaking can be reduced to a procession of great orators or that the transformative power of stumping can be understood solely as the product of personal talent or will. As we shall see, an apparent capacity for speech making was only rarely a mark of individual genius and was more often a collective product: schooled in comradely tutelage and partisan contest, promoted by institutions and press agents, acclaimed by supporters sometimes beyond its worth.

Nonetheless, if stump oratory was never a purely individual performance, then it is also true that the form and meaning of the stump speech pivoted around the career of a relatively small number of notable orators: Davy Crockett, Henry Clay, Charles Gavan Duffy, Graham Berry, and William Gladstone, among some other, lesser, lights. In remarkable appearances, these and other practitioners became widely known; in the cultivation of distinctive styles, they embodied new possibilities of democratic eloquence; in the achievement of political celebrity, they became models, for good or ill, of what the stump speech might be. To consider these orators in some detail is not necessarily to celebrate a canon of great men but rather to explore how oratorical reputation and example helped shape subsequent practice.[7] It is in a careful study of how major stumping careers were made, sustained, remembered, and exploited that we might best recapture the complex rhythms of political change.

Dramaturgical, culturalist, transnational, and biographical, the book departs from the procedures and frameworks of much earlier political history. *On the Stump* follows a temporality and historical dynamic that will be unfamiliar to many students of nineteenth-century politics. Readers should be warned of these departures from convention in the pages to come.

First, the book differs in temporality. Traditional political history was organized around the nation, considering the reigns of kings, prime ministers, and presidents; challengers have suggested an alternative periodization, structured around national "party systems"—moments of sustained contest between Federalist and Republican, Democrat and Whig, Liberal and Tory, and so on. Seeking to track the history of stump oratory, I have organized this study according to quite different principles. The narrative divides into three separate parts.

Initially, I consider the beginnings of the practice, its close association with the American frontier, and its gradual rise to prominence through the thrilling and controversial careers of Colonel Davy Crockett and Senator Henry Clay. Second, I trace the diffusion and transformation of stump oratory within the United States, a process advanced by its use in party struggles that reached a new intensity from the fifth decade of the nineteenth century. Finally, I narrate how developments in the United States shaped the British world, influencing British understandings of both radical and partisan speech, inspiring agitational performance, and framing the growth of a more vigorous and open practice of electioneering. The volume closes by establishing the ways in which stump oratory was eventually accepted across the Anglo-American world and by more systematically considering its influence on the character of modern politics.

The book's concern with political performance also offers a comparatively novel approach to the examination of political change. Earlier studies of performance have emphasized the relatively fluid and relational character of social identities, challenging the more familiar understanding of such social categories as gender and race as rigid or fixed. They have further confirmed that performances change, for the apparent repetition of an action invariably implies some degree of reinterpretation, reinvention, and instability. If behaviors and events are "performances," then this means that they are ineluctably re-presented or remade. This, in turn, is thought to open up the possibility that they might be deliberately reoriented and transformed.[8]

These insights also apply to the political domain. In the performance of the stump speech, a distinctive understanding of the political order was enacted. In the diffusion and refashioning of the stump speech, new political identities were asserted, and new claims were made. The history of the stump is therefore the source of distinctive insights into the unfolding of politics in the nineteenth century. Through the close examination of a political perfor-mance, the book also offers a novel perspective on the process of democratic change.

Although this historical study has no direct precedents, I am nonethe-less able to draw upon generations of important scholarship. There is a rich body of research on the nature of nineteenth-century elections in the United States and Britain, and the best of this work often acknowledges the role of the stump speech. We have many excellent histories of such subjects as the presidential campaigns, the political parties, the suffrage, the act of voting, election rituals, electoral fraud, the hustings, and the platform.[9] Much of this work informs my own study of the stump speech, but no previous scholar has granted this performance his or her primary attention. None has traced the stump speech beyond the electoral contest, considering its impact on cultural debates. For the student of modern electoral politics, stump oratory features most often as a subordinate aspect of some other history.

Likewise, fragments of this story have been told before in fine studies of the development of oratory in modern Britain and America. Important work in this field has explored a range of overlapping topics: the connections between revolution and public speech, the rise of radical oratory, conflicts over the meaning and form of language, the emergence of a "democratic elo-quence," the connections between oratory and the culture of public life. But electoral persuasion (described by one scholar as "notorious" for its "literary in-significance") has understandably received only limited attention in works of these kinds; canonical texts, literary compositions, and celebrated rhetoricians have occupied a more central place.[10] In consequence, the rhetorical forms of the stumper have not yet been closely examined; no extant study has sought to systematically interrogate the complex history of the rhetoric of the stump.

Finally, several earlier scholars have previously examined the influence of the United States on British political discussion and practice. The tradition reaches back at least to the 1950s, and it has recently been energized in stud-ies of the revolutionary years, the early Republic, and of even broader spans. Little of this work closely examines the period between the Revolution and the Civil War, however, and none of it attempts to examine the experience of the Australian colonies alongside the "Mother country."[11]

Modern democracy has been shaped by many forces, and stump oratory is only one aspect of its complicated history. I do not wish to deny the import of other factors or to proclaim a new orthodoxy regarding the politics of the past. Rather, I aim merely to recover the history of the stump speech and to consider its usually overlooked role in the forging of political change. By recapturing the historical significance of the stump, this book aspires to better understand the unfolding of the great democratic adventure. I hope, thereby, to nurture and to extend it.

ON THE STUMP

INTRODUCTION

GEORGE CALEB BINGHAM AND
THE PROBLEM OF DISCOVERY

Somewhere on the American frontier, a large figure, well clad in brown trousers and vest, white shirt and black bowtie, great long cream coat, stands on a stump, hatless, speaking to a small group. He is a man of some years but still rude vigor. In the act of making a point, he leans forward from the waist: his left palm is open, beseeching, and the forefinger of his right hand lays across it, pressing downward in emphasis. This is not a back-woods demagogue: the gestures are restrained and relatively graceful; the eyes do not blaze with fury but possess rather a still energy and concentration; the clothes and bearing suggest wealth and some confidence but balk just before outright showiness.

Neither is the stump simply the base of a fallen tree, for it has been wrought into a more elaborate structure. Two branches provide supporting struts on left and right sides, and a thick plank completes a makeshift lectern, just below the hips. The speaker's papers and red handkerchief rest on one side of this flat board; a discarded top hat, brown, is on the other. Behind the rostrum sit two men. One is corpulent, big-bellied, gruff: the yellow waistcoat and green jacket barely contain an ample girth. His legs are spread apart, and a thin walking stick rises from his left hand almost half way up his gut. The prominence he is accorded implies formal duties: perhaps this is the chairman of the meeting? The second figure is animated by a thin concentration: his crossed right leg providing the balance for a notebook and pencil, the gaze downward, the brows knit. This is probably the opposing speaker, and his scribblings will form the basis of a reply.

George Caleb Bingham's *Stump Speaking* (1853–1854) is among the first and most celebrated images of American electioneering. The painting's title signals the intention to represent an activity and a scene rather than an individual portrait, and Bingham's rich depiction of the listeners is one of the great pleasures of the canvas. Collectively, at least fifty men have gathered at the stump. Some are clearly workers of the land: like Pieter Bruegel the Elder's *Harvesters*, they are fleshy, animal, red-cheeked, and open-shirted. Their hats are small and sometimes battered. Most stand surely, legs apart, coatless, attentive; some sit, resting heavy heads on strong hands. Others turn to their neighbors, anxious to contest a point in a whispered aside. There are also knitted thumbs, cradled chins, appreciative or perhaps glazed smiles, and bored and sleepy listeners, lost beneath the shadows of their tilted hats. All the men have pale skin. There is not one woman to be seen.

Although the stump is encircled by the large crowd so described, a series of particular figures immediately attract the eye. Sunlight illuminates only part of the assembly, running from the height of the speaker upon the rostrum on the left of the canvas to a gentleman in almost identical dress, gazing back from the far-right side. The two seem to be facing one another. The mirroring is not complete, and the divergences imply a possible tension. While the orator stands tall and bare-headed, his counterpart is seated, crowned with a substantial top hat. He sits, straight-backed, left hand resting on his hip, right hand clutching at a thin branch or walking stick. There is an implication of skepticism as well as influence. Behind him, two men pass comment on events.

In the right center of the painting stands a figure of more complete opposition to the man upon the stump. The apparent antagonist is dressed in dark fabric, from top to toe, and the clothing is shabby and excessive. This auditor stands, whereas most others sit; his face is partly obscured. Could he be about to intervene? The stump speaker seems to look beyond him, yet smaller figures draw attention to the possibility of tension: two dogs face off near his right leg—like the stump orator and the dark interloper, their coloring and postures serve as opposites—the black hound presenting his back to the viewer, the apparent antagonist marked by a white snout and jowls. Farther to the left, the same arrangement is mirrored in the interaction of two boys: one extends his hands in request or demand; the other's strained expression and folded arms suggest resistance or possibly alarm.

Stump Speaking forms the middle part of a triptych of paintings that represent the beginnings of mass democracy in the United States. Bingham was a child of Missouri, a mostly self-taught artist, and a local Whig politician of some note. He imagined *The County Election* (1851–1852) in the years immediately preceding his pictorial study of the stump, and he followed these

George Caleb Bingham, *Stump Speaking* (1853–1854),
oil on canvas, 42.5 x 58 inches. (Courtesy of Saint Louis Art Museum.
Gift of Bank of America 43:2001. Photography by Jean-Paul Torno.)

with *The Verdict of the People* (1854–1855). Together, the paintings constitute
an "Election Series"—a treasure trove for the historian anxious to document
the democracy of the past. What, precisely, do the paintings suggest?

First, Bingham depicts "stump oratory" as central to the life of the Republic. Across the three paintings, the artist narrates the very happening of
American democracy. This includes a study of the act of voting and another
of the announcement of results. But alongside these official moments of political decision, he also devotes a full canvas to the less recognized activity of
public persuasion. Through Bingham's painting, stump speaking is formally
registered as a significant moment in the process of self-rule.

Bingham's work has often been compared with Englishman William
Hogarth's four paintings that illustrate the election of a candidate for the
seat of Oxfordshire, almost exactly a century earlier. Like his American successor, Hogarth viewed *The Humours of an Election* (1755) as encompassing
the act of campaigning, the moment of voting, and the joys of celebrating.
He identifies a quite different series of political performances, however. Of
the two canvases devoted to electioneering, *An Election Entertainment* depicts
the first moment of the campaign, replete with well-stocked tables, overflow-
ing goblets, and raucous conviviality. *An Election: Canvassing for Votes*, the

William Hogarth, *An Election: Canvassing for Votes* (1754–1755).
(Courtesy of Sir John Soane's Museum.)

second, pictures the act of electoral persuasion as nothing more than the offering of bribes and the whispering of entreaties. The tone is darkly satirical. Of oratory, and orators, there is nothing at all.

Placed in this pictorial context, Bingham's representation of *Stump Speaking* emerges as a strong statement of the distinctiveness of American politics. On the Missouri frontier, the stump speech has supplanted more shadowy and malign influences: it now occupies a primary position in the acts of election and representation. The offering of inducements has given way to the trading of arguments; if democracy in America is something new and important, then stump speaking is a defining element of that new and better way.

Giving voice to Bingham's paintings, I argue in this book that stump speaking was a central presence in the life of American democracy. But I reject Bingham's mythological treatment of stumping as an always noble practice, unconnected with the venal or malign. The "stump orator," as we shall see, was more often presented as an ambitious, thrusting, and vulgar presence. Bingham's canvas is a misleading portrait of the practice and an unreliable indicator of its reputation.

Perhaps just as controversially, Bingham also depicts "stump oratory" as an activity of the frontier. From the left side of the picture looms a clump of great, green trees, their many branches blocking out much of the blue sky. The ground is littered with sticks and stones, and the mud is baked hard. We might be on the very edge of wildness. But as the eyes move right, there are definite signs of human progress: a barn, standing two full stories; a group of men on a horse-drawn carriage; in the far distance, larger buildings and a few riders making their way abroad.

The artist's imagination of stumping as a frontier practice may elicit dissent from some readers. Certainly, the scramble for office was evident across the Republic: upstarts challenged their social betters in New York as much as Tennessee. As we shall see, however, the earliest news reports unequivocally identified stump speaking with the frontier, what were typically labeled the "western states" or the "southern and western states." Stump oratory was at first thought to be a narrowly "south-western" mode of "conducting a political campaign."

The geographical referent is imprecise, although it can perhaps be specified. Historians of the Early Republic have previously noted the import of "spouting" in Virginia and of "stump oratory" in Maryland. Kentucky was more commonly celebrated for its oratory in this period, however, and, along with its neighbor, Tennessee, was at first most often identified as the home of the stump speech. Davy Crockett and Henry Clay—national representatives of this region in Congress—were the first major figures to symbolize the practice of stumping to the nation as a whole.[1]

While it would be inaccurate to claim that only frontier elections encompassed persuasive speech, it would be equally misleading to overlook the repeated and insistent association of "stump" with "frontier." Bingham's canvas forms but one part of a widespread and powerful cultural pattern. It is an association that demands scrutiny: if the meaning and the character of the stump speech are to be fully registered, it is necessary to pursue Bingham's insight and to more deeply examine its relationship to life on the frontier.

As generations of American historians have disclosed, the frontier was not a single place but a point of distinction: the space where land could be appropriated by white men and women from America's first inhabitants. "Free land," it was called, an expression that compressed a thrusting unconcern for prior occupants, an opportunity for the most hardy and determined, and a comparative absence of social and political restraint. The acquisitive impulse invested the frontier with a dynamic quality; the continuous recession of free land drove a movement westward. Likewise, the process of settlement was itself punctuated by the rhythms of change: the first European hunters gave way to what would be called more "civilized," "plain," and "frugal" farmers; men of capital and enterprise followed in their path.[2]

Doubtless, the experience of frontier life encouraged activities and values that would find expression in the scene that Bingham so artfully records. Migrants to the Southwest were ambitious for personal advantage, and their experience as hunters and farmers would have confirmed the priority of individual effort and reward. For white men, hereditary station was manifestly unimportant. Personal networks of authority were stretched and then snapped by great travels westward; governments and their agents had less opportunity to enforce their will. In this kind of environment, the social capital of the gentleman depreciated rapidly, and older practices of deference and preferment were replaced by new customs of "coarse familiarity." It was a cultural world conducive to new forms of political authority and appeal.[3]

The school textbooks of innumerable Americans have imparted something of the flavor of this hard life. The physical demands of settling the land were great, with practical capacities much more useful than the niceties of abstract learning. None of the frontier states provided adequate schooling, and the curse of illiteracy continued to haunt much of the United States for the bulk of the nineteenth century. Moreover, a sparse population of readers was not well served by a local press, and publications from elsewhere in the Republic took many weeks to reach the hands of the pioneer. Political exchanges were often especially vigorous around occasions of community assembly: militia musters, court days, markets. In consequence, the power of the voice retained a central place in the passages of public life.

Of talk, there was plenty. Untutored, relatively unconstrained, grappling with a sometimes hostile new world, the people of the Southwest traded stories, insults, and even new words. Writing in the middle 1820s, one western correspondent suggested that the "peculiar modes of life" of the frontier had also produced a distinctive form of language: "singular," "copious" and "amusing" new phrases, along with "strange curses" and repeated profanity. It was a frequently echoed claim. Later on, more critical spirits would distinguish western speech in other ways: an apparently "wordy" and "theatrical" approach to public address, along with a "directness," "enthusiasm," and "playfulness." Subsequently, historians would identify a cluster of additional qualities: a capacity for "free invention" and "mock pompous words," a facility for "storytelling," and a "marked tendency" toward "vulgarity of style." Deprived often of the privileges of the pen, western creativity was most commonly expressed in the art of speech. Here might be found one source of the strange orations that would one day be given from the heights of a stump.[4]

Improvisations in the king's English were but one part of a broader challenge evident on the fringes of the new Republic. Transformations in social life and behavior were also reflected in the boundaries of the polity. Within the original thirteen states, the years of revolution had already expanded the franchise to include between six in ten and nine in ten white males, depending upon one's precise location. In the years that followed, barriers to participation were further dismantled. From the 1790s, the new state of Kentucky dispensed with the property qualification entirely, and a powerful group of Ohio Valley states soon followed this example. This new democratic frontier placed a competitive pressure on the more established and less inclusive states; the inhabitants of the western counties of the older polities led the charge for constitutional revision. Reform followed in the first few decades of the nineteenth century, extending the vote to nearly all white men, although also depriving free black men and women of property of these same privileges.[5]

Importantly, this was a process of oppression as much as emancipation. America's first professional court historian, Frederick Jackson Turner, famously presented the life of the frontier as the unambiguous source of American democracy: "It came stark and strong and full of life, from the American forest." Although once one of the pillars of national self-understanding, it is an interpretation that has long been overturned. Turner failed to examine the frontier experiences of women, Native Americans, and African Americans. His arguments overstated the individual freedom of the frontier and understated the import of the state. He downplayed the ubiquity of racist violence and the structural power of slavery. He overlooked the presence of democratic struggle in other parts of the Republic. He equated "democracy" with a still narrow political order that privileged the white male alone.[6]

Contrary to Turner's celebrated thesis, the frontier where stump oratory was first identified was therefore far from equal or free. The white men who traveled across the Appalachian Mountains to Kentucky sought land rather than political freedom. The fields of cane and the forests they found were cleared by slave labor; the courthouses that symbolized order and government were often adjacent to spaces where human beings were bought and sold. If the privileges of the would-be aristocrat were most strongly assailed, then those below the simple white man were thrust even more firmly into a subordinate place. The rude republican of the Southwest sought to scramble his own way to the top: the ideal of the frontier was not the plain citizen or the friend of the excluded but the rising fellow, the "self-made" man. The poor white's pursuit of elective office was an opportunity for distinction as much as a challenge to the powerful. It was individual advancement, not the quest for abstract equality, that spurred the first stump orators.

In his *Recollections of the Last Ten Years* (1826), Timothy Flint thought this unaccustomed opportunity for political advancement among white men the source of the "unblushing effrontery" that soon came to characterize the elections of the frontier. As Flint saw it, in the "scramble for offices" within a new state, all the elements of "vanity," "ambition," and "aspiring consequence" once contained by social restrictions could finally burst forth. Alexis de Tocqueville, the celebrated French observer of local customs, strongly agreed: only in the Southwest, where the "body of society" was formed but "yesterday," had "speculators" and "adventurers" truly managed to achieve a public eminence. It was here, in the states of Kentucky and Tennessee, that self-nomination for political office was first accepted; self-promotion followed in its wake.[7]

But the political awakening of the frontier was not a purely secular process; it was equally commanded by a strange revolution of the soul. The new method of stump speaking also owed a usually hidden debt to slightly earlier changes in the forms of religious observance. In an odd and troubling inversion, the calumnies of the stump were at least partly inspired by the revelations of "Our Lord": the frontier politician traveled on a track first beaten by the rural preacher.

In the first years of the nineteenth century, a great religious revival gathered strength. At a meeting of Presbyterian ministers at Cane Ridge, in upper Kentucky, those gathered were touched suddenly by what seemed a heavenly power, moving them to tears and cries of mercy. Some auditors were deprived of the capacity to speak or hear; others lost consciousness of anything at all. The assembly was extended for weeks, and its extraordinary happenings were communicated to parts of Tennessee, Virginia, and what would become Indiana; many thousands tramped or rode across the land to see and hear for themselves.[8]

The Cane Ridge meeting became the model for annual "camp meetings" organized across the frontier by Methodists, Presbyterians, and newer Christian denominations. On the verge of unbroken forests, men and women blazing with a righteous energy would build altars and platforms of pine, enclosing them within temporary sheds large enough to protect thousands from the wind and the rain. These camp meetings were likened to "festivals" of the people. The daily grind of farm work and commerce was briefly suspended, and an isolating life became overwhelmed by intimacies of revelation. It was experienced as a moment of friendship and unity.

Meetings lasted for many days and nights, and sometimes even for weeks on end. Hams, legs of mutton, eggs, and chickens were shared, along with corn dodgers and preserved meats brought from home. Teams of preachers testified, one following another, separated by only the briefest of intervals. Then occurred what could only be considered small miracles: some worshippers professed to fall into trances and to receive visions of the divine; they were known to run, to jump, and even to bark. Others were arrested by jerking motions that could be allayed only by the activity of the dance. One young woman was possessed by an angelic spirit, and her face was briefly "too bright and shining for mortal eyes to gaze upon." Another thought "the final day had come." Ebenezer Stedman, a bluegrass craftsman, described these scenes as a perplexed outsider to the atmosphere of heightened exultation:

> We listened [as] one Man was Don preaching and they commenced Singing & Shouting. One young Girl jumpt on a Stump & Shouted [and] Clapt hur hands. Then another fell on the ground & to all appearance fainted. I Bact out of the Croud. . . . All the people ware going Crazy.[9]

Critics alleged "courting" and "nocturnal depredations" under the cover of religious fellowship, the "insidious lips" of preachers murmuring entreaties that would tinge the pale cheek of the innocent with scarlet. Others recoiled at the emotion and abandon of the gathered crowds.[10]

But regardless of contemporary alarm, historians have since identified a lasting political import of these meetings. The religious awakening challenged the leadership of the established churches and thereby undermined religious hierarchies. In this way, it contributed to the democratization of American society. Poor and untutored men without instruction of any kind began to speak to their fellows of the love of God and the fires of hell. The new preachers used the ordinary language of the backcountry. They spat into their hands, as if they were about to grab an axe or a spade, and their voices rang out with great volume and power. They did not compose and memorize elaborate sermons but expounded the word of God without note or manuscript. Some questioned the virtue of "educated preachers" and demonstrated by their own clear eloquence the value of another way. Their orations were animated with bold gestures and directed to the conscience and the feelings of the assembled. They denounced enemies and debated doctrine, and they preached on and on until compelled to cease: "Glory to God in the highest."[11]

Revivalist culture was only one expression of frontier life, and "rowdies" often disrupted camp meetings, anxious to defend the unholy pleasures of the bottle and the flesh. There was also a great tension between the boozy conflicts of election day and the temperate moralizing of the revivalist church. Despite these quarrels, however, the religious practices of an awakened Christianity undoubtedly contributed much to the rise of stump oratory. Camp meetings broke down social hierarchies, elevated emotion over education, and accepted the necessity of individual choice. Aspirants for office were sometimes present at camp meetings—reportedly to "electioneer, and gain popularity." Political gatherings were routinely organized at the place of former camp meetings and even used the language of "The Camp," on occasion. The energy of religious revival also encouraged the movement of itinerant preachers or "circuit riders" across the land in a manner that prefigured the later trek of the rural stumper. In these ways, the quest to save souls anticipated some of the methods later used to win the votes of frontier people. Quite unexpectedly, the religious life of the Southwest thereby helped nurture a distinctive form of political address.[12]

Lawyers were much closer to the messy world of electoral competition than the blessed realms of heaven, and the frontier attorney also played a role in the creation of the political stump. Unlike the citizens of a contemporary democracy, the pioneers of the Southwest relied upon county courts to complete many of the tasks of local government: the collection of taxes, the maintenance of roads, the authorization of construction, the regulation of probate, the administration of poor laws, the appointment of public officers. Local courts sat infrequently, and lawyers traveled from county to county in a regular circuit that linked the major towns of the frontier.[13]

The steady migration of attorneys limited the scope for research and preparation, for few heavy legal books could be brought on the long trek across a southwestern state. At the same time, the need to appeal to juries of practical and hardheaded men shaped the tone and temper of the bar. Common sense rather than the black letter of the law prevailed, and "it was popular in the courts to be very democratic," as one memoirist recalled. A quick tongue proved the best means of attracting clients, and legal oratory was marked by plentiful metaphors, bombastic harangues, florid images, and gross inaccuracies. Weapons forged for the contests of the courtroom—invective, ridicule, and sarcasm—were also adopted by the stump speaker. In these ways, the arts of attorneys helped establish the oral tradition of the Republic's frontier.[14]

Bingham's imagination of *Stump Speaking* therefore contains important and sometimes concealed historical clues; in the contemplation of his famed painting, a story of American beginnings might be more fully disclosed. By setting his painting on the frontier, Bingham may have overlooked the rise of democratic challengers in other parts of the Republic. As later chapters of this book show, stump oratory would eventually be understood as a national rather than a regional practice; the hungry pursuit of office was never simply an oddity of the Southwest. Nonetheless, the language of the stump clearly implied backwoods simplicity much more than sophisticated urbanity, and Bingham's association of "stump" with "frontier" was at one time widely held. The composition of Bingham's canvas also clearly resonates with aspects of frontier history as well as myth. The exclusion of African Americans is quite accurate. So is the apparent informality of the scene. Is it possible to deepen the search for historical foundations?

Bingham's painting also discloses deeper lessons concerning the beginnings of stump oratory, although these are of a more allusive and metaphori-

George Caleb Bingham, *The County Election* (1852),
oil on canvas, 38 x 52 inches. (Courtesy of Saint Louis Art Museum.
Gift of Bank of America 44:2001. Photography by Jean-Paul Torno.)

cal kind. The original title for *Stump Speaking* was *County Canvass*, which
was the artist's preferred term while working on the picture. Doubtless, there
were personal and commercial reasons for the earlier designation: Bingham
had just completed a successful study called *County Election*, and a title that
invoked "the County" would draw attention to the similarities between the
works. The artist had also depicted a now-lost painting of the *Stump Speaker*
in 1847, and he might at first have sought to distance the later from this earlier and less successful attempt. Whatever the motivation, the nomenclature
is revealing, for it draws necessary attention to one of the most important
historical sources of the stump speech.

Before the stump, there was the "canvas," or (British spelling) "canvass."
To "canvass," *The Oxford English Dictionary* records, is "to solicit; *esp.* to solicit votes or support previously to an election"; the term was used in this way
as early as the sixteenth century. Historians inform us that canvasing could
encompass acts as dispersed as the act of taking "the rounds" of a district; the
venturing of personal recommendations; the providing of hospitality, especially in the form of alcoholic "treats"; the greeting of citizens as they traveled
to record their votes; and the organizing of election meetings, marked, on
occasion, by speeches or debates.[15]

Robert Mumford's revealing play *The Candidates; Or, the Humors of a Virginia Election*, drafted around 1770, imparts something of the flavor of the canvas in the years immediately before the American Revolution. Herein Mr. Wou'dbe does battle with Mr. Strutabout and Mr. Smallhopes for the suffrages of freeholders Guzzle, Twist, Stern, and Prize. It is a dispiriting contest for even the most community-minded of men; for the noblest of the trio, Mr. Wou'dbe, the rewards of service seem to pale before the purgatorial labors of the canvas itself:

> Must I again be subject to the humours of a fickle croud? Must I again resign my reason, and be nought what each voter pleases? Must I cajole, fawn, and wheedle, for a place that brings so little profit?[16]

Nevertheless, these were inhibited and constrained forms of campaigning as compared with the unabashed, tooth-and-nail contests of later years. Until at least the beginning of the nineteenth century, candidacy for public office remained the preserve of a patrician elite. America's gentry battled among themselves for the opportunity to serve community and nation; the limits of the competition and the principles that underpinned the polity served to contain the schemes of the electioneer. The methods of the canvas did not extend to the devices of the stump.

Why this restraint? Formally speaking, it was the claim to a "superior status and culture" that entitled America's elite to the exercise of authority. Political leadership was considered a social obligation, not an opportunity for private elevation. The ideal statesman of republican desire was distinguished by a physical and moral courage and a dedication to public service. Such a leader did not court popular favor directly but attended instead to the claims of truth. Executive competence was considered less important than possession of the cardinal moral virtues. Neither personal ambition nor affection for power was permitted to intrude.[17]

Americans formally praised leaders who did not court favor and were seemingly unambitious, but in reality, most fell far from this standard; the figure of the statesman loomed still as the aspiration of the citizenry and the paradigm of the candidate. Apparent proximity to the qualities of disinterested service promoted any campaign; identification of moral failure undermined public reputation and fitness for office.

Unsurprisingly, in these circumstances the personal character of a candidate itself became the central issue in most electoral contests. Denunciation of office-hungry opponents was a familiar manoeuver; conversely, the disclaiming of overt ambition habitually appeared as a preamble to the announcement of any bid for power. Reflecting on his first campaign for Congress, future president James Madison confessed to an "extreme distaste" for any "steps having an electioneering appearance." Moreover, he considered that "any step" that expressed eagerness or "solicitude" on his part would "be as likely to operate against as in favour of my pretensions." Self-advertisement, in short, was unlikely to appeal to a community that hungered for the rule of the wise aristocrat. The aspiring statesman had practical as well as moral reasons to desist from the open advocacy of his own cause.

Madison's was a judgment shared even by the fictional Mr. Woud'be, challenged by Messrs Strutabout and Smallhopes in Mumford's imagined Virginia election. Mr. Woud'be was convinced that the very tendency of his rivals to "fawn and cringe" before electors would ultimately alienate them from public affection—"they'll soon be heartily despised." Speaking through his most attractive protagonist, Mumford made it obvious to his audience that restraint in the presentation of one's own claims was ultimately the most effective, as well as the most virtuous, of public acts:

> *The prudent candidate who hopes to rise,*
> *Ne'er deigns to hide it, in a mean disguise.*
> *Will, to his place, with moderation slide,*
> *And win his way, or not resist the tide.*
> *The fool, aspiring to bright honour's post,*
> *In noise, in shouts, and tumults oft, is lost.*[18]

While Mr. Strutabout and Mr. Smallhopes intrigued and postured, Mr. Woud'be and his eventual running mate, Sir John Worthy, adopted only the "properest methods" of public persuasion. Sir John organized a breakfast for the "principal freeholders" of the community. An honorable candidate was permitted to "shew" himself at such a gathering, but not to adopt the more brazen and maleficent techniques of the market-square hawker or the self-regarding braggart. The priorities of decorum bound the overt actions of the most judicious and respectable of nominees.

This is not to imply that the aspirant for public office lapsed into fatalistic inactivity; rather, the most favored electioneering tools rested upon the concealment of personal concern. The most prominent gentlemen in a community typically pledged their support (or "interest," as it was known) to a particular individual or slate of candidates. This ritual served to protect the nominee from accusations of self-advancement; it also delegated the tasks of public advocacy to others. Further measures extended the distance between the arts of promotion and the apparent knowledge of the candidate. For these purposes, the power of the pen was especially adept. Pamphlets and newspapers might be turned to the support of an aspirant's cause, as might campaign tracts and handbills of various kinds. The nominally "private" letters of candidates could also be deliberately circulated to a more general audience, thus more fully exposing their character and principles.

Other agencies might be exploited. Public meetings could be organized, citizens assembled, and resolutions passed. The candidates were customarily absent from gatherings of these kinds. But if the arriving statesmen deigned to address the citizenry, as they sometimes did, then such talks were typically imagined as "oration" rather than "speech": a public display of superior personality, virtue, and independence, not a direct appeal for the suffrages of the people. The candidate appeared here in the guise of statesman; the voter's attention implied due deference to a social superior.[19]

The canvas and the stump were therefore separated by a sizeable cultural gap. A candidate's ascension to the stump involved not just the adoption of one weapon of campaigning over its alternatives; this was also a challenge to the fictions that had guided and organized American public life. Bingham's decision to title his electioneering study *Stump Speaking* therefore not only drew attention to the oratorical act itself and to the pertinence of a distinctly American terminology; it also identified the scene as a departure from a political tradition that had been governed by deference and restraint. Although the continuities with earlier performances were evident, the sense of new beginnings was stronger still. Indeed, the action of naming the picture may itself serve as a kind of metaphor for the beginnings of the stump speech: a new practice slowly improvised, documented, and recognized; an unforeseen creation of the New World gradually supplanting a time-honored feature of the Old.

The coining of the term "stump speech" in the early decades of the nineteenth century reflected a dawning American awareness that this practice was something new in political life; earlier terminology was no longer apt. The growing use of the label across the Republic marked the diffusion of the practice and the acceptance of this change. Seen in this light, Bingham's preference for the title *Stump Speaking* over *County Canvass* serves as a valuable historical marker. As French historian Marc Bloch argued in *The Historian's Craft*: "The advent of the name is always a great event. . . . [I]t signifies the decisive moment of conscious awareness."[20]

Still, Bingham's painting invites further scrutiny. His election pictures have been described as forms of "contemporary history painting." If that is the case, then the precise identities of those sovereign people who have gathered at the stump obviously demand clarification. Is the imagined scene of *Stump Speaking* based on a particular person or event? The very vitality and conviction of the picture raises the question of its precise historical roots.

Bingham first ran for the Missouri State Legislature in 1846, and some have been inclined to identify the protagonists of his picture with real participants in frontier political life. The stump orator has been variously named as James S. Green, a former U.S. senator from Missouri; Erasmus Darwin Sappington, the man who opposed Bingham's own campaign for office; and even Bingham's friend and patron, James S. Rollins. Some have suggested that the assiduous notetaker who sits behind the rostrum might be Bingham himself. Attempts have also been made to identify others within the crowd.

The painter's own letters here provide only a dim illumination. Although Bingham's correspondence contains one plan to use the Missouri politician Thomas Benton as the subject for another picture (never completed), the painter never explicitly acknowledged a direct historical source for the scene around the stump. Writing to his closest friend in the heady throes of composition, Bingham noted only:

> In my orator I have endeavored to personify a wiry politician, grown gray in the pursuit of office and the service of party. His influence upon the crowd is quite manifest, but I have placed behind him a shrewd, clear[-]headed opponent, who is busy taking notes, and who will, when his turn comes[,] make sophisms fly like cobwebs before the housekeeper[']s broom.

Later commentators have interpreted this passage as a proof that Bingham had no particular subject in mind. Still, the possibility of another reading persists. Bingham's excerpted description was included in a missive to his close friend, Rollins. The latter had not yet seen the canvas, and its author might have looked forward to a moment of surprised recognition, for now deliberately deferred. Certainly, the resemblances of the speaker and the notetaker to Sappington and Bingham are almost disarming. If they served as the models for the stump speakers, then the references to a "wiry politician" and a "shrewd" opponent could in fact be read as ironic nods to their public characters; Bingham's correspondence certainly included self-deprecatory humor of this kind. Now cut off from the world of the frontier, we cannot be completely certain of Bingham's exact inspirations. Ultimately, the history that lies behind the representation can never be definitively known.[21]

But here again, a close examination of the painting promotes recognition of an intriguing and important metaphorical truth. Like the enigma of Bingham's canvas, the history of stump speaking resists complete discovery. We do not know who first clambered atop the stump and began to address his fellows on the urgent questions of the hour. The time and the place of this democratic revolution was not then recorded, and it cannot now be rescued. Writers of the nineteenth century thought of stump oratory as a creature of "tradition," lacking the necessary gravitas to qualify for the elevated chronicles of "history." As a result, the task of recovery is particularly difficult. Many, perhaps most, speeches simply eluded notation of any kind. Those reports that do survive are often tainted by partisanship. Reporters were "pressed upon and elbowed" by the crowd. And even a faithful scribe could struggle to capture the twinkling humor and artful flourishes of the best stump speech; correspondents were known to discard their pens, declaring any written record an "injustice" to the charms of the moment: "To appreciate them, they must be heard."[22]

In consequence, the happening and the form of the first stump orations are lost to history. The newspapers of the Early Republic trace only the shadows cast by a world now long since passed away. Reports published in the first decade of the nineteenth century might include references to speeches given from "the stump of a fallen tree," the "top of a stump," or the "top of a hogshead." These happenings are novel and yet recorded with an unromantic matter-of-factness. The person of the stump orator is identified only from the second decade, alongside equally intriguing but more evanescent figures, such as "slang-whangers" and "spouting" orators. It was not at first apparent that speeches given from a stump might be deserving of more than a passing interest.[23]

It is always the historian's burden to be left with traces of the past; this is the basis of history's challenges, and its pleasures, too. But for the historian of the stump speech, the weakness of the source material is particularly vexing. The chronicler of the stump does not have access to the experience of the authentic speech: the ringing of a baritone in the open air, the sting of the interjection, the flash of the retort. Rather, this is a history that must be composed of representations: letters, reports, reminiscences, paintings. The beginnings of stump oratory can be rescued only from looking between the lines of news reports, or, indeed, by asking questions of celebrated works of art. Like the story of Bingham's canvas, the history of stump oratory cannot be completely reclaimed. Yet this is an aspect of democracy's past about which we can and should know much more.

If the search for the history of the stump necessarily implies a study of images and representations, then the history of Bingham's paintings itself divulges one final lesson. Within the career of Bingham's own "election paintings" might be found a kind of metaphor for the broader history of the relationship between the stump orator and the American nation. In scrutinizing the public life of Bingham's works, we might also learn something of the processes that shaped many other images of the stump speaker in action.

Bingham's paintings were the children of the frontier, born of rough experiences in the rude democracy of Missouri. Yet the "election series" was eventually to achieve national recognition as an expression of self-government in the new world: a symbol of the American Republic as a whole. This designation was no accident of popular taste. Bingham had quite deliberately designed earlier paintings to appeal to prominent art buyers in the East, and his political canvases were also imagined with a national audience in mind. The Missourian organized an engraving of each of the "election" pictures so that they might be most widely diffused. In preparing for the engravings, he worked to change the details of paintings, removing local references (such as the newspaper title, *Missouri Republican*) and replacing them with national allusions (such as a continental daily, the *National Intelligencer*). Rollins, Bingham's patron and friend, strongly emphasized the national scope of each scene in his attempts to promote sales. Writing of *County Election* to Eastern art patrons, for example, Rollins called the canvas "pre-eminently a National painting, for it presents just such a scene as you would meet on the Aroostook in Maine, or in the City of New York, or on the Rio Grande in Texas, on election day."

We cannot be sure whether Bingham's quest for a national audience expressed a noble hunger for political mission or a less elevated pursuit of personal enrichment. In private correspondence, he unashamedly anticipated that the "election series" would lay "the foundation of a fortune." Yet there is no reason to think that as a member of the Whig party and a proponent of the market, he would admit to any tension between a bulging pocketbook and a celebration of the democratic creed. On the contrary, the cultural market and the national imagination were considered firm friends. For Bingham, it was as though an invisible hand promoted the image maker from an individual artisan to a servant of the Republic. In pursuing the maximum number of sales, he could act also to create a national myth; the promotion of a canvas like *Stump Speaking* could serve community as well as self.[24]

Critics might question the virtue of this general relationship, but they cannot doubt its cultural power. The career of Bingham's paintings is but one expression of a general process. Over the middle decades of the nineteenth century, stump oratory was transformed from an apparent child of the Southwest to a republican symbol of democratic action. In pursuing their personal objectives, students of the stump speech acted to transform American public life as well as to promote themselves.

The rise of stump speaking was surprisingly slow and uneven. From its identification in the earliest years of the nineteenth century, the practice remained at first relatively secured to the frontier. Certainly, stump speaking did not sweep across the Republic in the manner of a prairie fire; it cast at first only a flickering, uncertain flame. One veteran lawman from Indiana dated the "fashion" for stump speaking only from the middle 1820s. The term was still deployed with great uncertainty in private correspondence around this time (*"stumping* it, as he calls it," read one explanatory letter to Daniel Webster, New England's great politician, in 1826). Northern journalists disclaimed acquaintance with the "technical meaning of the term" as late as 1839. And the "political tactic" of stump speaking was still considered to await confirmation a year later, during the presidential campaign of 1840.[25]

It is only really from this point that stump speaking was considered a genuinely national phenomenon. From the second half of the nineteenth century, the term was increasingly included in American dictionaries or guides to local usage, alongside a range of Yankee and Southern slang. English correspondents, anxious to explain the strange and misunderstood ways of the new, democratic world, also offered definitions at this time. By the beginning of the century's seventh decade, the term and the practice were widely known. Indeed, in some eyes, they had come to symbolize the Great Republic itself. In 1860, London's *Punch* summed up the new attitude, noting with simple certainty that "elections in America are principally carried on by a process called 'stumping.'"[26]

The passage from frontier to nation was complicated and sometimes confusing. It forms one of the major themes of this book. In appreciating the particular career of Bingham's paintings, we learn something of the devices by which this transformation was wrought. The rise of stump oratory was the product of deliberate cultural labor. Individuals sought to advance themselves. Some used stump speaking to win elections. Others took up the stump orator as an object of pictorial or literary composition or even dramatic performance. In cross-cutting and often confused attempts at self-assertion, a new form of public activity thereby attained an increasing prominence: the alleged child of the frontier became a symbol of the nation.

Who were the men who first championed the methods of the stump to a national audience? And how did they themselves become the object of cultural imagination? That is a story taken up in the succeeding chapters. It begins with two products of the mythologized frontier: Colonel Davy Crockett and Senator Henry Clay.

1

FRONTIER STUMPING

Davy Crockett and Henry Clay
as Orators and Symbols

Stump oratory was originally imagined as a "frontier" rather than a national practice. The first politicians to win continental renown as stump speakers hailed from the neighboring states of Tennessee and Kentucky: Davy Crockett (1783–1836) and Henry Clay (1777–1852). Americans came to understand the nature of "stump oratory" through the medium of these two substantial careers. Controversial and divisive, the southwestern pair not only demonstrated the capacities of the "stump speech"; they also symbolized the method to the Republic as a whole: its meaning, its challenge, its disruptive force.

Crockett was the "giant of the stump," in the words of the *Times* of London. Vigorously promoted by the partisan press, he would come to embody to northern Americans that "mode of itinerant preaching" and those "stump and tavern-door-step speeches" that found favor among the "wild" and "gaming" characters of the South. For many years, "the regular Davy Crockett line" would be a byword for persuasive election oratory. And illustrations of "Colonel Crockett Making a Stump Speech" would adorn his famed autobiography through countless print runs.[1]

More esteemed and refined, Clay was sometimes ranked among the greatest of American orators (more extravagant admirers even compared him to Cicero, Demosthenes, Edmund Burke, and Lord Chatham). Clay was the first American leader whose parliamentary eloquence was considered worthy of collection and publication. On the stump, his appearance incited tremendous demonstrations across the land ("an irrepressible curiosity to hear me

Speak"). His platform speeches were often transcribed and his utterances widely read ("the whole country is familiar with them").

Clay was most often imagined in the pose of the orator. Handbills presented him as a tall figure on a stump: mouth open, bugle in hand (to denote the trumpeting voice). Illustrated newspapers featured engravings of the Kentucky statesman "standing on a stump": coatless, arms free, liberated to "give full scope to his gesticulation." Supporters of Clay's nomination for the presidency even dug up the stump of a fine tree from his family farm, "Ashland," placed it in a box, and sent it to his party's convention as a kind of talismanic or mystical offering. Opponents, too, acknowledged the import of Clay's stump speaking in their coining of derisive epithets: the "Pilgrim Orator," "the Table Orator." the "Travelling Speech Maker," the "itinerant political preacher," and the "Hero of Barbecue Dinners and Stump Orations."[2]

Yet if they emerged simultaneously as national symbols of the stump, then Crockett and Clay owed their prominence to distinctive political trajectories. Clay was a high officeholder and a major partisan leader from the first decades of the nineteenth century. Central to the rise of a national party system, he used stump oratory to defend one presidential administration, to pull down another, and to seek a third. Crockett, by contrast, won his fame as the object and the author of tall tales of hunting, drinking and voting on the southwestern frontier. He became a symbol of the "stump orator" by acts of cultural imagination and false attribution as much as by personal achievement. Clay was a great stump orator, while Crockett was a dominating image of what stump oratory signified. But their careers were linked, and, as we shall see, their versions of stump oratory contained a similar challenge to class, honor, gender, and political order.

In the pages that follow, I closely consider the lives, struggles, and speeches of these first Americans to achieve national renown as champions of the stump. My account draws from diverse primary sources: speeches, letters, newspapers, memoirs, fiction, drama, painting, and burlesque. Concerned with capturing the environment in which stump oratory was first publicized, I lay out the complicated context of national politics and individual biographies. Attentive to the meaning ascribed to stump oratory, I give substantial attention to myths and tall tales alongside established facts. Drawing on these materials, I establish how stump speaking first became visible to a national audience and how this troubling performance was initially understood.

Over a half century of active politics, Henry Clay served as speaker of the House of Representatives, secretary of state, and senator. His contributions as a legislator, party leader, and wielder of national compromise are well remembered; his capacities as an orator and electioneer were recognized from a precocious youth, too.

Successful in the Kentucky courtroom from the age of twenty, the young man attained wider public attention in the last years of the eighteenth century as a critic of alien and sedition laws that restricted freedom of speech. No account of these first public orations, however imperfect, has survived, but Clay's eloquence in the cause was memorialized in one early biography as "difficult to describe." Another suggested that these speeches "laid the foundation of his reputation as a public man." His letters written to the *Kentucky Gazette* (adopting the Latinate pseudonym "Scaevola") do remain: in them, he celebrated annual elections, exalted the popular will, and expressed confidence in the power of truth. It was also from behind the mask of "Scaevola" that Clay first considered the election campaign. Breaking with the deference of electors and the intrigue of committees, he boldly called for the candidates' open declaration of principle and position.[3]

How Clay first presented his own case from the stump, we cannot know. His most devoted biographers chronicle merely "few" and "well directed" remarks, "ingenuous" appeals, and subsequent acclamation. But although the details of his apprenticeship must necessarily remain a mystery, historians have adjudged Clay a brilliant student of the raucous arts of the frontier election. Importantly, by the 1820s, stumping was no longer merely a local practice: he began at this time to apply the techniques of the stump in political struggles that had a national profile. And from this point, too, many sources disclose his powerful political style.[4]

The immediate cause of Clay's deployment of stump oratory across the nation was the presidential election of 1824. No candidate had won a clear majority of electoral votes, and the election was ultimately decided by a vote of the House. Although Clay had himself held hopes of personal victory, he was instead placed in the position of a kingmaker: the block of votes Clay controlled was sufficient to decide the issue between General Andrew Jackson of Tennessee and John Quincy Adams of Massachusetts. Clay had established his career in criticism of Adams's father's deployment of executive power, and Jackson had won more than 40 percent of the popular vote. Kentucky's legislature urged state delegates to support Jackson.[5]

Violating expectations, however, Clay sided with Adams. In a considerable lapse of judgment, he also accepted the position of Adams's secretary of state. "Intrigue, corruption, and sale of public office is the rumor of the day," wrote the defeated general; Clay's behavior appeared to him to display a "want of principle" and a devotion to "self aggrandisement." Jackson's supporters likened Clay to a traitor and even to the devil himself. Brooding over his exclusion from office, Jackson's sense of righteous anger grew. In flaming letters, he excoriated Clay's actions as a "barter" of the "rights of the people" and a horrible "precedent," leading probably to "the destruction of our Republican institutions."[6]

Long celebrated as an embodiment of national virtue and newly confirmed as both the people's choice and the victim of intrigue, the general's arguments won strong support. He was an "idol" to the "unsophisticated" and "less informed," mourned one antagonist; his popularity was "most extraordinary." An array of tough-minded political leaders across the country now also lined up behind him. Jackson's name and popularity were used to create new political organizations, and his managers forged alliances between previously disparate or antagonistic political machines.[7] Even their opponents admitted that Jacksonians were animated by superior "zeal," "activity," and "management." The party's deployment of the newspaper press was especially notable: "not a column in their Newspaper is ever printed," wrote one admirer to Clay, "which does not contain an attack upon you."[8]

The intensity of this political assault shocked Clay into some kind of response. In private missives, he conceded that the principle of attack "generally succeeds" over that of defense. Clay's adversaries, as he also emphasized, "never give up, but make defeat a new point for fresh exertions." If opponents had profited from their aggressive electioneering, then surely some kind of rejoinder was essential? So the secretary of state advised his ally, William Plumer:

> The system, on the other side, is one of manoeuvres & demonstrations, & I regret to believe in the necessity of counteracting it, by a like system on our part.[9]

Clay's greatest power lay in his capacity for oratory rather than in the organization of "manoeuvres" or "demonstrations." Pained by repeated strokes against his honor and hoping to retain his power, Clay therefore took to the stump. In consequence, the methods long associated with the Kentucky frontier now won prominence far beyond the southwestern state.

At first, Clay's national campaign of speech making appeared genuinely spontaneous. As the new secretary of state made his way homeward from Washington, he was met by unmistakable and apparently sincere expressions of popular support. Writing from the Ohio River in late May 1825, Clay related events to his friend Charles Hammond:

> My reception West of the Mountains so far has exceeded my expectations. I was invited to a public dinner at Union town, which I was obliged to decline, in consequence of previous engagements at Washn.

& Wheeling. In all the villages through which I passed[,] crowds of decent orderly citizens visited me and with much kindness & cordiality welcomed me. Public dinners, well attended and accompanied with warm and enthusiastic sentiments, were given me at Washn. & Wheeling.[10]

Within little more than a fortnight, invitations followed to similar entertainments in Maysville and Frankfort, Lexington, Nicholasville, Winchester, Louisville, Lancaster, Norristown, and Irvine's Spring. These were frank declarations of personal and political support, deliberate rejoinders to the unrelenting vigor of the Jacksonian persuasion. As Maysville residents explained, the "calumny" of Clay's "secret enemies" justified a public expression of confidence in Kentucky's leading man.[11]

The banquets and the barbecues offered Clay a fine opportunity to defend reputation, career, and political cause. His speeches at these events were widely reported. And although they were perhaps at first the unthinking reflex of the assailed, Clay's public performances soon took on a less exculpatory and more aggressive form. As planning began to succeed impulse, the deliberate stumping tour emerged.

The secretary's annual return from the nation's capital to Ashland quickly became the occasion of speech making at banquets, dinners, and barbecues in every year in which he held that high office.[12] By the third year of his tenure, signs suggest that the practice had become routine. Increasingly, Clay seemed to solicit requests to stop and speak ("it will be quite convenient for me to pass by . . . if I should become satisfied that my visit . . . will not be unacceptable"). Clay now "procured himself" invitations, or so his critics would allege. With Jackson's looming political success more obvious by the day, Secretary Clay more frankly and openly embraced the politics of the stump. In a remarkable speech delivered in Baltimore in May 1828, Clay declared his willingness to brave criticism ("all imputations") in the quest not merely to vindicate his past choices but even more to keep the vengeful general from the presidential chair:

> I would visit every State, go to every town and hamlet, address every man in the Union, and entreat them, by their love of liberty, for the sake of themselves and their posterity . . . to pause—solemnly pause—and contemplate the precipice that yawns before us![13]

Clay's speech making did not halt Jackson's thundering advance. But although he had been bested in the contest for power, Harry of the West now strengthened his determination to deploy his oratory in national political campaigns. Only a few months after Jackson's election, Clay now claimed a "serious cause of alarm" in the general's ejection of public servants from their employment. The Kentucky orator argued that it was his "painful duty" to speak out against this danger: the perilous health of the Republic made platform appeals an absolutely necessity. At a speech in Fowler's Garden, Lexington, in May 1829, he urged his "fellow citizens" that it was the "duty of all" to "exercise their judgment freely and independently on what is passing":

> None ought to feel themselves restrained, by false pride, or by any part which they took in the late election, from condemning what their hearts cannot approve.[14]

By this time, Clay's speeches had been confirmed as a major feature of an increasingly national political struggle. Through this politician's pained and often disappointed exertions, the stump oratory of the frontier was made familiar to citizens far beyond the boundaries of the bluegrass state.

The contrast with Davy Crockett is here revealing, for the Tennessee hunter won renown less by the profusion and persuasiveness of his speech than by processes beyond his control. Unlike Clay, Crockett's legislative career was relatively undistinguished, and his quest for higher office unfulfilled. The child of a poor family of Tennessee farmers, he was at first notable merely for the unorthodoxy of his path to Washington. Elected to the U.S. Congress in 1826, Crockett seemed to many to symbolize incipient transformations of the new Republic: the vitality of the Southwest, the possibility of upward mobility, the challenge of General Jackson to the elites of Virginia and Massachusetts. His status as a symbol of these changes seemed to inspire the greatest share of initial attention. Newspaper commentaries, theatrical depictions, novelistic treatments, and popular songs all identified Crockett as an often comic outsider to the civilized and straitened conventions of the northern social and political round.

But Crockett soon broke with Jackson's government, which elicited a changed but still more attentive interest. Now Jackson's opponents increasingly promoted the colonel as a western soldier to match the hero of New Orleans. A popular volume, drafted anonymously by the clerk of the House of Representatives, shared *Sketches and Eccentricities of Col. David Crockett* with an appreciative northern audience. Apparently composed for "amusement," it claimed also a fidelity to the facts of the new congressman's life.[15] Although it praised Crockett's marksmanship, generosity, and seemingly inexhaustible fund of anecdotes, the backwoodsman expressed dissatisfaction with the account and resolved to compose an autobiography. An attempt to correct the record and to gain a direct share in Crockett's own growing commercial appeal, *A Narrative of the Life of David Crockett of the State of Tennessee* helped the congressman attain a genuine national celebrity as frontier politician, hunter, and purveyor of tall tales. Seldom out of print, it would eventually be recognized as a classic of early American literature.

While President Jackson waged a war with the banks, America's financial elite turned increasingly to Crockett as a counterweight to the general's common appeal. Crockett was dispatched on a speech-making tour of the North and the East in late April 1834. Journeying to Baltimore, Philadelphia, New York, and New England, and then returning southward as far as Indiana, Ohio, and Kentucky, the hunter from Tennessee was greeted by variously curious and adoring onlookers and an eager partisan press; the events were recalled and embroidered in a rapidly ghosted memoir.

Echoing Clay, Crockett justified his speech making on tour as a courteous response to spontaneous invitations ("I was surrounded and called upon for a speech"; "I had not the least idea of addressing you") and as a necessary departure from convention in a moment of political crisis. In Louisville, he told auditors that he would normally have "refused" an invitation to speak and explained that only "recent occurrences" (the actions of Jackson's government) had imposed "the duty" upon him of addressing "the people" on the "real and true situation of our once happy country." In Cincinnati, he announced to those assembled:

> The time has come when every public servant is indebted to his country to speak out and sound the alarm, and let the country know the situation it is in.[16]

The ghosted memoir of the tour was published under the elaborate title of *An Account of Col. Crockett's Tour to the North and Down East, in the Year of Our Lord One Thousand Eight Hundred and Thirty-Four. His Object Being to Examine the Grand Manufacturing Establishments of the Country; And Also to Find Out the Conditions of Its Literature and Morals, the Extent of Its Commerce, and the Practical Operation of "The Experiment," Written by Himself.* Crockett's name was also soon afterward affixed to a poisonous biography of Jackson's ally and presumptive heir, *The Life of Martin Van Buren, Heir-Apparent to the "Government" and the Appointed Successor of General Andrew Jackson.*

But although he was prominent on tour and in print and even touted on occasion as a potential nominee for chief magistrate, Crockett's political career increasingly faltered. Crying foul at the dirty tricks of opponents, the colonel was defeated at the 1834 polls. Deflated and apparently embittered, he swiftly followed through on a threat to clear out for Texas.

Returned now to the very edge of the frontier, Crockett and his fellow adventurers met with unexpected resistance. The advance of the Mexican army checked the encroachment of the European. As General Santa Anna led his troops northward, Crockett gathered with other Americans at a former Roman Catholic mission, the Alamo. Under siege, cannon fire, and then outright assault, they perished in its defense on March 6, 1836. But Crockett was hailed as a martyr of Texan independence, allowing him to enjoy an afterlife at least as significant as his earthly span. A fabricated memoir claimed to induct the reader into the smoky mystery of his final battle:

> Pop, pop, pop! Bom, bom, bomb! Throughout the day.—No time for memorandums now.—Go ahead!—Liberty and independence for ever![17]

These and other apocrypha circulated widely. A series of popular *Crockett Almanacks* was also continued for some two decades, although their ostensive author had expired; ghosted works proliferated. Liberated by the ending of the man himself, writers and artists were now free to make his image anew. The elements of fantasy that had always formed a part of Crockett's self-presentation were increasingly exaggerated, their comic implausibilities stretched with great ingenuity. Crockett persisted as an American legend and as an enduring symbol of frontier life and politics. Reinterpreted by modernity's culture industries, he survives in this form, still.

Crockett's notoriety as a stump orator therefore reflects the creativity of political patrons, newspaper editors, and anonymous scribblers as much as the speech making of the man himself. Scholars have long recognized that the "real" Crockett is necessarily elusive.[18] It was as a "legend" rather than a "man" that the hunter from Tennessee came to symbolize a new kind of politics.

In seeking to register the image and the symbol of the frontier stumper, I therefore necessarily look beyond Crockett's actual contributions, giving equal attention to those who appropriated his identity and spoke in his voice. For the historian of stump oratory, it matters not whether the real Crockett spoke or acted or whether the hunter and politician served as a kind of ventriloquist's dummy. The legendary Crockett became a symbol of stump oratory. It is therefore in the close study of this (sometimes false) image that the initial meanings attributed to stump speaking might be more fully understood.

Owing its prominence to quite divergent agencies, the stump oratory ascribed to Clay and Crockett nonetheless bore important similarities. Ascended upon the platform—or imagined in this position—the two frontier politicians both proclaimed humble origins, adopted demotic speech, projected masculine power, and reimagined the electoral contest in novel and confronting ways.

Some of these themes were evident in other political interventions. Deployed in combination, as part of an unfamiliar political performance, they represented a powerful challenge to prevailing political assumptions. They also established the stump orator as a political actor of a new and troubling kind.

The first characteristic Crockett and Clay shared was the proclamation of humble origins. Crockett was born in Tennessee, the fifth of what would be nine children. "I was pretty *well born*" the first *Crockett Almanack* ironically notes of the frontiersman's origins: "My size . . . is over six feet." *A Narrative of the Life of David Crockett* frankly disclosed a humble birth, a poor education, business failures, and a simple home. According to political tradition, these social facts should have barred the aspirant from public prominence. As Crockett himself conceded, "all great men" had tended to rest their "hopes" on a "noble ancestry." The contrast with his own background was stark: he "stood no chance to become great in any other way than by accident."[19]

But although he was questing for public eminence, the child of the backwoods did not obscure his uncelebrated background. Rather, Crockett worked to reorder the meaning of his origins. The humbly born were widely thought to be inferior. Crockett identified this judgment as a form of snobbery. In this way, the frontiersman's well-connected opponents for office were reimagined not as social betters, justly habituated to the exercise of authority, but as a maleficent elite that aimed to deny the common folk equal status or respect. Understood in these new terms, Crockett's candidacy became an episode in a social drama, as the principles of democracy and equality vied with the aristocratic principles of hereditary birth and rank. It was a narrative becoming popular in other electoral contests. Crockett developed this rhetoric in his circulars and stumping anecdotes; his supporters then elaborated it, sometimes misleadingly.

As his memoir relates, Davy's first electoral contest was for the post of colonel in the local regiment. Approached by a Captain Matthews to form a joint ticket—the captain seeking the position of colonel, with Crockett to run as his major—Crockett's running mate allegedly revoked this initial arrangement and instead supported his own son for the lesser position. Angered by the betrayal, Crockett resolved to run for colonel: his superior's literal favoring of heredity over merit stung Davy into action and thereby into the beginnings of a public life.[20]

Crockett's account of how he came to run for the legislature adheres to a similar pattern. This time, the backwoodsman sups with three local notables: Doctor Butler, a nephew to General Jackson; a major in Tennessee's militia;

and one other man. Encouraged to run for office, Crockett at first declines. Then, a week or two later, a newspaper announces his candidacy anyway. Davy is convinced that this report is an attempt at mockery—"a burlesque on me." He determines "to make it cost the man who had put it there at least the value of the printing, and of the fun he wanted at my expense."[21] The condescension of elites drives the colonel to compete for respect as well as for office.

Crockett's subsequent campaign explicitly invoked social distinction as a means of winning support. Competing with Doctor Butler, he confronted his more fancied opponent at a public meeting. Crockett publicly raised the centrality of money to the political process, admitting that Butler "had many advantages over me, and particularly in the way of money." Deliberately dramatizing his impecunious state, the farmer and hunter explained that his "industrious children" would "hunt every night till midnight to support my election"; while they planned to kill coons, he proposed to shoot, skin, and scalp wolves—"good to me for three dollars." In this way, the colonel explicitly introduced the theme of wealth into the campaign. Money was no longer bracketed out of political contest; the poor man identified his own deficit, and this also became one important basis of his appeal.[22]

It was a method often applied. In a later announcement of his intention to run for Congress, Crockett described himself as one who had "no superior claims upon the people," who had "shouldered his knapsack and gun" in defense of liberty, and who now had "the daring impudence" to oppose the "immaculate" officeholder. Apparently ignored in public debates between candidates, the colonel effectively accused his chief opponent of snobbery: "I told him that he had not had the politeness to name me in his speech." "I envy no man his wealth," Crockett argued in another letter, although he did object to the tendency of "monopolizing institutions" to deprive the poor of "our rights." The colonel claimed to be "the poor man's friend"; after all, "I am poor myself."[23]

Clay's origins were less obviously plebeian. Although Clay was bereaved as a child, his departed father legated his seventh-born child the ownership of two slaves; his mother's second husband boasted wealth and good connections, and young Clay was inducted into the law by none other than George Wythe (a signatory of the Declaration of Independence, an earlier mentor to Thomas Jefferson, and a professor of law).[24] Nonetheless, Clay revealingly aimed to obscure these advantages and claimed a much more humble birth.

The politician described his status upon arrival in Lexington as "pennyless [sic]," orphaned, "without friends," and unblessed by "the favor of the great." This was to be an image assiduously promoted by publicists of Clay's party and person. The *Henry Clay Almanac* (1843) recalled his first years as "oppressed by poverty." Partisan propaganda presented him as "the great

Commoner"—a "man of the people" and an "orator of the people," a hale fellow who first impressed as a "hardy backwoodsman," accustomed to the toils of the frontier.

With Clay long famous and contemplating another tilt at the presidency, his biographers recovered (or invented) the story of young Hal once riding a pony to a distant mill to procure his family's daily bread. They called him the "Millboy of the Slashes," and the image was reworked in many party pageants. Here, and in later forms, the lawyer and orator was depicted as a man of the land. The *Daily National Intelligencer* dubbed him "the farmer of Ashland," for Clay had planted his property with favored ash trees and had adopted Ashland as the name of his family's home. Party banners also portrayed their champion as a plain tiller of the soil. Campaign literature assured readers that Clay "delights" in agriculture and was a "practical," "industrious," and "methodical" farmer. Indeed, he was even described as the "Cincinnatus of the Age."[25]

Whether such privation was imagined or endured, the frontier stump orator sought to claim rather than obscure apparently humble origins. Likewise, he employed an openly demotic and rambunctious style. Crockett, as obituaries recalled, possessed a loud voice, "well suited to stump oratory." Among other nicknames, the colonel attracted the sobriquet of the "Ringtail Roarer," and none doubted the power of his strong lungs. The pitch and tone of his speech were less certain. A notoriously unreliable melodrama from the 1870s portrayed Crockett's utterances as "clear as a bell" and "as sharp as the crack of a rifle." In contrast, an equally dubious witness, British traveler Captain R. G. A. Levinge, deplored the Tennessean's voice as "so rough it could not be described." Was he a tenor or a bass? We cannot know. But his portraitist, John Gadsby Chapman, recorded an appreciation of Crockett's "clearness of diction," "command" of "expression," and "emphatic" and unrestrained speech.[26]

Loud and emphatic, the style was neither grammatical nor graceful. Crockett's speech was described as "blunt," "rude," and "unpolished." Not merely deploying the "simplest language possible," he used also the "slang," the "coarse figures," and the "phraseology" most common in the West. As presented in reportage and in fiction, his method rested also upon anecdotes drawn from frontier life: stories of lazy boys who "called the dogs and set them a-barking" and of farmers who ploughed crooked fields. The natural world was similarly a rich fund of metaphor: politicians were a "hungry swarm"; enemies were "chicken-bred," "toad-hoppin," and "bristle-headed." Crockett warned his listeners to beware of "political weasels" and "caterpillars of corruption." He feared the poverty of "a turkey fed on gravel stones" and embraced "hull hog patriotism." The metaphor of the "whirlwind," like the "airthquake" and the "chain of lightning," was used often to symbolize and to convince. All of this was far from the studied allusion or the charming vignette that had so distinguished the parliamentary orator of earlier generations. It lacked, too, the discipline of the classical model. Critics called Crockett vulgar. Even the colonel himself admitted, "I have not pretensions to be an orator."[27]

Matching the absence of oratorical pretension, Crockett spoke in a "blunt way," his language "bold" and "strong." His speeches have been described as "forcible," "sensible," and "unpolished." The colonel, for his part, claimed to speak "without trimmins" and as "straight as a gun-barrel." "I a'n't used to oily words," he explained. "I am used to speak what I think, of men to men." Crockett was but a "plain, blunt, Western man," he wrote to the *Daily National Intelligencer*, so how else could he be expected to talk? The "plain homespun manner" was best, especially for one who did not "pretend to be a great politician."[28]

The claims to artless sincerity are regularly reaffirmed, although they suggest political affect rather than naïve repetition. Crockett began nearly every major speech on his northern tour with some reference to his "plain manner," "plain way," or "home style." Explicitly, he suggested that this trait made him more trustworthy than the conventional politician. "I know I speak the truth," he told auditors in New York, "and you know it too." In an address to some five thousand in Philadelphia, he made the connection between plainness and sincerity still more obvious:

> You shall have it in my own plain way; and of one thing I assure
> you—you will be at no loss to understand me, if I understand myself:
> for of all the despicable creatures on the face of this here God's globe,
> I despise most your non-committal skulking politician.

Crockett's boosters argued directly that his "frankness," "sincerity," and absence of "classic refinement" were best understood as a "voucher" for the "truth" of "the facts he relates." This argument was shared by parts of the press. "It is plain truth, plainly spoken," summarized the *New York Spectator* of one of Crockett's oratorical efforts, "coming directly to the point, without rhetorical flourish, or circumlocution."[29] In this and other appraisals, an apparent deficiency in formal speech was reimagined as a signal of deeper fidelity to the truth. The ignorant farmer had become the truest republican, the rude hunter the safest custodian of the citizen's trust.

Although Clay's speech making was much more sophisticated, it nonetheless shared a distance from classical tradition. Unschooled in Latin and Greek, he was conscious, in later life, of never having "enjoyed the advantage" of familiarity with the "dead languages."[30] His training in oratory came not from meditation on the example of Cicero but from a more practical discipline. From what he remembered as an "early period" in his life, Clay began the practice of "daily reading and speaking" the contents of "some historical or scientific book" in and around the cornfields, forests, and barns of his bucolic home. Private, apparently untutored, certainly effective, it was an exercise in self-perfection he would continue for some years. In Clay's view, this was the "one single fact" to which "I owe my success in life."[31]

Clay delivered his speeches extemporaneously from notes. As one assessor observed, he spoke "as the battle of debate demanded": instant, fervid, to the point of the moment. Although "copious," his vocabulary was "common" and the language "simple," "plain," and "unaffected." Even a child could understand one of Clay's speeches, it was said. There was simplicity of reasoning— "just enough to prove the point, and no more." And there was a "directness" and "precision." Overall, his speeches were characterized by perspicuity and force.[32]

This was a western oratory, and it was named as such. Clay's friends called him the "Cicero of the West" and the "Lion of the West." Clay was "the great Orator and statesman of the West," the "brightest" of "jewels" in the "crown" of Kentucky's glory. He was "Harry of the West" and the "consummate Kentuckian," celebrated in song as "Kentucky's noblest son," canonized in early reminiscence as the very "representative" of "the eloquence of the western country."

Clay's critics acknowledged his western character but dissented from the approbatory sentiments. Josiah Quincy of Massachusetts, severe and precise, criticized the "rough, overbearing eloquence" of the westerner, formed, he said, in contests with the "half-civilized" in "the county courts of Kentucky," quickened by "successful declamations" at "barbecues" and in "electioneering struggles." Others mockingly called him the "Stump Orator from Kentucky," the "Pride of Kentucky," and the "Western Cataline." The *Globe* newspaper dubbed Clay the "lord" of the "stump orators" of the West.[33]

The apparently untutored and demotic nature of this speech was evident most obviously in the common description of Clay as a "natural" orator. He was, so they said, an orator "formed," "made," and "by nature." Comparison with the natural world was sometimes more exact: Clay's voice was likened to "thunder," "earthquake," and "whirlwind." It "rolled like a torrent," poured "like a flood of flame," and raged like "the current of some majestick river."

Margaret Bayard spelled out the implications of these descriptions in her *First Forty Years of Washington Society*. Clay's "natural" power, she said, separated him from the eloquent statesmen of earlier American tradition (Bayard here cited Jefferson, James Madison, and William Crawford). Their intellectual strength was derived from "education" and "favoring circumstance." In contrast, Clay's "force of mind" owed nothing to such advantages:

> Whatever he is, is all his own, inherent power, bestowed by nature and not derivative from cultivation or fortune.[34]

Clay's natural oratory therefore stamped him as plainer and less cultivated, more American and more democratic than the great leaders of an earlier age. In their insistence on his natural style, commentators may not have grasped the studied art of his powerful speech. Still, their sometimes misplaced assessments served in their own way to register Clay's originality and his importance.

The third common characteristic shared by these frontier stump orators was an emphasis on masculine power. Crockett stood "about six feet high," journalists said, and was "stoutly built," with high cheekbones and a big nose. His hair was "long, dark, and curly-looking," uncombed and wild. Ben Perley, a Washington correspondent, remembered Crockett as a "true frontiersman," leavened by only a "small dash of civilisation." The clerk of the House of Representatives pictured him as "high and lofty," dressed only in homespun attire; armed with a rifle and a butcher's knife; stowing his effects in nothing but a raccoon-skin bag, carelessly slung over a great right shoulder.[35]

Chapman's notable portrait confirms the accuracy of these accounts. The artist placed the congressman not in a cramped studio but outdoors. Captured in an act of greeting or signal, the colonel stands tall. He holds a black, broad-brimmed hat in his right hand, upraised past his head. The left arm cradles a rifle that rises from the inside of his thigh: vast, straight, strong, unchallengeably rigid. He is armed also with a butcher's knife and a tomahawk. It is a picture of command: the wildness holds no terrors. Although twisted branches lay at his feet, Crockett's footing is firm. Two dogs bend to his gestures. Deployed often as symbols of domestication, these hounds are especially compliant, one following the movement of the hat and the other seemingly alert for some further signal. But although the frontiersman has tamed the natural world, a roughness seems to lurk in him, still.

Crockett's nose is arched, and his face has been described as "Indian" in shape. In truth, there seems to be little to differentiate him from an original American native. The colonel wears a linsey-woolsey hunting shirt, leggings, and moccasins. His skin almost takes on the tawny color of the outfit, and his hair appears to cascade to shoulder length. Chapman's Crockett does not belong in the Halls of Congress or even the streets of the city. It is the portrait of a wild frontiersman, seizing possession of the earth and its bounty, but also taking on something of the character of this Promised Land.[36]

John Gadsby Chapman, *Portrait of Davy Crockett.*
(Harry Ransom Center, The University of Texas at Austin.)

Neither were appearances deceptive, for the colonel was justly celebrated for his stunning masculine feats. He was a brave soldier. He fired a gun named Betsy. When the British threatened, he fought for home and hearth. At war with America's native peoples, he directed his fellow soldiers to seek out the enemy. And if he was respected as a soldier, Crockett was even more renowned as a hunter.[37]

"It requires a *man* to be a bear hunter," argued *Sketches and Eccentricities.* If this was the measure, then Crockett must indeed have been something of a man. His memoir kept a tally of slaughter: 15 bears in one fortnight, 17 in one week, 47 in a month, 105 in less than a year. He claimed to have used a gun, a tomahawk, and a hunting knife to kill a bear weighing six hundred pounds. Other species also suffered under his fire. Volumes of *Crockett's Al-*

manack included stories of moose and wolf hunting, the killing of raccoon, bear, bison, possum, and turkey. Crockett reported also on "rageriferous fights" with thirty-seven-foot alligators. Famously, one journal suggested that General Jackson had charged him with the task of mounting the Alleghany and wringing the tail of a passing comet. Another suggested that he could "vault across a streak of lightning" and "skate down a rainbow."[38]

Crockett's real or imagined boasts often emphasized his physical gifts: "I can kill more lickur, fool more varmints, and cool out more men than any man you can find." This superiority apparently extended also to jumping, squatting, diving, and running. He claimed the capacity to "whip my weight in wild cats," "wade the Mississippi," and "leap the Ohio." He could "eat up a panther," "hold a buffalo out to drink," and "put a rifle ball through the moon." He battled with a bear "as big as Kongress Hall." Crockett could "suck away at a noggin of aquafortis, sweetened with brimstone, stirred with a lightning rod, and skimmed with a hurricane." Joining his gargantuan appetite with more conventional racism, he claimed even to have the capacity to "swallow a nigger whole."[39]

As the expansiveness of Crockett's claims showed, manly dominance could also be won with words. The colonel's imposing masculinity was registered in his claim to "outspeak any man" on the floor of the Congress and even to "give him two hours start." His voice was also described in masculine terms on occasion, likened to "the growl of a bear" and the "spring of a panther." Speaking was itself a form of challenge and response, a ritualized struggle for ascendancy. Disparaged as "the gentleman from the cane" when first present on the floor of Tennessee's parliament, Crockett recalled the event as a test of his self-respect; the colonel "popped" to his feet "as mad as fury," put aside the legislative issues ("I don't know what I said about my *bill*"), and turned upon his assailant: "I jerked into *him*. I told him he had got hold of the wrong man; that he didn't know who he was fooling with."[40] In the parrying of attacks and the utterance of such threats, supremacy over one's fellows might be attained. Although a capacity for violence lurked behind Crockett's sallies of this kind, his genuine verbal dexterity served also as an independent means of projecting a manly power.

The battle between the parties could also be understood in these masculine terms. Crockett claimed to "handle the administration without gloves": like a man handy with his fists. When a Jackson supporter began "slang-whanging" for the administration, Crockett "let him have it, strong and hot as he could take." When he rebutted an opponent's slurs, he asked whether this man thought him so weak as to "passively submit" to so many slights: "Did you think," he asked, "that I would suffer myself to be squeezed to death like a mouse, without at least a squeak?"[41]

Stories of insults and challenges, fisticuffs and threats are usually considered somewhat distant from the world of democratic politics. But masculinity was important to Crockett's image and to his public appeal. In the rude republic of the United States, manliness was a means of establishing superiority over others. As one *Crockett Almanack* explained, "Men frequently fight when they are sober, for no purpose, except to ascertain which is the better man." And if strength truly made a man better than his fellows, then it also encompassed a claim to public position and to leadership. In this way, masculinity could become a political tool.

Crockettean literature explicitly muses on the relationship between physical dominance and electoral authority. In the noted play *Lion of the West*, a fight on a Mississippi steamboat ends not just with the victory of a character based on Crockett ("I put it to him might droll") but also with a promise of future political support:

Says he, stranger, you're a beauty anyhow, and if you'd stand for Congress I'd vote for you next [e]lection.[42]

Likewise, in *Sketches and Eccentricities*, Crockett won the vote of a Kentucky boatman only by besting him in fisticuffs. In one issue of the *Crockett Almanack*, the colonel narrated a fight with a stage driver that terminated not just in a victory for Davy but also in a promised new vote. The struggle for dominance is fierce and homoerotic: Crockett's opponent tears his trousers from him; Davy tugs at his adversary's whiskers until his eyes obtrude; the driver responds with a kick at Davy's bowels. As the story reaches its climax, Crockett eventually achieves dominance, but only by grabbing "a poker" that had been "in the fire" and then thrusting it hard "down his throat." Now "mastered," the driver turns from rival to admirer:

Says he, stranger you are the yellow flower of the forest. If ever you are up for Congress again, I'll come all the way to Duck river to vote for you.[43]

Violent and sexual, stories of Crockett's manly virtue were also marked by a revulsion of the feminine. The account "Col. Crockett's Adventure with a Grizzly Bear" claimed that its protagonist "was never skeered of anything but a female woman." Another included a female character with a strong sexual appetite and a petticoat of "brier bushes"—"I would as soon have embraced a hedgehog" as have penetrated her underclothes, Crockett informed his readers. Critics have discerned the frequent presence of "riproarious shemales" of this kind in the stories that came to cluster around the Crockett myth. They have also noticed a regular lampooning of the family unit.[44]

A manly fellow, a dominator of other men, a fugitive from the feminine, Crockett came to symbolize the rough masculinity of the frontier. In his violent and blunt actions, a new kind of superiority was established. If Crockett was no richer, he was certainly stronger. Martial vigor served to compensate for a humble birth. By feats of strength and victories in battle, Crockett asserted a claim to be a better man and thereby a right to rule over other women and men. In the form of the great and powerful hunter, the stump orator could hope to win votes as well as admiration.

Of course, this was not Crockett's path alone. Generals George Washington and Andrew Jackson also marched from battlefield to politics, and both shared a reputation for physical strength. Even in this company, however, the backwoodsman's gifts for shooting and brawling seemed impressive; they were not matched, moreover, by the wielding of command over many soldiers or by the possession of great lands and many slaves. The apparent slightness of Crockett's other claims to authority therefore drew even greater attention to his masculine capacities. In his assertion of a formidable manliness, Crockett helped inspire a distinctive and enduring basis of mass political appeal.

Clay did not succeed as a warrior or hunter. It was only upon the stump that the Kentucky statesman seemed to rise to a more substantial and imposing form. In his carriage and his bold declamation, Clay presented a model of oratorical manliness. Lacking the traditional markers of male power—physical bulk, bravery under fire, martial prowess—Clay established a distinctive claim to political authority through his masculine performance upon the stump. In the exercise of oratorical mastery, Clay hoped to win not simply the sympathy of his audience but also the authority to command them in political manoeuver. It was an inventive and a successful approach. The reputedly masculine character of Clay's style was noticed and commended by enemies as well as by friends.

In Clay's own self-assessment, he had neither "taste" nor "time" nor "talents" for lecturing or ceremonial oratory—comparatively decorative and feminine performances. His preferred arena was the clash of debate or the sustained political address. The speaker's voice was normally described in masculine terms: "deep," "commanding," and capable of wielding "great force." Clay's very brow, it was reported, gave the world "assurance" of the "man." The deportment was "manly." Epes Sargent, Clay's biographer, argued that his subject's "manners and address" were such as to "convey to everyone" the "conviction" that he "is a true man." The great orator's personal style was often linked to the qualities of "force," "energy," and "action," all suggestive of a male strength. "His mode of speaking is very forcible," read one account of

Matthew Henry Jouett, *Henry Clay.*
(Courtesy of Transylvania University Library.)

February 1820. Hearing a Clay speech could be an overwhelming experience for many listeners: a kind of mastering, attained by a potent and unyielding spirit. Clay "enchained" his audience, it was said; listeners would "resign themselves to his will."[45] In essence, this was the achievement of a manly dominance: in the vital force of his imposing style, Clay found a way to reach and to control the men of a mass democracy.

The Kentuckian's style was notable not merely for his effect on male listeners but also for his appeal to women. From the public platform, he often directed his attention to the "fair ladies" and "fair daughters" who flocked to their hero's cause. Clay called women "the fairest and sweetest flowers in the bouquet of Life," and promoters promised his female supporters "how Old Harry of the West loved their faces, and how it was his wont, on many occasions, to kiss the girls." Mawkish and highly unconvincing to later ears, testimonials suggest that this was a method then favored with some success. Female admirers requested autographs and locks of hair. William Milburn related that Clay was "loved by women as no man on this continent has ever been." His apparent popularity with women served to enlist voluntary labor and to enhance enthusiasm for his party and its leader. Perhaps more significantly, it also provided a distinctive form of masculine display.[46]

Like the gallant and flirtatious banter of the ballroom, the statesman's delight in female adoration was a proof of male success. A man loved by so many women was surely someone worthy of respect: in the desire of the nation's women, America's men saw also a confirmation of their own free choice. The importance of female support to Clay's public image as an orator is evident most overtly in the highly sexualized language often used to describe Clay's presence upon the platform. One biography drew attention to its subject's "small, white hand, with its blue veins apparently distended, almost to bursting," moving "gracefully," but with "all the energy of rapid and vehement gesture." Clay's appearance, we are told, was like a "pure intellect . . . brightly glowing through the thick and transparent veil of flesh that enrobed it." Similarly, Edward Parker observed how "the blood mounted glistening" in Clay's "broad, bright face" and the "gushing" of Clay's "burning" brain, as if a "halo hovered round his head." Less extravagantly, George Prentice described Clay's oratory as bringing "opposing spirits" together—"like kindled drops . . . mingled into one." Others gave more attention to Clay's erect and growing form. One later study identified a speaker "aroused . . . to his full height," towering "majestically over his audience," wiry and "virile." Another glimpsed a man growing "taller and taller with every new statement," until he reached "a supernatural height."[47] Not simply powerful or imposing, Clay seemed in these versions to be the very embodiment of manhood itself.

The effect of these interventions was that Clay came to be publicly recognized as a strong man and a worthy leader. Opponents described the Kentuckian as "every *inch* a *man*," complimenting him on his courage, readiness to assume responsibility, and strong will. Admirers celebrated his "sublime manhood" and "unmistakable," if "generously tempered," sense of "manliness."[48] It was from the platform that Clay most exhibited these manly qualities; it is in the contemplation of his public image as an orator that we can better understand the growing centrality of the stump in the establishment of a democratic authority. Without his manly stumping, how could Clay ever hope to rule?

The fourth and final characteristic shared by the first famous stump orators was a willingness to reimagine the electoral contest, and especially the role of public speech, in the quest for power. As already established in the Introduction, the traditional assumptions governing the electoral canvas implied a mostly inactive candidate, downplaying the role of political oratory. Quite misleading, they presented the ideal candidate as a moral servant of the community, mostly mute, summoned from the comforts of privacy (somewhat unwillingly) by the call of admiring electors.

Crockett and Clay rejected this conception of the electoral contest, although they did so in quite different ways. Clay offered the most idealistic reimagination, emphasizing the value and necessity of a candidate's speech. As early as 1803, Clay wrote to the *Kentucky Gazette* in precisely these terms:

> When an individual offers himself for the suffrages of the people, that people have a right to demand an honest avowal of his political opinions. As their dearest interests, their political honor and consistency are placed at his disposal, it is their right, it is their duty to make the enquiry, and he can have no negative right to dissent from it.[49]

It was a position strengthened across the decades. Indeed, as the years passed, the western speech maker increasingly presented his oratory as an exact manifestation of democracy itself. The closeting of high officials away from popular assembly could "hardly be deduced from popular representative government," he reasoned. And it was a misunderstanding of republican principles for a public officer to abstract himself from society or to adopt a "stiff and stately port." Was not a "frank," "friendly," and "free" intercourse with "fellow-citizens" a more consistent and estimable rule of conduct?

I am a "slave of the people," claimed Harry of the West. Their "summons" apparently brought him to the platform, their "expectation" that he address the crowd "I do not feel at liberty to disappoint." Clay would complain that he was "seized" by local committees and forced upon the stage.[50] In these and other pronouncements, he reimagined what others had considered to be vulgar self-promotion as an exhibition of democratic public service. From the heights of the platform, he declaimed upon the necessary connection between a state of freedom and the practice of debate:

> He was a free man, an American citizen, and would go wherever it suited him. . . . [H]e would meet any prominent man of the Democratic party, before the free people of this country and discuss his principles.[51]

From this perspective, every "freeman" possessed the "right" of speaking out in defense of their "conscientious opinions." Accepting that he would be "charged with improper motives," Clay claimed that this was a risk worth braving for the opportunity to perform a public good: in the practice of oratory, he also advanced the Republic.[52]

It was a hazardous path. The acceptance of stump speaking in later years blinds the observer to the radical and risky nature of Clay's undertaking. Kentucky's brightest jewel was excoriated and defamed. A series of abusive epithets summarized Clay's divergence from convention. Robert Walsh, the editor of

Philadelphia's *National Gazette*, coined the most memorable sobriquet: "The Table Orator"; it was rapidly adopted by Jackson's allies across the country. Clay's actions were widely presented as a moral failure: "selfish," "indelicate," "reprehensible," "bad taste," "contemptible," "cunning," "grossness," "coarseness." The language of descent was often prominent: Clay, it was said, "stoops to retail the lowest slang"; he was "willing to descend to the lowest expedients" to attain personal success. To "solicit" a "continuance in office," as he undoubtedly did, was to "forget" personal "dignity" as well as "the respect due to the people." To persist after ejection from office was to forget the "deference which is due" to the station of the president.[53]

The depth of the malediction undeniably damaged his career. But it also drew attention to the novelty of Clay's actions. The secretary had chosen an "unprecedented course," argued the *New-York Enquirer*. In "no country on earth," suggested the *Delaware Patriot*, had the "second man in government" run from "state to state" in eager distribution of "electioneering libels." The *United States' Telegraph* likewise searched in vain for some historical precedent. "Not one of our Presidents has been a great table orator," posited the *Richmond Examiner*. And no previous secretary of state had launched an "immediate public attack" on the "feeling and character" of the succeeding president.[54]

In the identification of Clay's break with tradition, his traducers found reason for his damnation as a man of honor and a figure of trust. The chronicler of stump oratory finds equal cause for the confirmation of Clay's importance to the rising prominence of the stump. The table oratory of public dinners ultimately became a kind of a "system," as one hostile newspaper would note: spouting speeches was rendered increasingly "common" as the years passed. Clay's energy and capacity helped bring about this change. For those enemies who felt his lash, Clay's "system of addressing the people" loomed eventually as an "example" and as a rationalization for like behavior. For those men who toured the country in later decades, Clay served as a comparator and even as a "patron saint."[55] Whether his actions warranted sympathy or condemnation is properly the matter of some controversy. But there is no question that they sustained a powerful challenge to the practice and the culture of American public life.

Crockett's apparent break with established political assumptions was perhaps even more radical and flagrant. Partly, this was a departure enacted by the man himself. More commonly, this was a challenge issued in stories and speeches that falsely appropriated the frontiersman's identity and voice. The Crockett "legend," not the "real" Crockett, most decisively challenged American political assumptions. And yet this was a "legendary" or "mythical" challenge of great importance, nonetheless.

Many of the most famous anecdotes attributed to the colonel concern the process of election itself. In these stories, the character of Crockett tore the veil that had often obscured the struggle for the people's favor; in conse-quence, he also helped redefine popular understanding of what democracy was and how it should be understood.

In one mocking story, "The Grin," Crockett satirized the untrustworthy smiles of questing candidates. In another, he admitted to alcoholic treating (the provision of free alcohol) as a successful means of besting a more elevated and rational rival for office.[56] In *Colonel Crockett's Exploits and Adventures in Texas* (a book long attributed to Crockett, although actually written by another), the narrator relayed his best "tricks of the trade," especially suitable for "young politicians" anxious to set out on the "highway to distinction." The advice was bitter, cynical, and partly tongue-in-cheek, and the portrait of democratic culture, harsh and bracing, bears repeating.

Unashamedly, the old hand of campaigning emphasized the importance of active struggle for office. Crockett urged the ambitious to "visit your con-stituents far and wide." On the stump, he advised, one must resort to bribery: treat electors "liberally" and "drink freely." Although this practice threatened both self-worth and public reputation, Crockett assured readers that this mat-tered little in comparison with the electoral calculus:

> True, you may be called a drunken dog by some of the clean shirt and silk stocking gentry, but the real rough necks will style you a jovial fellow—their votes are certain, and frequently count double.

Women and children should also be courted. The colonel directed the ambi-tious candidate to "kiss and slabber" the children of hamlets and towns, to "wipe their noses" and to "pat them on the head." This would win the favor of the female sex; although women could not cast a ballot, it was still impor-tant to enjoy their goodwill.

Crockett's advice to the orator was even more cynical. "Promise all that is asked," he suggested, "and more if you can think of any thing": roads, bridges, churches, rearrangement of territories, bestowal of offices. "Promises cost nothing," the old dog pointed out, and it would therefore be imprudent to deny them to anyone "who had a vote or sufficient influence to obtain one."

Crockett's suggestions cast doubt upon the moral basis of the republican order. Charity and care for others were considered by most to be emanations of virtue and Christian sentiment, but the colonel yoked them to the struggle for office: "If any charity be going forward, be at the top of it, provided it is to be advertised publicly; if not, it isn't worth your while." The public meeting was an exercise of treasured liberties and an expression of rude democracy, a spon-taneous gathering for the purposes of deliberative exchange. Crockett treated it as little more than an opportunity to secure individual prominence. "Attend all public meetings," he advised, and "get some friend" to "move that you take the chair" or, failing that, be "appointed secretary." In the event of further reverses, fabricate your own meeting ("two or three acquaintances, over a bottle of whiskey") and publish the resolutions ("no matter on what subject"). These devices could win public prominence. And with "your name" introduced to the public, the beginnings of a political career could be established.[57]

When a letter was published in the *United States' Telegraph* supporting Crockett for the presidency, he mocked the ritual by which such public invitations were conventionally accepted. Whereas aspirants for higher office typically disclaimed interest in such position, only to justify an acceptance by appeal to an alleged social duty or obligation, Crockett offered only the laconic: "If you think you can run me as President, just go a-head. I had a little rather not; but you talk so pretty I cannot refuse." Whereas a candidate's letter of acceptance was usually extended into an elaborate statement of political opinions, Crockett suggested that opinions "are not the things that they are cracked up to be, no how." He promised to "go in for *non-committal*," thereby leaving his supporters the liberty to "work the election" as they saw fit. Jackson's successor, and Crockett's likely opponent, was Martin Van Buren, a caucus intriguer renowned for his flexibility in matters of principle. Crockett's statement was therefore a pointed criticism of the prevailing flavor of democratic politics. Indeed, he explained, a refusal to disclose his opinions was the only effective means of opposing the man known as the Little Magician: "Running against the man I do, I can't get along in any other way."[58]

Van Buren's political career was often the pretext for Crockett's dissection of republican life. In *The Life of Martin Van Buren, Heir-Apparent to the "Government," and the Appointed Successor of General Andrew Jackson* (1836), the author—purported to be Crockett—attacked the very worthiness of electoral politics. Why, he asked, did citizens brave "violent angry disputes," risk "getting into a scrap," and break the family bond with the rancor of political exchange? What was it all for? "To elect a man to an office that does not benefit me one cent! . . . to put *Mr. Love-leisure* into a comfortable office, to *keep him from work*, while it does not *lighten my labor one stroke!*" In these interventions, and in others, Crockett criticized the very form of the political process. In widely circulated congressional speeches, he laid into the "political weasels" around him: spouting gas, chawing tobacco, spitting juice, spreading lies, drinking liquor, proclaiming "the good o' the nation," bringing naught but its "eternal bankruptification." They made "five acre speeches" and spread "slantendicular slurs"; they cared "for no one's stomach," save for their own "eternal internals." In popular writings, he (or those appropriating his identity) depicted congressmen as avaricious and self-serving, obsessed with "office, office," deliberately extending legislative proceedings so as to ensure greater pay, and "sadly calculating" their descent from the "heights" of "political dignity" to the ordinary depths of the common woman and man.[59] Such condemnations were then rarely heard from those who aspired to public office; the Crockett legend rested partly on antipolitical sentiment of this kind.

As an unfamiliar politician, Crockett was able to see the world of Washington with an outsider's eye or to serve as an imagined protagonist through which that world might be viewed. In his outrage at the corruption of the republican dream, the voter found a mirror to his own indignation and disappointed hopes. A critic of democratic failure, Crockett was also one of its first beneficiaries. In original and scathing condemnations of what politics had become, the man from Tennessee ironically appeared to be more trustworthy than the noble men he hoped to supplant. From the puncturing of illusions, his own political career was publicized and advanced. And from his frank depiction of democracy in action, the character of public conversation took on a distinctive, if less elevated, form.

Crockett himself left behind no overt disciples. Defeated in 1834, the colonel's abiding significance lay in his capacity to serve as a political symbol. Few had the opportunity to hear Crockett speak, and fewer still to vote for the hunter from the canebrake. Most read of the colonel's adventures and anecdotes in newspapers, plays, novels, and almanacs. A celebrity long before his death on the southern frontier, he rapidly became a legend afterward.

Although those distant from the frontier did not directly enjoy the colonel's stump speeches and unashamed treating, they increasingly became familiar with them through the stories of the man from Tennessee. His memoir became an American classic; ghosted works carried his legend and beliefs across the land. Northern newspaper reviews drew attention to Crockett's "stump oratory" stories; northern journals often reproduced them in part. Not always attributed to the colonel himself, they were also published as expressions of an unknown "Stump Orator," one of those "'half-horse half-alligator' Cicero's of the Western regions." Editions of *Crockett Almanack* enjoyed a national readership until the very cusp of the Civil War. Popular songs paid tribute to his life and career. And melodrama reimagined the hero of the frontier in new and surprising forms.[60]

Not only the subject of explicit treatment over many years, Crockett's literary example also helped foster a continuing current of humorous writing that ridiculed the political process. His influence was evident most obviously in Seba Smith's Jack Downing stories, famed accounts of a political innocent from "Downingville" who eventually rose to become a member of President Jackson's kitchen cabinet. Smith even composed imaginary exchanges between his own creation and the colonel from the southern frontier. At the same time, Crockett also helped inspire those comical "stump speeches" that increasingly featured in elocution exercises and in minstrel shows from the fifth decade of the nineteenth century.[61] Like the myth of the colonel himself, these mocking versions of political oratory retained popularity for more than a generation.

Crockett's biographers have struggled to reconstruct the precise outlines of his life and career. Liberated from the need to separate fact from fable, the historian of stump oratory is instead obliged to consider the circulation and the significance of his legendary form. An upstart practitioner of politics in Tennessee, Crockett was among the very first frontiersmen to win election to state and national politics. But his significance lies much less in the limited successes of his legislative career than in his willingness to articulate a rough vision of democratic politics, defined by the open struggle for power among ambitious white men. In Crockett's career, the stump orator and hunter scrambled for a share of political power. In Crockett's celebrity, the legend of this challenge to American elites became known across the land. Although the colonel himself never attained significant place or position, his life and reputation symbolized the emerging principles of a contested and sometimes grubby American democracy. The stump formed a part of this political world. Crockett endures as its first and perhaps most compelling myth.

Stump oratory emerged not as an abstract practice but as a political tool wielded by particular men. At first strongly associated with America's southwestern frontier, it became widely known across the Republic in the divisive and yet enthralling careers of Davy Crockett and Henry Clay. As practitioners of the stump speech, their successes confirmed its efficacy. As symbols of its meaning, they embodied, for good or ill, the disruptive character of the new technique. In their speeches from the stump, humble origins were proclaimed, demotic speech was employed, masculine power was projected, and the electoral contest was reimagined. In Clay's tours and in Crockettean literature, the assumptions of traditional politics were overturned.

This was a symbolic challenge that would be evident across the United States and in the broader British world, too. As we shall see, the figures of Crockett and Clay circulated across the Atlantic and even to Australia. They influenced the prevailing meaning of the stump speech far beyond Kentucky and Tennessee.

Within the United States, the methods and myths of the "frontier stumper" would be incorporated into national political habits within only a few decades. But how and why were the methods of the stump so diffused? And what were the means by which this broader transformation was wrought? These are the questions that dominate the chapter that follows.

2

PARTISAN ORATORY

An American Habit

Named on the frontier and identified at first with its inhabitants, the practice of "stump speaking" was eventually acknowledged in the towns and cities farther north and east. Its performance outside Kentucky and Tennessee was clearly registered in the election commentary of the antebellum press. As early as 1837, Cleveland's *Daily Herald and Gazette* recorded the "earnest" local adoption of this "south-western mode" of "conducting a political campaign": in a break with tradition, local candidates were now apparently eager to "down horse, and up stump." Two years later, Philadelphia's *North American* confirmed that the custom was "travelling northward," while the *Boston Times*, for its part, recognized this "fashion of electioneering" in the very cradle of the Revolution itself. At the beginning of the century's fifth decade, New York merchant and diarist Philip Hone noted the appearance of westerners and log cabins on the corner of New York's Broadway and Prince Street: "capital speeches" apparently delivered by "gentlemen" of Ohio, Indiana, and Kentucky to loud hurrahs. A number of New England's journals documented the obtrusive presence of stump oratory at this time.[1]

Still, this seemed a political manifestation at first uncertain and possibly ephemeral. Despite earlier reports, the *New York Herald* emphasized the novelty of stump speaking in 1844: "People stopped in Broadway and wondered what it all meant." Nearly a decade later, the *New York Evening Mirror* described the performance of stump oratory "throughout the nation" as a "revolution" only then "taking place." And four years later still, in 1856, *Frank Leslie's Illustrated Newspaper* implied that "stump speaking" was only beginning to reach the North, suggesting that the practice was at this time "becoming more and more prevalent" in the colder latitudes of the Republic.[2]

As one perceptive historian has noted, the identification of novelty was often a prelude to moralistic rejection: if stump oratory was framed as an unprecedented break with tradition, then it might be more easily and confidently dispatched.[3] Considered from this vantage, the narrative of a northern migration might be dismissed as misleading propaganda, an attempt to smear the techniques of political opponents as alien and therefore inappropriate to the communities of the North.

It is a hypothesis worthy of consideration. Certainly, it would be inaccurate to depict northern politics as less democratic or contentious than that of the frontier. On the contrary, northern politics had long been characterized by intense participatory struggles and defined by vigorous plebeian challenge. Respected historians have been inclined to depict the North as more democratic and less deferential than the slave-stained Southwest. And northern newspapers from the early nineteenth century did sometimes record the delivery of electioneering speeches, even if the term "stump oratory" was not at first deployed.[4]

Nonetheless, northern electioneering had traditionally taken on a quite different form than that of Kentucky or Tennessee, and consequently, speech making at first played a lesser role. The greater literacy of the North made public oration less necessary as a source of public information. Habits of organization developed more quickly, as did recognition of "the party" as an acceptable constituent of American life. The career politician and the boss emerged as archetypes of urban politics in those very years when Davy Crockett and Henry Clay came to define the political mythology of the far Southwest. If northern communities unquestionably developed a version of demotic politics, then it was at first more disciplined and less loquacious than the politics of the American frontier.[5] A revealing novel from 1834, William Alexander Caruthers's *The Kentuckian in New York*, artfully conveyed the principal differences.

The eponymous Kentuckian of Caruthers's novel, Montgomery Damon, has been identified as a partial portrait of Crockett. Blessed with broad shoulders and a "quaint, rude, wild humor," he strides the avenues of New York in "home-made cotton and woollen jeans," a heavy riding whip in hand. An inveterate hater of "tories" and "Indians," he is also an admirer of frontier elections. Damon's first acquaintance with the New York variety, however, comes as something of a shock.

Although the southerner's appetite for a "New-York speech" was "whetted," Damon's quest for electioneering entertainment leads him only to a "parcel of chaps" standing behind a "little counter." These are devoted partisans, anxious to thrust electoral tickets into his hands. Upon interrogation, they promise "plenty of drink" and even the opportunity for a "stomach full of fight," should the Kentuckian want it. But the organizational capacity of the urban machine largely renders oratorical persuasion redundant, and no speeches can be heard. "Smash me if I heard any speeches," says Damon, "nor saw any candidates either; they manage them things here after quite a different fashion." One of Damon's fellow southerners, the more elevated gentleman Chevillere, strongly agrees:

> The New-Yorkers never have what we call "stump speeches" and never personally know, or even see their representatives. These city mobocracies, composed as they are, principally of wild Irish, are terrible things.[6]

These are fictional observations, and yet they clearly express a familiar cultural opposition. They are also supported by persuasive contemporary evidence. Newspaper reports of the early nineteenth century often lamented the prevalence of violence and fraud in New York elections. The roles of organizational discipline and partisan journalism were also frequently discerned.[7] In contrast, oratory was much less often identified. And, as we have seen, when "stump oratory" was finally recognized, it was generally depicted as an importation from the political world of the frontier.

Of course, this does not mean that northern communities simply imitated the frontier practice. On the contrary, the process is better understood as one of adaptation or transformation: the particular version of stumping that came to encompass the Republic differed greatly from the simpler form at first identified with the nation's Southwest. The practice had first been described as an improvised means of courting the people's suffrage, and frontier speeches were initially delivered on occasions of routine social contact: market days, militia musters, court assemblies. Stumping had attained wider notice at public dinners organized for Crockett and Clay and in the literature that surrounded these divisive archetypes of the frontier. None of these versions of stumping implied great ceremony: preparations were limited, and organization rudimentary. Indeed, the very verb "to stump" implied a kind of primitive simplicity: the felled tree suggesting roughness and informality. Although it was undoubtedly a break with tradition, the stump oration itself was at first relatively unadorned.

By the middle years of the nineteenth century, this was no longer the case. New political appeals were now launched at special moments of public life, sharply distinguished from the daily round. At mass conventions and political camps, tens of thousands specifically gathered in fields and on plains

to listen to political addresses; their travels and assemblies extended sometimes for more than a week. The thriving cities of the Republic were similarly
overtaken by mass gatherings that spilled out of civic buildings into crowded
streets and squares. These speeches were delivered from elevated platforms,
not coarse tree stumps. Listeners marched in formation, waving banners to
and fro. Bands played, songs were sung, and fireworks illuminated the sky.[8]
Overall, this was complicated political theater, marked by careful planning
and sometimes elaborate choreography. The management of the voice and
the fluency of the peroration figured less prominently than in the stumping of the frontier, for the orator was now merely one player in a grand and
imposing company.

The purpose of the oration was also much changed. Whereas the speaker
had once addressed himself to "Fellow Citizens" of uncertain affiliation, his
auditors were increasingly identified by the marks of partisan preference:
fellow Jacksonians or Whigs, those already confirmed as followers of a candidate and party. Although the quest to reach the undecided did not entirely
disappear, the speaker now mostly aimed at arousing existing supporters from
lethargy and encouraging them to get to the polls.[9] Inclinations were assumed
rather than courted, and exhortation jostled with persuasion. The continental spread of stump oratory therefore involved much more than the political
transfer of a frontier practice: this movement encompassed also a profound
alteration in what it meant to take to the stump and to orate for the cause.

Why was the national diffusion of the stump speech apparently so slow
and interrupted? Why was it matched with such a deep alteration in theatrical form? The answers to these questions propel the historian beyond
individual biography, for this was a process of change neither driven nor
symbolized by a single American politician. In the following pages, I argue
that the extension and transformation of stump oratory was a product of a
complicated mixture of political forces, events, and individuals. It involved a
central dynamic, a jagged rhythm, and three stages. It can be best narrated
through the lives of no fewer than five central players.

The overriding dynamic was the competition of the parties, which im-
pelled persistent acts of invention and emulation, as rival organizations quested for dominance. The historical consequences of this dynamic were jagged
rhythms of political change, as first one party and then another perfected
a new political strategy, only for its chief rivals to bridge the gap and then
develop their own original political techniques.

The historical unfolding of the process effectively encompassed three
broad stages in the national deployment of stump oratory: first, a Jacksonian
persuasion, with which the Democratic Party succeeded over the late 1820s
and 1830s with only limited use of stump oratory, instead exploiting a range

of alternative methods; second, a Whig challenge that succeeded in 1840, partly replicating Jacksonian methods but also combining these with powerful oratorical appeals, so as to develop a new version of partisan stumping; and third, a Democratic response, which incorporated recent Whig techniques and established a version of partisan stump oratory as the dominant American political form.

The nature of this process made the stump orator a more routine and unremarkable political figure, and so a collective portrait is more apt than a singular biographical study. Nonetheless, the political forces at work are still helpfully illuminated by the examination of individual political careers. The following pages give special attention to General Andrew Jackson, Governor Thomas Corwin, John W. Bear, Senator Daniel Webster, and James K. Polk. In the rise and fall of their fortunes, one may also detect the uneven ascension of the politics of the stump.

The most comprehensive study of American eloquence has argued that "the new political oratory" was "pioneered" by "Jacksonian politicians and journalists" in the late 1820s and early 1830s, a claim that has been supported by less notable studies. It is a historical assertion that lacks supporting evidence. As established in the preceding chapters, stump oratory emerged earlier and was brought to public notice by Jackson's opponents much more than his associates. Not only on the frontier but also in New York and New England, the earliest uses of stump oratory were usually ascribed to "Federalists" and "Whigs," not to partisans of the general from Tennessee. Careful examination of Jacksonian campaigns suggests that stump speaking was at first relatively marginal. The electoral machine that supported Old Hickory rested mainly on a range of alternative techniques.[10]

The meeting, the machine, the pen, the press, patronage, and the collective celebration of Jackson himself proved sufficient to win electoral success for the general. Far from a pioneer of new political oratory, the warrior from Tennessee was slow to embrace the method, and his political success without recourse to the stump provided a practical argument against its rapid spread.

Jackson's allies and friends typically preferred alternative forms of electoral appeal. In the quest for the popular suffrage, they chiefly arranged meetings, passed resolutions, and formed committees. Meetings decided upon a candidate, resolutions proclaimed his superiority, and committees worked to secure victory. Although they were obviously conducted through the exchange of opinions and the exercise of speech, such events did not rest upon great oratorical performances. A meeting's success was chiefly established by the size and composition of its attendance, the unanimity of its decisions, and the publicity accorded to its actions. As recent research has disclosed, party gatherings were often relatively small and lifeless affairs, routinely managed from behind the scenes. Supporters emphasized the "large and respectable" status of those assembled; opponents delighted in apparently fragmented or disreputable gatherings. News reports of the 1820s and early 1830s seldom acknowledged that speeches were delivered on these occasions; even if noted, they were still more rarely transcribed. The performance of the orator at first ranked far below the rude facts of assembly and decision.[11]

Neither were those committee members empowered to organize electoral campaigns necessarily distinguished by their oratorical facility. Contemporary observers discerned instead the centrality of the "rowdy" or "professional" partisan: graduating often from prizefighting or gambling and therefore persuasive for reasons other than dexterity in argument or address. David Ross Locke's darkly satirical imagination of the "Dimekrat" Party hack, Petroleum V. Nasby, memorably codified the archetype. Nasby apparently "rallid 2 the poles" from early morning—"bringin in the ajid and infirm" to vote, "knockin down the opposition voters," and sharing alcoholic treats: "No man hez drunk more whisky than I hev for the party," he boasted; "none hez dun it moar willingly."[12] Oratory—even demotic and informal—seemed marginal to this kind of election campaign.

As with the most penetrating satire, Locke's portrait was largely verified by contemporary observation and has since been confirmed by impressive historical scholarship. The Nasbys of the campaign—"petty agents" of electioneering—gathered up the names of qualified voters, tallied their preferences, and turned the screws on those who might be pressured or cajoled. They distributed the "electoral tickets" then necessary for voting, ensured that supporters exercised their rights, and challenged the would-be voters brought forward by opponents. This political contest was most often waged with "bone and tissue" rather than persuasive utterance. Whig numbers man Thurlow Weed was convinced that the shadowy labors of committees greatly exceeded the value of even the most accomplished oration: "a perfect Poll list in each town and ward is worth more than twenty speeches."[13]

In any case, a candidate's appeals were predominantly framed in ink: for most, the pen was thought mightier than the voice. Meetings resolved to publish their proceedings "in the several newspapers." They typically arranged for the drafting and the publication of a written address rather than the delivery of a subsequent speech. Letters, pamphlets, and handbills were widely circulated in the collective cause. Active campaigners considered these publications "combustible materials" or "ammunition" for the battles that raged.[14] In many parts of the country, they were highly favored over speeches delivered from the platform or the stump.

Newspapers exerted a still greater appeal. For the bulk of the nineteenth century, the press was the principal purveyor of political information. A majority of newspapers were openly attached to specific political parties, and new ventures were launched even for the duration of a single electoral campaign. Editors became major public figures; exchanges between them helped construct a genuinely national political network. The most Machiavellian of party leaders identified the numbers and affiliations of newspapers when calculating their chances of electoral success. Local worthies urgently requested bulk copies for distribution to "our most active friends." In private epistles, they remonstrated that "without a press," it was impossible to make "Victory complete"; provided with newspapers, they pledged to "safely meet and conquer" the most despised and vigorous who blocked their way.[15]

Duff Green, a Jacksonian editor of the *United States' Telegraph*, directed the general's first successful presidential campaign, in 1828. Exploiting the reach of the U.S. mail service, he brought Jackson's image and his message to hungry readers of newsprint from across the land. It was, one acute historian has noted, a "far-flung media blitz," embracing a "galaxy" of "strategically located" newssheets. Green's success confirmed the power of the press and the greater facility of Jacksonian leaders in exploiting its possibilities.[16]

In the cause of power, other techniques were as ardently embraced, and their adoption further marginalized the methods of the stump. Oppositions perennially mourned the abuse of government patronage; officeholders seemed less vexed by the bestowal of official largesse. Defeated by what he considered a "corrupt bargain," Jackson had railed in the 1820s against "the influence of patronage" wielded by President John Quincy Adams and his secretary of state. But once ensconced in the White House, Old Hickory soon became notorious for his elevation of the loyal and the untalented to the payroll and for his brutal ejection of those considered Adams's men. "If my personal friends are qualified and patriotic, why should I not be permitted to bestow a *few* offices on them?" the general now reasoned to friends.

Jackson called it "reform" and invoked a classical precedent: "trying to cleans[e] the Augean stables." But the stables of the Republic ended up far from pristine: the number of federal offices rose from just over eleven thousand to a little more than eighteen thousand in the decade from 1831. Officeholders and office seekers increasingly became "the most active agents" in elections for county, state, and national positions. Foreign observers identified the activation of a new and nefarious principle: "to the victor belong the spoils." General Jackson and his lieutenants first used this method to systematically extend and reinforce a national party. In the wake of Jacksonian labors, the parties became "patronage machines."[17]

Political approaches of these kinds were at first counterposed with the techniques of the stump. New York's *National Advocate for the Country* praised the "caucass"—the symbol of disciplined party politics—as a means of keeping out "barbecues, barrels of whiskey, and stump oratory." According to this logic, the "good systems" developed in the North apparently offered protection from the threatened invasion of the southern forms. Certainly, the caucus was widely accepted to be a northern creation, and allegiance to party was considered the "first commandment" of leading politicians from the Empire State. Those defeated by the Jacksonian system did not blame stump speeches; rather, like the wealthy merchant Hone, they bemoaned the "lying," "cheating," "corruption," and "false-swearing" of urban machine politics. Partisan newssheets lamented Jacksonian "zeal," violence ("Jackson rioters"), and fraud. But although Jackson's supporters untiringly attacked the stump oratory of Henry Clay (as shown in Chapter 1), his opponents almost never returned the accusation with some counterclaim. This was a revealing silence, for it confirmed that the general's success was largely won without those flamboyant and open forms of oratory that Clay so capably deployed.[18]

Of course, this did not mean that Jackson's associates in the North or South shunned all innovation. In fact, those who supported the great hero's candidacy organized some important and effective new electoral appeals. But these experiments in mass persuasion rested principally on the presence or evocation of Old Hickory's physical being, not the exercise of his capacity for speech. Alternatives to direct advocacy from the stump, they helped promote the Democratic Party without jeopardizing the muteness and apparent disinterestedness of the leader himself. They represented early forms of image management and collective celebration: this was public display rather than public speech. In the short term, these methods delayed the national deployment of stump oratory. Over the longer term, as we shall see, they created a context for its diffusion and its transformation, too.

"I Recollect Jackson I thought was the Roughest Man in his Speech I Ever hear"—so remembered the bluegrass craftsman Ebenezer Hiram Stedman, himself, one suspects, not the most fluent of speechifiers. The general made no claims to eloquence, admitting in 1826 that "having lost many of my teeth," it was only "with great dif[f]iculty I can articulate." The magnetism and dignity of the hero therefore rested not on the projection of the voice or the grace of the gesture but in a life of national service and in a body strained and even impaired in the Republic's successful defense. Whatever the precise cause— and it was ultimately unknowable—the effect of his presence was tremendous: Jackson's very being inspired acclamation and enthusiasm. "The President is certainly the most popular man we have ever known," lamented the New York Whig Hone; "Washington was not so much." He was "the idol of the people."

Surviving accounts registered a spontaneous popular excitement: the people "pressed forward for an introduction," and "he was greeted by every mark of applause," recorded the *Richmond Enquirer*. Margaret Bayard, a Washington memoirist, remembered the "eagerness" of citizens to shake the great militarist by the hand—so great that Jackson was "nearly pressed to death" and "torn to pieces": "Ladies fainted, men were seen with bloody noses and such a scene of confusion took place as is impossible to describe." The subject of the tumult sometimes himself appeared surprised at his own charismatic power: the "feeling of the people" in contact with him "surpassed any thing I ever witnessed," Jackson wrote to his son from Philadelphia, 1833; "never before have I witnessed such a scene of personal regard," he wrote from New York of a new episode, only a few days later.[19]

Jackson's associates well understood the potency of Old Hickory's appeal and worked to press it to partisan advantage. In the aftermath of his second electoral victory on February 5, 1833, a committee from Hartford, Connecticut, invited Jackson to visit the "institutions of Republican Freedom" that allegedly defined the New England states. His public acceptance encouraged many more invitations, and the first formal and official presidential tour since the journeys of James Monroe soon began. It was an enterprise of "party origin and management," the *National Intelligencer* warned, and subsequent scholarship has confirmed the allegation. The hero was paraded in a barouche drawn by white horses, toasted at grand dinners, and saluted by the discharge of great guns. The streets filled, and Jackson claimed to have "bowed to upwards of two hundred thousand people" on a single day alone. Critics complained that the president was exhibited "as if he were a wild beast." One satire imagined the general's companions as being tired by the continued display: "To be bamboozled about from four o'clock in the morning till midnight, rain or shine . . . if this aint enough to tucker a feller out, I don't know what is." Another comical writer exaggerated the physical rigors of this strange form of electoral demonstration:

> I've got the rumatiz now all over me—I ha'nt had my hat on for nearly three weeks. As soon as we go out, I take one side and the Gineral t'other, and once in a while we change sides, and keep it up, bowing right and left.[20]

But whatever the mockery and the trifling humiliations, the fervor of the people was never in doubt.[21] Although he remained largely silent, Jackson's very presence served to excite and to persuade. Public display proved to be a powerful weapon for the Democratic Party, surviving the general's own political career into succeeding campaigns.

In any case, the talismanic power of the Hero of New Orleans extended far beyond his physical form. The very name "Jackson" was sufficient to attract Americans to assemble and combine. "Jackson Dinners" brought further recruits. Political supporters celebrated the anniversary of the general's triumph at the battle of New Orleans with the discharge of artillery, partisan toasts ("Henry Clay: When he can be elected President of the United States, the Allegany Mountains should be turned into roast beef and the Potomac run whiskey"), and public entertainment. Portraits of the great hero decorated partisan gatherings, and a cannonball found on the battlefield of New Orleans was even presented at one substantial Democratic meeting.[22] Most important of all, the hickory tree eventually became an embodiment of the man and even of his capacity to inspire.

Jackson had received the nickname "Old Hickory" from troops in 1813, apparently as a tribute to his toughness. An American growth, the hickory tree suggested a contrast with the "Royal Oak" of England, thereby associating the general more strongly with the natural life and the equality of the New World.[23] With the bestowal of the sobriquet, Jackson's qualities were more fully defined: the hero was confirmed in the character of indomitability, stiffness, and strength. As the *Pittsfield Sun* showed, the joint characteristics of the tree and the American general could also be interpreted as symbols of masculine political authority in peace and war:

In upright majesty and grace[,] it is distinguished from all other trees. It flourishes in every soil. . . . A species of the Hickory furnishes a wood peculiarly beautiful for cabinet work; and as for musket stocks and ram-rods, both friend & foe have been forced to acknowledge it.—Huzza then for the Hickory tree.[24]

But if the general seemed to embody the hickory, then the tree also came to symbolize and stand in for the presence of the great man. Jackson's supporters could not always look upon or shake the hand of the hero and the statesman. The tree, however, was invariably accessible for public display.

In the presidential campaigns of 1828 and 1832, hickory trees were cut and trimmed in the woods and hauled and raised in city and town. With only a tuft of green foliage at the top, they resembled a pole. Pole raisings had been used to express opposition to the Crown and the love of liberty in earlier years. The French visitor Michel Chevalier therefore compared the raising of the hickory pole to "festivals" of the Old World: "stopped involuntarily" by the "solemn entry" of several "gigantic" hickory poles into a middle-class neighborhood of Philadelphia, he was struck by the sound of "fifes and drums," the enthusiasm of people waving flags ("Hurrah for Jackson"), and the sight of many Democrats "bearing no other badge than a twig of the sacred tree in their hats." The trees were raised at the sites of Jackson Clubs and the centers of Democratic Party campaigning, such as Tammany Hall. But they increasingly appeared elsewhere: one correspondent from the *New York Evening Post* claimed to have been "met by a flag waving from the top of a Hickory pole" nearly "every few miles" of a long journey; in later years, Henry Clay would complain of the "hickory poles" and "boughs" that "obstructed" his travels, especially "when it was previously known that I was to pass on a particular road." The physical labor to raise a hickory pole was challenging and could require more than a score of strong men. Several hundred supporters often attended such events. Children hurrahed, booze was liberally shared, and critics bemoaned the dancing and "delight." But the trees were also used in other political contexts: the coaches and wagons of Jackson men were adorned with "hickory brooms" and "hickory trees" in election season, and when Jackson came to visit, the streets were decorated and lined with hickory branches and boughs.[25]

Campaign songs orbited often around the object, reflecting the identification of leader, nature, nation, and party. *The Pennsylvanian* publicized "The Hickory Tree":

> *Raise high our proud emblem—the Hickory Tree*
> *Which, Jackson, thy country makes sacred to thee;*
> *With rapture we hail it, & hallow the name;*
> *To belong but to Jackson is glory and fame.*
> *All shall yield to the Hickory Tree;*
> *Bend to thee, blest Hickory,*
> *Matchless is he*
> *We name after thee,*
> *And thou, like him, Immortal shalt be.*[26]

In this complex metaphorical exchange, party supporters shared in the qualities of military hero and native tree—Americanness, glory, immortality. The *Vermont Gazette* made the exploitation of national sentiment for partisan logic more obvious, still:

> *Here's a health to our own country's Friend,*
> *The friend of the weak and the poor,*
> *Who never will suffer a tyrant to plant*
> *His foot on Columbia's shore.*

It's good to be grateful and true,
It's good to be honest and free,
It's good to support the Republican cause,
And stick to the HICKORY TREE.[27]

More critically, the *Commercial Advertiser* mocked the deference of Jackson's partisans to their leader and his symbolic form. In "Tammany Pledges," it satirized the bended knees before the hickory pole and the alcoholic camaraderie of the Democrat electoral machine:

Round about the hickory staddle,
In the beer tubs let us paddle,
With the folks with whom we're banded,
Who were born to be commanded.[28]

The savagery of the burlesque disclosed the bitterness of repeated defeat. In presidential elections from Jackson's breakthrough in 1828 until the cusp of the Civil War in 1860, Democratic candidates would be defeated only thrice. The Jacksonian persuasion was remarkably successful. While the Democratic press savaged the stumping expeditions of Clay and Crockett, the Jackson party's functionaries applied their own disreputable and effective electioneering tools. The general remained mute, rendering political oratory at first relatively marginal to his cause. Democrats' repeated victories, secured by these means, helped explain the delayed adoption of stump oratory across the polity.

Why, then, was stump oratory ever adopted at all? Its increasing use was largely explained by the dynamics of party competition, for the regularity of Democratic triumphs did not entail a complete dominance. From the mid-1830s until the late 1840s, the popular vote for each major party was more or less equal. Moreover, there was no state in which one of the parties possessed no electoral strength of any kind, and Whig candidates for president were victorious in 1840 and again in 1848. The closeness of the competition and the significance of the stakes fostered an especially intense tussle for advantage. America's politicians effectively inverted Carl von Clausewitz. If the German strategist suggested that war was the pursuit of politics by other means, then for the partisans of Jackson and Clay, electioneering was war by other means: parties "arrayed their forces" and deployed their "troops," generals commanded operations, "champions" engaged in close contest, and the bested vowed to "keep on our armor" for the battles that were yet to come. Earlier historians have already identified the prevalence of this martial terminology.[29] It was in the heat and clamor of these almost military conflicts that the rise of stump oratory across the Republic may be most fully explained.

Devoted to victory and watchful of opponents, the struggle of one party invariably promoted the countermobilization of the other. If the relative "zeal," "activity," and "management" of antagonists were the best indicators of likely success, then only the most persevering could anticipate a victory. The allegedly "unexampled energy" of rivals therefore prefaced many a call to action. Party meetings resolved that the "exertions," "efficiency," and "energy" of opponents justified "corresponding efforts" among "friends." The *Louisville Public Advertiser* enunciated the guiding principle as early as 1828: "They have been at it for months. . . . We should follow their example."[30] The technicians of mass persuasion quested always after some advantage. In this way, advances in the art of electioneering were rapidly emulated and often as swiftly surpassed. The dynamic of desperate competition drove the use of more direct and unashamed forms of electoral appeal. Eventually, it would compel the adoption of stump oratory. And because stump speaking was pressed into service as but one element of an intense partisan conflict, it was undoubtedly changed by this process, too.

The diffusion and transformation of stump speaking unfolded over several years of struggle and experiment. First, Democratic victories realized with enhanced organization and Jackson's symbolic power incited a review of Whig failure. The lessons seemed simple enough. As Clay wrote to William Browne, the practices used to secure the election of General Jackson appeared to demonstrate the "necessity" of "appealing to the feelings and passions of our Country men, rather than to their reasons and judgments." Clay put it more directly from the stump in North Carolina, 1844: the Democrats had been "our masters" in "employing symbols and devices to operate upon the passions of the people." Another Whig, James Kent, the great jurist of New York, framed the issues more generally:

I find from the Experiences of 40 years in Politics that the more levelling, violent, democratic & unprincipled side of the electoral Contest for Power is generally successful.[31]

These and similar resolutions presaged a transformation of Whig electoral techniques. The prestige of the great general from Tennessee had provided perhaps the strongest basis of Democratic appeals. Seeking their own military hero, the Whigs therefore confirmed Ohio's General William Henry Harrison as their presidential candidate for 1840. If Jackson was "Old Hickory," then Harrison was "Old Tippecanoe," a sobriquet that sprang from military conflicts with the Shawnee. Harrison's more dubious martial successes were now as ardently celebrated, and his glories were extolled in biography and song. This was clearly an attempt to "make a second Jackson," as the *Ohio*

Statesman alleged, and historians have correctly identified a certain mimicry of Jacksonian appeals.[32]

But overall, this was an elaboration of Democratic Party methods, and it is more accurately understood as an improvement, or even a "revolution," than as a simple repetition of the Jacksonian forms. As perhaps the premier historian of party campaigning has argued, the Whigs now employed "techniques" of persuasion and mobilization "never seen before."[33] Whatever hopes were nurtured by party leaders, the general from Ohio lacked Old Hickory's genuinely charismatic power. Popular enthusiasm for Harrison could not be taken for granted; it needed to be sponsored and provoked. To address this need, the Whig Party experimented with original modes of electoral persuasion. The Whigs propagated new campaign slogans and symbols, exploited the power of song, and organized processions and mass meetings of unprecedented size. These, in turn, provided a context for the diffusion and transformation of stump oratory. Stumping only became a central tool of party electioneering when used alongside these important innovations. In understanding the full panoply of Whig appeals, we shall therefore gain a necessary insight into the conditions that made stumping more ubiquitous and effective.

The origins of Harrison's 1840 success lay in an error by his opponents. A Virginian newspaper had dismissed the Ohioan's claims for high office in a rash paragraph early in the campaign:

> Give him a barrel of hard cider, and a pension of two thousand dollars, and our word for it, he will sit the remainder of his days contented in a "log cabin."[34]

Harrison's supporters immediately embraced the derisive dismissal as a badge of pride. Long cast as the defenders of privilege and the opponents of democratic feeling, "Log Cabin" and "Hard Cider" Whigs might now disclaim aristocratic pretensions and project them upon Jackson's successor as president, Martin Van Buren. Seizing the opportunity, Whigs reimagined Harrison's patrician home as a humble frontier dwelling, and the figure of the log cabin became the party's preferred symbol of the campaign. It served as the title of Whig newspapers and the leading slogan of candidates. The technique worked "as the hickory poles did for Jackson," recorded the metropolitan diarist Hone: "It makes a personal hurrah for Harrison." Thurlow Weed, the shrewd manager of the New York Whigs, outlined the stark simplicities of his party's propaganda:

> The log cabin is a symbol of nothing that Van Burenism knows, or feels, or can appreciate. It tells of virtues that dwell in obscurity, of the

hopes of the humble, of the provisions of the poor, of toil and danger, of perseverance and patient endurance, of hospitality and charity and frugality.[35]

Common and simplified appeals of these kinds were not unprecedented, but the unwavering propagation of the log cabin symbol nonetheless appeared to violate expectations; its strident repetition certainly provoked critical commentary. Even Whig statesman Daniel Webster was forced to admit: "It appears to some persons that a great deal too much use is made of the symbol of the log cabin." Alongside press and oration, campaign songs insistently contrasted the rustic simplicity of the general with the allegedly royalist leanings of the Democratic president:

In a cabin made of logs,
By the river side,
There the Honest Farmer lives,
Free from sloth and pride,
To the gorgeous palace turn,
And his rival see,
In his robes of regal state
Tinsell'd finery.[36]

The untiring delivery of the message was matched by the great creativity of the medium: this was the first time when songs were systematically deployed as part of a political campaign, and countless editions of log cabin songbooks were widely sold. Song sheets were also struck off by party workers and distributed to crowds. One Whig operative remembered that the songs "attracted large meetings everywhere" and "awakened much enthusiasm." The New York editor Horace Greeley, another devoted partisan, suggested that the parties were evenly matched in most respects but that the Whigs were "far ahead" in "singing" and in those "electioneering emblems and mottoes" that "appealed to popular sympathies." Historians have suggested that the Whigs' 1840 campaign made the partisan song a standard feature of political contests.[37]

The public procession served as the chief occasion not only for the performance of song but also as a wider ritual of collective affirmation. It would become crucial to the widespread adoption of stump oratory. Clearly indebted to Jacksonian pole raisings and presidential tours, the Whig processions of 1840 were nonetheless cruder and more raucous than anything that had come before. Upward of ten thousand participants were often claimed, in convoys that spread out over several miles. Enthusiastic Whigs carried banners and party symbols: log cabins up to twelve feet in span; ballot boxes, helpfully labeled "The People's Panacea"; representations of Old Tip, "by the side of his log cabin, with flail in hand, the very picture of comfort and kindness." The raccoon functioned as a party emblem, and the caged animal was conveyed in dug-out canoes and exhibited from log cabin roofs. The skin of the animal was dangled from the heads of partisans. Owls, buzzards, dogs, and possums were also displayed, and the national symbol of the American eagle was trapped and presented to Harrison himself.[38] This was political theater of great, vulgar energy. It provided an outlet for popular involvement and a means of inciting heightened enthusiasm. And it afforded a new context for the delivery of public speech.

Whig processions were most evident as the prelude to large partisan assemblies, which were another remarkable feature of the log cabin campaign. Evangelical religions had long gathered at camp meetings and mass conventions as a means of spiritual awakening and organization. Political partisans had also used these types of gatherings for some years. In the quest for electoral advantage in 1840, the Whigs developed these occasions as moments of mass politics. Established often on the sites normally reserved for spiritual meetings, political encampments and mass conventions carried on for two days or even longer. Their basic elements would endure for many decades: the appointment of party champions as star performers; assiduous promotion in the press; the election of local delegates to attendance; sometimes long journeys to camp, enlivened by songs and displays of banners and partisan symbols; frequent alcoholic refreshment; tremendous processions upon arrival and departure at assembly grounds; the rotation of speakers to multiple stands across the meeting; laudatory reports ("without parallel," "a splendid affair," "thronging Whigs poured into the public square"); and inflated estimates of crowds to signal the party's growing popular appeal. Importantly, these and other gatherings also welcomed the presence and even the limited participation of American women.[39]

Whig conventions and encampments constituted only the most extravagant expressions of a general impulse to collective gathering. In cities and towns, the rival parties organized meetings as places of speech and interaction. The custom of assembly had, of course, been established in earlier decades, but the heightened contests of the early 1840s provided an impetus to larger and more elaborated congregation. Log cabins raised in tribute to Harrison's imagined origins in town and city centers served as enduring sites of fellowship and speech—sometimes fifty by one hundred feet in size—and in later campaigns, the Whigs would also establish Clay Clubs and reading rooms and even build large wigwams as places of campaign oratory. Rented rooms also served as party headquarters.[40]

In the late 1820s, political gatherings of some six thousand had seemed to informed New Yorkers to be entirely without precedent, with Tammany Hall apparently "crowded to breathless suffocation" by the crush of the mob. But fewer than two decades later, many thousand Whigs would spill out onto the great boulevard of Broadway itself. Now the national and party emblems of eagle and raccoon looked down at swelling crowds, bands played, glee clubs performed, and a fine silk banner waved above:

> *Get out of the way, you are all unlucky,*
> *Clear the track for old Kentucky.*[41]

The implication of southern invasion was widely considered apt, but no part of the Republic was left undisturbed by the changing forms of electoral appeal: it was a truly national rather than a sectional transformation. Driven by the quest for party advantage, Americans in the North and South increasingly gathered in large numbers to affirm their fealty to party and leader. The convention and the campaign song, the procession and its demotic display, the repetition of party language and its symbols were all established and then confirmed as features of the modern electoral campaign. The adept combination of these many performances was the great achievement of the Whigs of 1840. In this context, stump oratory was extended and transformed.

Crockett and Clay had previously demonstrated the power of the stump speech in the service of self-defense and self-promotion. Not surprisingly, many Whigs were therefore already predisposed to the use of oratory as a partisan political tool. But the joint effort to bring Harrison into the White House created new opportunities for stump speaking. In the campaign to unseat Van Buren, northern newspapers first began to identify the practice of "stumping" in the Republic's North and East.[42]

The new collective gatherings of 1840 required not just the assembly and display of partisan commitment but also the distillation of a public message. Local committees across the Republic courted the most acclaimed Whig speakers. Their celebrity attracted larger audiences, and their proficiency ensured the adroit management of popular enthusiasm. The orator formed a central element of the spectacle. Clay, perhaps the most famous of all, complained: "If I could divide myself into a hundred parts, I could find full employment for each." Daniel Webster, his only rival as a Whig orator, was "pressed so hard to show myself in important and doubtful places" that he felt "obliged to give a strict account, almost upon oath, of my engagements every day." In such hurried times, Webster considered repose impossible: "If I said that I intended four days for a hunt . . . they might shoot me."[43]

Clay and Webster were already the most prominent enemies of the Democratic machine, but the heightened enthusiasm and activity of the campaign illuminated scores of lesser political lights. The careers of two Ohioan politicians—Thomas Corwin and John W. Bear—perhaps most fully illustrate the process by which the party struggle of 1840 propelled the stump orator into a new and unexpected prominence. In a compressed study of their political lives, it becomes possible to comprehend how the practice of electoral speaking was diffused and transformed.

B orn in Kentucky in 1794, Corwin had been reared on an Ohio farm, fought with Harrison as but a youth, prospered as a lawyer, and entered Congress against the Jacksonian tide. When a Michigan Democrat questioned General Harrison's military honor on the floor of the House, Corwin shot to prominence with a coruscating, sarcastic reply. It became a favored campaign document, and Whig congressmen used their free postal privileges to dispatch hundreds of thousands of copies across the land. Corwin's fearsome reputation as an orator helped win him the Whig nomination to be the governor of Ohio in 1840. One party member argued at a county meeting that

> the nominee would be expected to take the stump through the State, and . . . those who desired the candidate to be possessed of "stump talent," would throw their influence for Thomas Corwin.[44]

Stumping for his own election as well as for Harrison, the Kentucky native was diligently promoted by the party apparatus throughout the year. Several "acre meetings" were organized for June 1840, and twenty-nine speaking engagements were advertised for August and September alone. Over the entire span of the campaign, Corwin claimed to deliver more than one hundred "regular orations" to crowds of "at least seven hundred thousand people, men, women, children, dogs, Negroes and Democrats." Man, woman, and dog were understandably drawn by Corwin's gifts as a public performer: surviving descriptions suggest a genuinely funny and entertaining presence. The *Boston Times* identified a "keen sense of the ludicrous," and New York's *Harper's* magazine noted also a beguiling humor, pouring forth from an essentially "exuberant" and "jovial" nature. According to the *Daily Evening Bulletin*, Corwin was simply the "prince of wags."[45]

But although his eloquence was deemed "natural" and seemed spontaneous to many, a political address from the candidate was actually much more than a succession of witty anecdotes. As a congressional debater, Corwin had drawn heavily upon John Milton, Lord Byron, and Edward Gibbon for illustration; he turned often to the Bible in his efforts on the stump. The range of the orator is perhaps the most frequent theme of close examinations: Corwin could move with celerity from the "playful" to the "serious," Ohio's *Scioto Gazette* observed. The *New Hampshire Statesman* agreed:

He will exhibit the sunshine, shower and wild sweeping storm of the human passions. No man can wear a darker cloud on his brow, or more certainly overwhelm an opponent with humorous ridicule.[46]

The evocative notices threaten to sweep up the historian's own enthusiasm and overwhelm a necessary skepticism. But it must be remembered that the newspaper reports that attested to Corwin's tremendous gifts were not the objective impressions of detached observers but rather the vigorous interventions of skillful partisans. Accounts of Corwin's eloquence on the stump illustrate the attempted management of an oratorical reputation at least as much as the undoubtedly substantial talents of the politician and performer. Certainly, not all observers were equally enamored of the candidate's proficiency. Democratic newssheets presented Corwin as dumbstruck and continually bested in debate, "disgusting the people wherever he goes." Such reviews must be set beside the overheated descriptions of those Whig journalists who recorded a "power of eloquence" literally beyond imagination and "excellence" beyond comparison or paid tribute, like the *Cleveland Daily Herald*, to Corwin's capacity to inspire a "breathless silence" among the multitude:

The quivering lip, the starting tear—flushed cheek and the beating heart, told [of] the orator's power . . . as he hurled back the vile slanders of the corrupt and profligate.[47]

The likelihood of slanted reportage is no reason for scholarly lament, however, for the production of partisan stories formed an important element of the delivery and success of any Corwin stump speech. In effect, the journalist and speaker worked in harness, with the Whig orator providing excellent copy, and the newspaper furnishing advanced notice and worshipful reviews.[48] Corwin's sweeping progress across the state cannot be understood apart from the modern machinery of the mass party: the procession and the press, the collective assembly and the panoply of popular enthusiasm. The methods that popularized "Old Hickory" and "Old Tip" also functioned to promote this lesser statesman.

Magnified reports of Corwin's eloquence were matched by additional measures calculated to enhance his appeal. Young Corwin had driven wagons across dangerous and unsettled territories in the War of 1812. Recalling and doubtless exaggerating the courage of these exploits, Whig partisans dubbed their candidate "the Wagon Boy." The image was frequently celebrated in party processions; in many parts of Ohio, it was often found beside the more ubiquitous log cabin. In the town of Warren, twenty thousand watched "Tom Corwin's Buggy" drawn by thirty-two yoke of oxen, carrying some two hundred passengers. At Zanesville, another version of Corwin's wagon was also widely displayed: "rudely constructed" on large timber wheels, inscribed "No English Coach," drawn by a yoke of thirty oxen, and carrying a "fine band of music" to entertain the crowds. Campaign songs also turned the youth's martial adventures into a political parable, as Corwin was presented in the guise of a skilled tracker, hot in the pursuit of his Democratic prey:

> *Tom Corwin the wagon boy, stuck to their trails,*
> *And tracked them until he got close to their tails—*[49]

Later appreciations have acknowledged that the promotion of his boyhood militarism "contributed largely" to Corwin's becoming "an idol of the people."[50] Those who ventured to open fields to experience his eloquence were inspired also by tales of his youthful valor and by the excitement of vast processions that might entertain and divert. The stump orator of 1840 did not stand alone.

If Corwin's actions in 1840 serve as a symbol of the growing importance of stump oratory, then an examination of his career deepens our understanding of its collective production. The speaker's formidable talents were exercised at party gatherings, romanticized in song and procession, and proclaimed by a partisan press. Although he was a child of Kentucky, Corwin's stumping differed greatly from the improvised utterances of the backwoods screecher. This was stump oratory for a party cause before mass crowds of excited partisans. The very forces that promoted the stump speech also embedded it in a quite different political context. But whatever the relative contributions of oratorical brilliance, organizational preparation, and journalistic management, the collective outcome was undoubtedly difficult to resist. Corwin was elected the governor of Ohio in 1840, mirroring the national triumph of his old commander, General Harrison. The Whigs won a slashing victory, and Corwin himself would one day be hailed by students of political rhetoric as nothing less than the "King of the Stump."[51]

Bear's ascent was equally remarkable. Certainly, its origins in the campaign to elect Harrison were more obvious even than in the case of Ohio's governor-elect. "The Buckeye Blacksmith," as he came to be known, was born at the very beginning of the nineteenth century, in Frederick County, Maryland, of "poor but respectable parents." Put out to service with a tavern keeper at age ten, inspired by personal contact with a passing Clay, and driven from employment after a pugilistic victory over an employer's overbearing son, Bear was distinguished by his respect for African Americans, his opposition to slavery, and his determined capacity to master his environment.[52]

The orator's autobiography resembled Crockett's more famous memoir in its sensitive chronicling of the slights and struggles of the self-made man, but it differed in its more sober tone and repeated declaration of principle. In Bear's own words, on the cusp of 1840, he was but a common blacksmith in a small village just south of Columbus, Ohio, the "best posted man" in the county concerning public affairs but experienced only in "small meetings" about the county or in "holding friendly talks" with neighbors and friends. The upheaval of the Harrison campaign provided an unforeseen opportunity for him to exercise previously unrecognized talents. Caught up in the partisan excitement, the blacksmith attended a "grand ratification meeting" in support of the Whig candidate for chief magistrate:

I started with my leather apron on and my face all black just as I came out of the shop, and arrived in Columbus just as they commenced speaking at the main stand.[53]

Recognized by local customers as a naturally eloquent opponent of the Democrats and a "first-rate speaker" at county gatherings, Bear was unexpectedly called to the stage. His address raised more than one appreciative shout from the crowd and provoked vigorous exchanges. Congratulated on his descent, the blacksmith was invited to speak again, this time from the "main stand" of the convention. A still greater triumph led to further invitations to speak from county committees within Ohio, and then he was dispatched to Kentucky, Virginia, Pennsylvania, and New York.[54] Almost by accident, it seemed, his career as a stump orator was launched.

The popular appeal of the boy from Maryland lay partly in his untutored clarity and perhaps equally in his unchallengeable status as a masculine craftsman and small-town shopkeeper. Again echoing Crockett, Bear claimed to know only "a half dozen of those big words that most speakers use" and to offer nothing but "plain talk" to the people: "the plain, unvarnished truth, and nothing else."[55] Personal experience and exaggerated bluntness were blended in performances of concentrated and apparently authentic passion. But now the rough craftsman spoke out not for himself but for the cause of the party and the claims of its platform. The blacksmith's speeches in favor of Harrison were quite literally an embodiment of the Whig Party's promise to offer hope to the respectable laborer of enterprise and ambition. He contributed greatly to its collective success.

The unprompted eloquence of Bear and the serendipity of his public emergence were strongly emphasized by the orator and his party: the apparently miraculous arrival of the "blacksmith stumper" served as a kind of guarantee of his political authenticity. The more spontaneous his speech, the more powerfully he seemed to personify the people's will. But Bear's unprecedented success should not be seen simply as a happy collision of man and moment. The public career of the Buckeye Blacksmith was a deliberate product of organizational design. Bear's tour was financed by the Whigs, and he would receive the greater reward of an official appointment in the aftermath of Harrison's triumph. Party committees passed him from one prepared engagement to another, and leaders furnished him with written documents ("I had half a cart load"). Upon Bear's arrival in town, Whig worthies also provided a full account of the local gossip that swirled around those Democrats who might be expected to disrupt his oration:

> Whenever any of them said anything regarding myself, I would pitch into them on private matters, that would generally floor them.[56]

The blacksmith's appearance was equally rehearsed. The preference for a leather apron might at first have betrayed merely an innocent personal choice, but it soon became a genuine uniform of political labor. Already, from his second major speech in Ohio, Bear incorporated his leatherware and tongs into central elements of an elaborate public performance. In Maryland, he made a horseshoe in the presence of a large crowd. By the time Bear reached Pennsylvania, Whig committees had rigged up platforms with forge, bellows, anvil, and tools, so that their prized champion might demonstrate his mastery of craft and thereby his authenticity: "the multitude could see for themselves that I was a blacksmith." When he held up a horseshoe "as good as any other man in the country could make," Bear remembered that the response of twenty-five thousand people was "the greatest shout of applause I ever heard."[57] This was a success not won by Bear's plain words alone.

Like Corwin, Bear's talents were clearly singular, but his efforts nonetheless marked out an increasingly common path. Alongside the Buckeye Blacksmith, the Whig press also promoted F. W. Kellogg, the "whole souled Tippecanoe mechanic from Pickaway county." Less remarkable orators also claimed to have been propelled from the audience of camp meetings or conventions onto the public stage, their "bosom" apparently "so full of inspiration" that the urge to speak out could no longer be contained. The national press recorded the emergence of "*new-light* itinerant preachers or *exhorters*" in many places at this time. Others also attained an unexpected prominence in the campaign to unseat the Democrats. The roster of Whig speakers in these years came to include what one historian has called an "impressive listing of personalities, none of whom fit a common mold." Nathan Sargent, a Whig congressman, estimated that at least five thousand Whig speakers were "on the stump" in the great struggle for Old Tip and his party.[58]

The structuring force of the party was perhaps even more strongly expressed in the transformation of already celebrated orators than in the emergence of the heretofore unrecognized. Massachusetts senator Daniel Webster was the "star performer" of the Harrison campaign, according to one of the most insightful students of antebellum politics.[59] Born in New Hampshire, graduated from Dartmouth College, and able advocate before the higher courts, Webster would serve in the House, in the Senate, and as the secretary of state to three presidents. In plotting Webster's oratorical accomplishments, we might gain a new perspective on the rise of stumping across the Republic.

Webster's career owed much to the more traditional and restrained forms of public address. In 1825, he won laurels for his ceremonial oration on the fiftieth anniversary of the Battle of Bunker Hill. In the presence of the Marquis de Lafayette, the great Revolutionary veteran general, the Massachusetts statesman had canonized the "distinguished dead"; commemorated the "great public principles of liberty"; and celebrated the "guarded, regular, and safe" containment of Revolutionary enthusiasm. It would later be recognized as a model of nineteenth-century American literature. Five years after the Bunker Hill address, his reply to the South Carolinian Robert Hayne on the floor of the Senate would confirm Webster's status as an ornament of the legislative chamber and perhaps the most articulate of America's conservatives. The speech would become the most widely read political document of its time. Webster's closing words—"Liberty and Union, now and for ever, one and inseparable!"—would ring out across the ages.[60]

This was an oratory of stately and dignified power. Close observers emphasized Webster's "high, broad" forehead, "dome-like" in its vast span—almost a "national ideal of personal grandeur," as one historian would claim. His eyes were described as "dark," "penetrating," "piercing," "philosophical," and "majestic"; his voice was variously identified as "clear," "firm," "deep," "resonant," and possessed of a "thunder roll." Webster's tastes were "very English," and his dress was full and formal. The overwhelming impression he gave was "leonine," "godlike," and "majestic"; the manner "cold," "didactic," "earnest," and stern; the speeches an appeal to "reason" rather than to "feelings"; the language "cultivated" (a model of "exactness"); and the style very different from the extravagance of the backwoods or even the fluency of Clay:

His speeches have nothing of gaudiness or glitter. Words with him are instruments, not ends.[61]

This was a method well suited to the high courtroom or closed chamber but less well fitted to the tasks of popular persuasion. Even his admirers identified an apparent want of "passion and enthusiasm" in Webster's performances. When supporters organized for the senator to address large crowds in New York in 1837, his critics dismissed the address as too "long" and "elaborate," "an uphill effort." The contrast between the statesman from Massachusetts and his rival and fellow Whig from Kentucky did not reflect well on the former, at least according to somewhat slanted press reports:

Mr. Webster is not happy in such popular attempts at excitement. Compared with a speech of Mr. Clay, in the same place, on a former occasion, it was a failure.[62]

A later tour of the western states merely confirmed the impression. Appearing at a frontier barbecue in a buff vest, the embodiment of New England stiffness seemed anything but comfortable. Webster's vaunted eloquence was widely reported to have fallen flat. The *Missouri Democrat* was unimpressed by what it dubbed the northerner's "inflammatory harangues."[63] The *New Orleans Bee* thought Webster's hopes for higher office could draw no comfort from the rush of dinners and speeches:

He has talked a good deal, and been talked to, in the West, but that is all. No one has breathed a whisper favorable to his claims upon the Presidency.

"Daniel Webster cannot be made to 'take' with the people of the West," summarized *The Globe* in late July.[64] When the Whigs came to find their champion, General William Henry Harrison instead took the title.

Suppressing disappointment, Webster worked with much purpose for the party and its chosen candidate. Apparently on the advice of senior Whigs, the orator forswore the elegant speech that had brought him renown and adopted a much more demotic and vulgar appeal. One perceptive biographer identified a changing style at this time; another suggested that Webster appeared to the people in an entirely new light. Drawing on the wisdom gained from his disappointing western tour, the senator's solemn and lofty manner was lightened, his language simplified and burnished with wit. The memorialist of the American Revolution, who had celebrated its restraint—"guarded, regular, safe"—now exulted in the "spectacle" of grand processions, the energy of a "great movement of the people," and the prospects of a new kind of American Revolution, embodied in the Whig campaign:

The revolution should be one which should last for years, and the benefits of which should be felt forever. Let us, then, act with firmness. Let us give ourselves entirely up to this new revolution.[65]

In Baltimore, the legislator of English tastes and the speaker of precise economy now hurrahed for the "hard cider" that he suggested might be a remedy for "hard times." From the platform in Saratoga, he disclaimed the methods of the polished address: "I come to play no part of oratory before you." His speech recalled the "sneer" of Democrats against the "humble life" of the "log cabin" and tried rather desperately to assure his listeners of his own deprived beginnings:

Gentlemen, it did not happen to me to be born in a log cabin but my elder brothers and sisters were born in a log cabin, raised amid the snow-drifts of New Hampshire.[66]

In Richmond, Virginia, the declared opponent of slavery promised that no "General government" was empowered to interfere with "the institutions of the South." In Syracuse, he clambered atop a peddler's wagon to harangue the crowd for more than two hours. In Long Island, New York, the Massachusetts senator responded to Democratic taunting about his wealthy connections with an unexpected and ferocious simplicity: "The man that says that I am an aristocrat *is a liar!*" Stirred by the tremendous cheering of forty thousand, he even issued a challenge to his most persistent harasser, the New York senator Silas Wright:

The man that will not meet me fairly with argument, and uses idle and abusive declamation instead, and then will not come within the reach of my arm, is not only a liar but a coward![67]

It was a complete transformation. The most authoritative students of the American presidential campaign would eventually number Webster among the great stump speakers. Indeed, the New England traditionalist now campaigned with the bluster and exaggerated declamation of the Kentucky tub-thumper. What once appeared as a frontier practice had now become a national paradigm.

Although conservative in philosophy, the Whigs had proven to be true radicals in the struggle for office. Writing from Ohio in the aftermath of

Harrison's triumph, an intimate of Clay's observed that the "political tactic" of stump oratory had now been fully vindicated. A widely read reflection on "stump speaking" at this time argued that "the demagogue of coarse tastes" was not the primary figure to speak "from the Stump"; this privilege went instead to "the accomplished and refined orator" who had leveled "his art" to the "general capacity," "who plays the humorist, and even the mimic, before the multitude." A certain Daniel Webster came to mind. The "secret of the stump-speeching business" lay in the efforts of Whigs to "DESCEND" to the popular taste, and to "COURT THE PREJUDICES OF THE PEOPLE," the *Dover Gazette* agreed.[68] It was an allegation that seemed difficult to refute. Just as the opponents of Jackson appeared to pioneer stump oratory in the South, so they loomed as especially prominent in its national preeminence.

Whiggish prominence does not, of course, imply complete Democratic disavowal. The same competitive pressures that drove Jackson's opponents to embrace the stump eventually compelled the Democratic Party to rethink its original indifference. For some, the bell tolled early: the evident closeness of the 1840 campaign and the nascent success of the Whigs alerted the most perceptive Jacksonians to the need to revise their tactics. Writing from Tennessee in the early months of the election year, Crockett's old rival Adam Huntsman warned future president James K. Polk that the Democrats needed to recruit a different kind of representative:

> Instead of selecting men for nomination of great goodness—a Lady Rachel kind of man, select men who are able and capable and willing to present and discuss the principles of democracy upon a Stump and to do it if needful.[69]

In Harrison's own state of Ohio in 1840, Democrats claimed, somewhat misleadingly, that the "thrilling eloquence" of their own "stump speakers" was "driving the coon skin drivellers to the wall." At the Democratic National Convention in the year of the log cabin, one leader promised delegates that he "would take the stump" and "exhort the people not to desert the principles of their fathers." Elsewhere, Democrats also claimed to have "taken the stump" in an attempt to hold back the Whiggish tide. Historians have recognized the greater prominence of public speaking at party meetings of all kinds at this time.[70]

The hunger to reverse unaccustomed defeats provoked more wide-ranging change. Contemplating their ejection from office in 1840, leading Democrats embraced the performance of stump oratory even more fully: "Our Candidates for Electors should have taken an early and active part in the canvass," one dejected operative advised a party leader, "and have met their opponents upon all and every occasion." Another recommended that although Jacksonians could not "reenact the disreputable scenes" of the Whig campaign in 1840, the party needed to consider taking "the same course as that adopted by our opponents, to bring to our support men who cannot or will not be controlled by the dictates of reason." Remembering the way that Whig "orators" had "patrolled the country" in successful pursuit of victory, Democratic speakers underlined the necessity of expanded operations:

> Let us be organized, vigilant, determined. Let us fight the battle, inch by inch. We must resume the offensive. We must carry the war into Africa.[71]

It was a resolution fully enacted. The Democratic Party settled upon Polk, a former Tennessee governor, an able lieutenant to Jackson, and a redoubtable stump speaker, as its new presidential candidate. Convinced that the "superior organization and industry" of the Whigs lay behind their recent success, he ably cajoled and schemed to ensure that his own supporters swiftly bridged the gap. Contemplating the mammoth conventions for Harrison in 1840, Polk himself suggested a "great mass-meeting" of "the whole Democracy" for 1844, to be convened on the sacred ground that abutted General Jackson's famed homestead, the Hermitage:

> Thousands would seize the occasion to make a pilgrimage. . . . The moral and political effect, too, of bringing together the great men of the nation would be incalculable.[72]

His bold conception was pursued, and the Democratic press would claim fifty thousand in attendance at "Camp Hickory" in August of that election year. Every road to Nashville was overwhelmed with "battalions" of proud Jacksonians, "mounted and on foot, with their bands of music, their banners and their mottos." The camp reputedly extended over a great grove, fifty acres in extent; the dinner table was two miles in length. Democratic newssheets paid fulsome tribute, calling it "the largest assemblage of the people ever convened," "one of the greatest and most brilliant popular gatherings ever known," and a "great encampment of the sovereign people."[73]

But this was not a purely western innovation. "We hear of nothing but great mass-meetings (as they are called) in all parts of the country," noted Philip Hone, from the streets of Manhattan. Democratic orators thundered forth from the portico of the City Hall, from the front of Tammany Hall, from the Hall of

Records, and from many other places. What the *New York Herald* called "small fry orators"—lawyers, "bar-room spouters," and "old hacks"—criss-crossed the city in the hope of holding forth. The *Herald* discerned an entirely new urban phenomenon, as "cabmen deserted their stands," "omnibus drivers stopped short," and passengers "jumped out to mingle with the multitude":

> Such an outpouring of democratic oratory certainly never ascended up to the heavens from the same space of ground before.[74]

The efforts of Whig newspapers to promote Corwin and Bear were now as ably deployed by the Democratic press in the service of its party's leading speakers. When a young New York Democrat named Gansevoort Melville (brother to the famed Herman) emerged as an orator of some talent, his addresses were reported at length, promoted in an "extra cheap edition" of the *Herald*, and circulated across the country. William E. Cramer, another New York Democrat, worked to sponsor Melville's stumping tours. Cramer would write to Polk from the offices of the *Argus* in Albany that Melville was "one of the ablest Stump Orators we have." Subsequently, the "Tammany Hall Orator," as Melville became known, would be dispatched to Camp Hickory in Tennessee, to Ohio, and to New Jersey. Melville returned to the platforms of the Northeast in late 1844 not only with his capacities as a popular speaker vindicated but also with new stories of his time in the charismatic presence of Jackson himself:

> If any thing had been wanting to relume the first of democratic impulses in my breast, the glance of that old man's eye, the pressure of that old man's hand, the patriotism instinct in every line and lineament of that old man's countenance, would have done it all.[75]

The references to Jackson were highly recognizable from the late 1820s and 1830s, but the sustained performance of political oratory was much less familiar. Stump oratory was now more widely deployed in the Democratic cause. Northern leaders of the Democratic Party now proudly informed their southern comrades that they were "fast getting into your southern fashion of 'stump speeches.'" The superiority of Whig persuasion, so recently acquired, was rapidly ceded. "The Whigs complain bitterly that we have stolen all their music," one delighted Democrat rejoiced.[76] Jackson's disciple Polk gained the White House, and Clay was forced to admit another personal defeat. The logic of party competition had driven the near-universal adoption of the methods of the stump.

For the participants in these struggles, the bare facts of votes won dominated assessments and future plans. Striving for success, the overall shape of the election campaign mattered less than the eventual results. Stump speaking merited discussion as a weapon of battle and increasing promotion as a means of securing advantage. Sharing in party triumphs and defeats, newspaper editors only rarely offered wider perspectives. Perhaps for this reason, the diffusion of the stump speech never became a subject of sustained debate. The timing of the spread of the performance to areas of the Republic outside the Southwest remains slightly uncertain; the cause of its growing application must be reconstructed from scattered and imperfect clues.

From the distance of nearly two centuries, the overall dynamic is nonetheless clear. The rise of stump speaking was the product not of a single actor or institution but of a compelling logic of ruthless partisan competition. Stump oratory had emerged on the frontier and had been publicized from the 1820s by its most outstanding and peripatetic politicians. But although Clay and Crockett popularized the form, they did not initiate its immediate spread. The successes of the Democratic Party rested at first on alternative techniques. Only the campaigns of the late 1830s and early 1840s witnessed the more sustained use of the stump oration in the North and the East. Deployed most successfully by the Whigs in 1840 and increasingly applied by the Democrats in 1844, it eventually became an important tool of electoral combat. As the party contest waxed warm, partisans of all kinds took to the stump.

This interpretation is not usually ventured; one earlier study, in fact, suggested that the party system "checked the growing tendencies towards stumping."[77] But the evidence suggests that the contest between the parties did promote the quest for advantage and the impulse to emulate the most successful techniques. Not only that, but the structures and resources of the parties were necessary to the organization and diffusion of campaign oratory in several important ways. Political parties and their functionaries created new opportunities for the delivery of partisan speeches. Conventions, camps, and meeting rooms hosted party orators. Processions excited large crowds. Party networks facilitated the movement of speakers across the land. Their presses advertised, recorded, and promoted the most notable orations for the collective cause. As a result, the migration of stump oratory also encompassed a substantial transformation. Henceforth, stump speeches were mostly made for party rather than for an individual candidate. They were complemented by mass entertainment. And speakers more often addressed existing supporters than appealed to the wavering or uncommitted. If stumping was now common practice, the meaning of the action had substantially changed.

Party operatives did not always recognize the logic or the import of these transformations, but the increasing prominence of stump speaking was nonetheless acknowledged in the work of the writer and the satirist. Over the middle years of the nineteenth century, exaggerated versions of stump oratory became staple features of national whimsy. Their amusing dimensions offered an important historical index of the growing currency of the politician on the stump.

Of course, the habit of stump speaking had been the object of mockery from at least the early 1830s. Davy Crockett's writings and apocrypha served as masterpieces of comical fiction as well as important political interventions; burlesques of backwoods screeching circulated in newssheets and fiction. But as the method was applied more widely, parodic treatments took on a more dispersed geography. The subjects of satire were soon by no means limited to the frontier but instead ranged over the entirety of the North American continent. Humorous writings came to reflect and to consolidate the status of stumping as a genuinely national practice.

Especially from the 1840s, newspapers printed exaggerated and comical stump orations not just from "Wolf's Creek, Arkansas," or other mythical frontier locations but also from communities in other parts of the United States. One parody was attributed to a nameless stump candidate from San Francisco, and another representative sketch showed a "promising genius" of Congress not identified with any state or district. Seba Smith's wildly popular fictional portrait of Major Jack Downing reflected the new political forms. Smith's character had appeared in the 1830s as a small-town Democrat hailing from Downingville in rural Maine. In a series of newspaper sketches and books, he had been propelled into the kitchen cabinet of Andrew Jackson and was thereafter an enduring presence in the Democratic machine. At first, Smith was largely neglectful of stumping, but by the second half of the 1840s, this caustic observer had clearly noted the ubiquity of the oratorical practice. Commenting on the 1848 presidential elections, Smith cast Downing as an itinerant campaigner for the Democratic Party, traveling "all round the lot," sometimes "by the steamboats," sometimes "by the railroads," sometimes "by the telegraph," and, "when there wasn't no other way to go," trudging across the continent by foot.[78] The man from Maine was now a national stumper.

Smith's writings not only were widely read; they also served as a model for Charles Farrar Browne's equally notable character, Artemus Ward. A child of "Injianny" and a veteran of "show biznis" rather than party politics alone, Ward symbolized the emergence of stump oratory as a truly national practice, used in conjunction with a range of other nefarious and persuasive electoral tools. Browne's imagination of a July 4 oration in Connecticut, delivered by Ward, was a withering re-creation of demotic American oratory of the nineteenth century and a sharp description of the repertoire of electioneering at that time:

> Be shure and vote at leest once at all elecshuns. Buckle on yer armer and go to the Poles. See two it that your naber is there. See that the kripples air provided with carriages. Go to the poles and stay all day. Bewair of the infamous lise whitch the Opposishun will be sartin to git up fur perlitical effek on the eve of eleckshun. To the poles and when you git there vote jest as you darn please.[79]

Comedy's mission as a mirror of society was here fully honored. Alongside creative political fiction and its close cousin, the newspaper satire, a range of other popular arts also distinguished the American Republic. Chief among these was the minstrel show, which also reflected the changing patterns of political address.

Conventionally, the minstrel show was a series of songs and comical sketches, performed by a small group of white men blacked up with greasepaint or burned cork to appear to be African American. Growing out of a much longer tradition of blackface performance and resting upon the exploitation of the musical traditions of the enslaved, minstrelsy emerged from the late 1820s as the most popular entertainment of the Jackson era. It has been called the "first American mass culture."[80]

Although not identified in the earliest performances, burlesque versions of political stump speeches eventually became standard elements of a minstrel show, usually appearing midway through the program at the end of the first act or in the middle of the second. A man in blackface would attempt to address the audience on some public question of the hour. His apparently serious purpose would be undermined by verbal infelicity: malapropisms, grandiloquence, tortured metaphors. In the gap between black aspiration and achievement, the white audience would find amusement. A contemporary guidebook outlined the staging and context of the imagined oratory:

> *Stump Speeches* are always very popular, if original in thought, and well delivered. . . . In delivering a stump speech, let your costume be as comical as possible. If you are tall, wear a tight fitting suit, which will make you appear taller yet. . . . Some stump speakers come on in a ragged suit and damaged "plug" hat, carrying an old-fashioned valise and huge umbrella. A Negro stump speech, being only a burlesque[,] admits of any peculiarities you may choose to introduce.[81]

As the overt designation "stump speech" clearly signaled, this form of minstrel performance took the politician's oratory as an object of satire. Noted monologues of these kinds included John Diamond's "Negro Speech in Congress," Billy Arlington's "Labor vs. Capital," and Frank Brower's "Definition of the Bankrupt Laws." Byron Christy's "Burlesque Stump Speech" was perhaps the most renowned example of the form, for it was identified as a "celebrity" performance, widely anthologized, and delivered across the United States. The orator's first words gave a fair sample of the style:

> FELLER CITIZENS:—Correspondin' to your unanimous call I shall now hab de pleasure ob ondressin' ebery one of you; and I'm gwine to stick to de pints and de confluence where by I am myself annihilated.[82]

Unsurprisingly, blackface minstrelsy was a contentious art. One angered commentary in *Frederick Douglass' Paper* described the best-known minstrel troupes as nothing more than "the filthy scum of white society," those who had "stolen from us a complexion denied to them by nature" as a means to "make money" and "pander to the corrupt taste" of other white Americans. Another newspaper even posited an inverse relationship between the performance of blackface and the status of African American civil rights.

Quite rightly, many historians have emphasized the form's reliance on racist caricature and its explicit defense of slavery. The minstrel show rose to prominence just as the struggle for black emancipation also gained in strength. The language of "Nigger Minstrels" was used to mock the organization of antislavery conventions ("clear the track, white folks, the niggers are coming"). The popularity of the form has been interpreted as an expression of white assertiveness and as an attempted bulwark against the increasing mobilization of black protest.[83]

But while recognizing the racial hierarchy implicit in the form, revisionist scholarship has also identified its sensitivity to the richness of African American culture and a kind of "transgressive glee" that subverted accustomed categories and divisions. Some minstrel performances included antislavery themes and arguments. Burlesque stump speeches could be "radical" and "inventive." Their targets included pompous preachers and greedy capitalists. One historian has even interpreted minstrelsy as a challenge to upper-class Americans, encompassing a search for political alliances that might cross the racial divide.[84]

The capacities of black Americans were undoubtedly abused, yet the customs of the powerful were regularly mocked, too. Minstrel stump speeches poked fun at the deployment of national symbols in the orator's more personal cause ("Jest look at de great 'Merican Eagle! Look at him!"), the absence of rational argument ("logically speaking—yes, speaking logically, I see one-half geographically and climatrically, or in other words, climatrically and geographically"), the untrustworthiness of the parties ("de Democrats, de Aristocrats, de Autocrats, or any other *rats*"), the failures of political representation ("We as constituents of our representatives, we find—we find—yes, that is if we're lucky to find"), and the weakness of the stump oration itself ("how many stump speakers know what they'r talkin about?"). A notable minstrel song, "Money a Hard Thing to Borrow," further ridiculed the cupidity of the political class:

> *De polotician stares, office costs a mighty lump,*
> *And de mouf of his purse am so narrow;*
> *It was jest to raise de cash, he got upon de stump,*
> *Findin' money was a hard ting fur to borrow.*[85]

Even if the precise meaning of these performances remains the subject of great scholarly controversy, the appeal of the minstrel show is not open to serious dispute. A "minstrel fever" seized the country over the 1840s, so that it became the most popular form of entertainment in the United States. Through the repeated staging of minstrel shows, the performance of "stump speeches" in blackface became a conventional feature of American life. The "stump speech" was no longer tethered to the moment of election and the enfranchised white male. Carnival-esque capers embedded "the stump" in popular culture and demotic mockery, and the reproduction of minstrel "stump speeches" in literary anthologies carried the texts of these performances further still.

From the late 1850s, popular readers and guides began to include the most celebrated and admired of burlesque speeches. From Robert Kidd's *Vocal Culture and Elocution* (1857) and the formidably named Worthy Putnam's *The Science and Art of Elocution and Oratory* (1858), the custom extended to *Christy's New Songster and Black Joker* (1863), *Beadle's Dime Patriotic Speaker* (1863), *Spencer's Book of Comic Speeches and Humorous Recitations* (1867), and Nathaniel K. Richardson's *One Hundred Choice Selections in Poetry and Prose* (1868), to select only a few representative titles. Oliver Optic's collection, *Our Boys and Girls* (1868), even included detailed instructions on the use of gesture, along with its copy of the short comical address "The Bond Question: A Stump Speech." These minstrel texts were therefore models for domestic entertainment, diversion, and even training. They extended the reach and the form of the "stump speech" far beyond what exponents and commentators might have imagined only a few decades before.[86]

Driven by political struggle, the rise of stumping in the United States was then consolidated by cultural production. If its recognition was slow and uneven, it was also eventually complete. Even for those editors and journalists with their eyes on more immediate concerns, the national rise of the stump orator was ultimately beyond dispute.

As early as 1844, the *Charleston Patriot* was prepared to nominate "The Stump" as a worthy challenger to the more established rhetorical disciplines of Pulpit, Bar, and Senate, and as a "new power in the Republic." The "stump" is "deservedly considered an essentially 'American institution,'" *Frank Leslie's Illustrated Newspaper* agreed a decade later. A decade later still, the acceptance of stump oratory had even become an appealing theme for that safest of middle-brow critics, the Lyceum lecturer. General John L. Swift's address to the Middlesex Mechanics' Institute in January 1868 was revealingly titled "The American Stump." The once regional activity was now reinterpreted as a national achievement:

> The "stump" has become popular and one of the institutions of the land. It had an influence to educate the public mind upon matters of vital interest to our national affairs.[87]

The completeness of this shift may obscure its difficult passage as well as its political significance. First identified and named on the southwestern frontier of the American Republic, mocked and derided by elites, stump speaking had been confirmed as a key element of a distinctive national culture within only a few decades. By the middle of the nineteenth century, American politics was a symbol of popular self-government to the peoples of the world. And the act of stump speaking now appeared as a defining feature of this still strange and radical world.

But would this "American" performance be forever contained by the limits of the United States? Or would the powerful agents of popular culture and political competition propel it beyond the Republic's borders? In the next chapter, I take up the story of stump oratory's fascinating and important transnational career.

3

FROM AMERICA TO THE BRITISH WORLD

Stumping Translated and Reimagined

W hile Americans politicked and "stumped," the people of Britain looked on. The heart of the Empire, the United Kingdom, constituted in the late 1830s some twenty-one million souls; fewer than three-quarters of one million were then entitled to vote. As William Hogarth's justly famous engravings of the mid-eighteenth century remind us, the limitation of the franchise did not imply the tedium of the campaign: British elections were traditionally boisterous, corrupt, and occasionally violent affairs.[1] But what place did oratorical performance hold in this vigorous popular drama?

Traditionally, the British election was organized around "the hustings." The term was used in Old English to denote an assembly summoned for deliberative purposes. Later, it was deployed to refer to the court convoked in London's Guildhall and then, from at least the early eighteenth century, it described a temporary platform from which candidates for Parliament might be nominated and might then deliver an election address. Rich historical studies have disclosed the popular expectation that rival candidates would address their electors from the hustings. A notable satire, "The Election, A Poem," printed in 1701, confirms the performative character of these traditional exchanges:

> *When on the Rostra, as upon a stage,*
> *The Candidates their partizans engage;*
> *You'd think the Hall an Amphitheatre*
> *And these the furious Gladiators were.*[2]

Nonetheless, it would be misleading to equate these venerable public rituals with the procedures of the American stump. First, a British candidate's speech making was generally limited to this particular time and place; the oratorical tour and the public meeting were not initially embraced by the aspirant for office. Second, the political efficacy of the election address was doubtful. Historians emphasize that patronage, corruption, and violence were usually much more effective in a political environment still characterized by a restricted franchise and a culture of deference.[3]

Revealingly, Hogarth's four illustrations that make up "The Humours of an Election" depicted only election entertainment, the canvas, the poll, and celebration; unlike his successor across the Atlantic, George Caleb Bingham, the illustrator nowhere countenanced the delivery of an election address. Likewise, the words of British candidates of the nineteenth century mostly expressed revulsion toward the stump rather than an embrace of its forms. "We do not like a man to be always getting on a stump," claimed one British M. P. on the cusp of Christmas 1866; "Thank heaven," agreed the *Pall Mall Gazette*, the stump was, "as yet," a "purely American institution."[4]

Of course, this does not mean the historical judgments of the most conservative of Britons should be accepted. As we shall see, the words of the *Pall Mall Gazette* were themselves disingenuous or misinformed. The existence of "stump speaking" was selectively acknowledged within the British Empire as early as the 1830s. More importantly, by the 1850s, the "stump orator" had become a common epithet of political combat, its status the subject of genuine intellectual controversy. At the very moment when the *Gazette* proclaimed the stump's "purely American" character, the radicals of Britain increasingly took to it.

This is not to posit a simple identity between John Bull and Brother Jonathan. Proud of their traditions, largely scornful of Yankee innovation, and deeply divided over political reform, Britain's leaders looked upon the rise of stump oratory with almost uniform distaste. It was a judgment reflecting a very different political world. Washington and Westminster systems of government imposed distinctive pressures and implied divergent assumptions. In Britain, the status of the legislator as the representative of a constituency constrained the proper movements of the candidate to a small, bounded locality: the absence of presidential or gubernatorial contests denied the license to range more widely over the land. Moreover, the restriction of the suffrage and the dominance of the aristocracy limited the need for oratory, even to one's electors. And the survival of personal factions weakened the development of mass parties that had made "stumping" a genuinely national, American habit.

In any case, British understandings of the term and the practice of stump politics were at first unstable and far from reliable. As the London *Times* conceded, only the "most outrageous incidents" and "most offensive speeches" came "quickest" across the Atlantic; there, they were the "most repeated" of all news. Even British radicals most interested in the American Republic often failed to understand key issues or events.[5] Britons learned of the novel practice of stump oratory from the travelogues of emigrants and political tourists, the diffusion of America's rich political satire, and the increasing visits of minstrel troupes. But none of these was a mirror of the complexity of republican political life or of its capacity for rational or moral debate. All tended to exaggerate the rowdiness, vulgarity, and radicalism of the American stump. Granted only a partial view of the stump orator, it was not surprising that Britons therefore came to understand this practice in distinctive and perhaps distorted terms. And this perception had important consequences not only for meaning but also for practice: the British stump, when it did emerge, was quite different from the original American form.

The history of stumping in Britain therefore requires a prior investigation of how American stumpers were first identified and described in these distant Isles. And this, in turn, rests upon a close study of transatlantic cultural traffic. In the movement of political tourists, agitators, performers, and texts, we might grasp the foundation of Britain's distinctive political stump.

Europeans traveled to America for a number of reasons: overwhelmingly for economic opportunity, but sometimes also out of political curiosity or utilitarian enquiry. The power of the steamship diminished the great gulf of the Atlantic, especially from the mid-1820s, and from this time, the leave taking and return of migrants became increasingly routine sights. As lavish steamers plied their trade, well-heeled gents joined the more humbly born on quarterdeck. Their letters, diaries, and travelogues soon appeared in the bookstores of the Strand: more than two hundred English visitors published volumes about the United States between 1815 and 1860 alone.[6]

Radical acclaim for an American utopia had illuminated the late eighteenth century, but this interpretation was soon overwhelmed by the contrary view. British conservatives sought to undermine the appeal of the new Republic. England's "aristocracy," it was alleged, was intent on bringing the "stronghold of Republicanism" into common "disrepute." Middle- and upper-class Britons were most likely to publish accounts of their American experiences. From the dawning of the Age of Jackson, the cascade of works was largely condescending and critical. America was depicted as dangerously egalitarian, governed by unprincipled democrats and characterized by the abandonment of decorum.[7]

For the well-bred English visitor, a trip across the ocean quickly confirmed the bitter fruit of universal suffrage: the democratic form of government was a weaker, degenerate version of the aristocratic form. In the land of the Yankee, "election fever" constantly raged, the "politician" had risen to a commanding height, and the "race of American statesmen" had dwindled remarkably in the space of fifty years. Importantly, the stump itself bore much of the blame for this apparent degeneration: it alone had a "wide echo" across the land, and its prominence had nurtured a "vulgarity" and "coarseness" that now dominated American life. The orators of the Republic were "shallow," "rambling," and "abusive"; Manichean in their presentation of a case; unwilling or unable to appeal to "truth," "goodness," or "justice"; exultant in their "rabid passion for aggression"; too "fond" of the word "Republican"; and inclined to substitute its magical qualities for the more reliable guides of "reason" and "common sense." America's speech makers were demagogues. Its elections were dominated by a "peculiar" sense of "rancour" and "indecency." The stump was not a tool of political discussion but a means to command the mob.[8]

Of course, not all Europeans who visited the United States were so opposed to the democratic experiment, and many British radicals remained supportive of the Republic and inspired by its democratic ways. Nonetheless, there is little evidence that even radical admirers were impressed with the possibilities of stump oratory. Thomas Paine and William Cobbett, Britain's leading radical publicists, largely wrote before the identification of "stump oratory" and passed no comment on this frontier form.[9] Likewise, radical Scotswoman Frances Wright won fame for her celebration of American progress, *Views on Society and Manners in America* (1821), but came eventually to reject American "electioneering" ("the very word breathing of vice and venality") and "party politics" (the pursuit of "quarrelling" over "knowledge").[10]

Frenchman Alexis de Tocqueville was the most influential of political tourists to visit America, and his commentary therefore warrants close attention. In *Democracy in America* (1835), the noble emissary found much to commend. Tocqueville recognized a tendency of democratic law to favor "the good of the greatest number"; a propensity for citizens to work for "the good of the state"; and, most notably of all, an incitement of "restless activity" and "superabundant force" among the people of America "never" before evident in the European lands. Nevertheless, this was no paean to republican virtue. Tocqueville was repulsed by the "shortage of guarantees against tyranny" and unimpressed by the disappearance of the "race" of "statesmen" who had won the Revolution of 1776. To the educated European's cold eyes, an unschooled people too often reverted to "hasty judgements" on significant public issues, and hence "charlatans" pleased the electorate more often than their "real friends." Superior men were envied, and the most distinguished were either kept from power or unwilling to pursue political careers. The social benefits of democracy were therefore balanced by the deterioration of governmental competence. And it was this darker side of Tocqueville's interpretation that was most widely taken up in British debate.[11] Overwhelmingly, the stump was understood as a dangerous, venal, vulgarizing force.

The publication of political travelogues was matched by the transmission of American fiction and memoir. Northeasterners of the United States had first learned of the ways of the stump through the real and imagined deeds of Colonel Davy Crockett of Tennessee. Beginning in the late 1820s, the people of Britain also learned something of his amazing and fantastical life. The anecdotes that enlivened *Sketches and Eccentricities* were reproduced in the United Kingdom's press and in the colonies, the book was widely reviewed, and James Hackett repeatedly brought a thinly veiled version of the colonel, Nimrod Wildfire, to theaters in London and the surrounding regions.[12]

By the mid-1830s, the Tennessean stumper was therefore widely recognized. He was, said the daily press, the "celebrated Colonel Crockett." His death, it was claimed, was "as sincerely lamented by the people of England as by his admirers in the United States." One British schooner bore his name, as did several notable racehorses. "Who has not heard of David Crockett?" London's *Examiner* asked in the early 1840s. The *Morning Post* thought his "marvellous adventures" highly familiar to the "English public," and his stock phrases and principles were often invoked.[13]

Significantly, the colonel's feats of derring-do received only a limited share of attention, and his political experiences were as commonly recalled. Stories of Crockett's violation of etiquette at a presidential dinner, his warning to electors regarding a candidate's untrustworthy grin, and his wooing of popular support through the gift of treats all featured prominently in British newspapers. The colonel's apocryphal Texas memoir, including his alleged advice to budding politicians, was especially reproduced. In consequence, when Britons heard of Colonel Davy Crockett, they learned of the stump politics that he embodied, too.[14]

Alongside the colonel, the fictional character of Major Jack Downing also gained some recognition across the Atlantic as well as in the British colonies of Australia and India. Australians even put the character to work as a commentator on local events. Although they were less popular, Petroleum V. Nasby's adventures were also recalled. His "Advice to Stump Orators" decorated the pages of more than one English daily.[15]

In addition to these well-defined American characters, another comical creation emerged to symbolize the new era of mass democracy and to captivate the British world. Sam Slick of Slickville was the product of Thomas Chandler Haliburton's fertile and conservative mind. Haliburton grew up in Windsor, Nova Scotia, the grandchild of a Yankee slaveholder. A colonial gentleman, a judge of the Inferior Court of Common Pleas, and, briefly, a member of the Nova Scotian legislature, Haliburton combined a direct acquaintance with the vulgarities of North American ways with a deep respect for the verities of English tradition. Inspired by the success of the Jack Downing stories, the judge took up his pen in September 1835. But an eager provincial audience also attracted the interest of enterprising metropolitan publishers, and from the late 1830s, his books became London successes, too. Between 1837 and 1840, Slick's first adventures went through nine separate printings; they rivaled, briefly, the *Pickwick Papers* of Charles Dickens. *Blackwood's Magazine* dubbed them the "happiest of all burlesques." "Everybody has heard of Sam Slick," agreed the *Blackburn Standard*, adding, "His sayings have become famous. They are 'GENUWINE' diamonds in the rough." London's *Daily News* invoked an explicit parallel with Dickens's much-loved character of Sam Weller; its *Examiner* claimed to "read him in a roar"; English earls cited him in public address.[16]

At the center of the judge's darkly humorous vision lay a Yankee clock peddler, now traversing Nova Scotia's beautiful British lands. Sam Slick was a boastful nationalist, anxious to proselytize for the superiority of American ways. Yankees, he assured the reader, were "go ahead" people (a revealing nod to Crockett's use of that same phrase): "We rise early, live frugally, and work late." Unimpressed with higher learning ("books only weaken your understandin', as water does brandy"), he purveyed instead the proverbial wisdom of the school of life. Slick's language was terse, cynical and evocative, and herein lay the character's undeniable charm: "It's as hard to teach grown up folks as it is to break a six year old horse"; "I see how the cat jumps"; "The littler folks be, the bigger they talk."[17]

Yet the politics of the clockmaker constantly obtruded. In the eyes of Sam Slick, African Americans were "thick skulled" and "woolly headed," fit for slavery and not much else. The privileges of the male were the inspiration for jarring, violent doggerel:

> *A woman, a dog, and a walnut tree,*
> *The more you lick 'em, the better they be.*

"Politicks" appeared in Slick's world only as a corrupting force: it "grinds away a man's honesty" and "TEACHES A MAN TO STOOP IN THE LONG RUN." Electioneering was a "poor business," marked by dishonesty. Politicians, by their nature, "know how to lay it on." Indeed, although Slick spoke in the rough diction of the common people, he held a remarkably conservative world view. Looking on at the natural and spiritual worlds, the clockmaker discerned a necessary hierarchy that should also regulate human affairs:

Nature ordained it so—a father of a family is head, and rules supreme in his household; his eldest son and darter are like first leftenants under him, and then there is an overseer over the niggers; it would not do for all to be equal there. So it is in the universe[;] it is ruled by one Superior Power.[18]

Political progress did not necessarily tend toward the democratic principle but rather toward a mixture of republican and monarchical forms. Here, the author's mask noticeably slipped.

Under his own name, Judge Haliburton had argued against the Liberal current of democratic "reforms." He believed the English constitution to be "the best that was existing or that had ever been constituted in any age." In this context, it is perhaps unsurprising that Haliburton's famed protagonist rejected America's apparently excessive freedom of speech and assembly or that he suggested that people talk "less of politics" and more of their own affairs. Radicals, he thought, were all "for levelin all down"—"dangerous" and "disaffected." The "true patriot," in the eyes of the imagined clockmaker, supported "existin' institutions, as a whole."[19]

Haliburton's readers were instructed that this was wisdom won in bitter experience. Slick claimed to have served a term in the "Sackville House of Assembly," where he himself fell into the habit of "talkin' nonsense," much to his later shame. As an elected representative, he had been "squashed to death" by the weight of "cares," the requests for favors, and the impossibility of reflecting the popular will: "I was fairly bothered, for not two thought alike, and there was no pleasin' nobody." Politics was an illusory "bubble," comparable to the waters that flowed upward from a natural spring. It benefited only those "hungry birds," the party leaders; its practitioners specialized in "talkin big" but were ill-fitted for the "real world." Taken in the round, clock making, it seemed, was "a better trade by half."[20]

The character of political oratory was the object of Slick's particular excoriation, and here the then unfamiliar concepts of "bunkum" and "soft sawder" were most memorably applied. Both would become common currency in Britain, largely through Haliburton's influence. The former term was coined in mockery of the wearisome speech making of Felix Walker, the congressional representative for Buncombe County, North Carolina, in an 1820 debate.[21] It circulated widely in the United States. In *The Attaché*, volume two, Haliburton transplanted Sam Slick as an observer to the British House of Commons, and there the former clockmaker explained the term to a largely ignorant crowd of Brits: "Well, when a critter talks for talk sake, jist to have a speech in the paper to send to home, and not for any other airthly puppus but electioneering, our folks call it Bunkum." Significantly, Slick assured his auditors, there were bunkum speeches in Britain, too. Moreover, they were overwhelmingly identified with the radical side of the chamber:

> Slavery speeches are all Bunkum; so are reform speeches. . . . Do you think them fellers that keep up such everlastin' gab about representation, care one per cent about the extension of the franchise? . . . [I]t's only to secure their seats, to gull their constituents, to get a name.[22]

Passages from this story were reproduced in British and Australian newspapers.[23] Clearly, the Nova Scotian and his Yankee protagonist had struck a rich and resonant chord.

If "bunkum" was a little-known term in Britain before its use by Sam Slick, "soft sawder" was Haliburton's authentic creation. As a clockmaker, Slick often used the soldering agent to bind up the broken parts of a time piece. "Soft sawder" reflected the Yankee pronunciation of "soft solder"; it could be considered a basic tool of the peddler's trade. But Slick also gave a "dose of 'soft sawder'" to potential customers, promising to convert those who "act ugly" and to "take the frown" of their "frontispiece." Perhaps more notably, he acknowledged that "there's all sorts of ways of soft sawderin'" and identified the "politician" as an especially dexterous practitioner of the art.[24] British press and politicians rapidly took up the term.

Like Crockett, Jack Downing, and their successors, the character of Sam Slick embodied for Britons the jostling energy of the American way. But while his cousins and precursors thrived only in the Republic of the United States, and the three characters were often linked and sometimes confused, the crafty clockmaker differed from the others in making the short journey across the water to the Canadian province of Nova Scotia. His journeys served as a metaphor for the export of American politics and culture.[25]

In Canada, Slick traveled about on a horse dubbed Old Clay, named for the table orator and American statesman ("a prime bit of snuff"); the horse was said to resemble Crockett as much as his more respected southern comrade: "half horse, half alligator, with a cross of the airth-quake." Haliburton's stories also referenced the "hard cider" that had become famous in the log cabin campaign of 1840, and his creation imagined that the British colony might be remade by the policies of Henry Clay. Slick explicitly cited some of Crockett's speeches approvingly ("there was no 'bunkum' in that"). Moreover, Slick rose over the course of his colonial adventures like a self-made man on the make. He was eventually appointed to the high position of attaché to the American Legation at the Court of St. James, and this unseemly elevation prompted new adventures in the heart of the British Empire.[26]

The clockmaker's satirical journeys across the British world reflected quite literally the possibility of successful migration. Perhaps for this reason, his account of vulgar stump politics enjoyed an equally remarkable transplantation to the British world. As we shall see, Haliburton's creation somewhat overshadowed his better-known precursors. And when Britons first thought of stumping, they almost immediately recalled the Yankee Sam Slick.

Importantly, the prominence of these admittedly slight comedies was not merely a matter of whimsy or popular entertainment. Ignorant of the realities of American life, the British mind often confused the satirical with the actual. In consequence, the exaggerated characters of American fiction often came to be seen as reliable guides to democracy in action. There was "reality enough" in Jack Downing stories to show "much that is highly characteristic of America," argued one British periodical. Sam Slick stories were likewise thought to contain "generally sound information," according to London's *Examiner*, and the *Morning Chronicle* commended Haliburton for the "real and useful information" his stories contained: not "sheer nonsense," they encompassed also "a basis of truth." The *Daily News* agreed: although Samuel Slick might "exaggerate," he was, nonetheless, a "creation" from which one "may learn something." The *Sydney Morning Herald* thought the clockmaker was the very "pink of politicians." Not all readers were so credulous, of course.[27] But the willingness to accept the caricature for the careful portrait was to have significant consequences for the history of stump oratory. Mistaking fiction for fact, many Britons came to hold a most embellished conception of the speaker on the stump.

The visits of Americans only confirmed these misconceptions. From the second half of the 1830s, minstrels began to cross the Atlantic, winning almost immediate acclaim. Major companies also toured the Australian colonies and were as ardently embraced there. Impressed by the blackface songs and skits, Britons formed their own troupes. These played to enthusiastic houses; the best-known performers joined a global circuit that encompassed much of the Anglophone world. The American form was adapted in other ways: stump speeches were reworked to include British or Australian allusions, and books of stump speeches and songs were also published for the local markets.[28] In this way, minstrelsy became a genuinely Anglo-American form of entertainment.

Minstrels appeared in music halls, taverns, and saloons, the haunts of the male working class. Rough swells and hoodlums enjoyed the mockery of social elites, the denunciation of politicians, and the defense of raucous living. The hidden theme of "protest" in some blackface performance may also have resonated with the marginalized and disenfranchised members of the British world. Its political effects are difficult to divine. Downcast at the spread of this "pestiferous nuisance," Frederick Douglass thought minstrelsy was an educator in nothing but the "slang phrases" and "contemptuous sneers" of racial prejudice. Historians have confirmed its inculcation of racial stereotypes and epithets, but they have also pointed to a reworking of minstrel forms to mock the pretensions and capacities of the electioneer. Recent studies have established that some minstrel performances in Britain encompassed abolitionist themes or literature, suggesting that minstrelsy's popularity owed much to the rise of antislavery sentiment.[29] At the very least, working-class men learned something of the stump speech through the rowdy tumult of the minstrel show. It may be no coincidence that they numbered among the pioneers of the British stump or that their first performances were distinguished by a vulgar and riotous force.

B y the middle of the nineteenth century, British audiences recognized the blossoming of stump oratory in the United States; many identified this strange flower as a symbol of the Republic's thrusting, degenerate, noisy political life. Overwhelmingly, Britons understood stumping as a debased version of proper public address; they regarded its exponents and admirers as radical, subaltern, and therefore, by definition, outside the boundaries of the formal polity. Perhaps for this reason, the relevance of stump oratory to the center of the Empire was by no means accepted: the migration of the technique across the Atlantic remained a novel, even startling idea.

Thomas Carlyle—translator, essayist, and historian—most fully and momentously challenged this dominant view. Although he was a fearsome critic of the stump, he propelled it, by the force of his denunciation and the power of his reputation, to the very center of British debates. Carlyle defined "stump oratory" more expansively than did his peers, and he identified its presence in a great variety of places and times. Violently opposed to its influence, he served, ironically, to promote its increasing recognition as a genuine presence in the political life of Britain, too.

By the midpoint of the nineteenth century, Carlyle was perhaps the most controversial and admired figure in the life of British letters. The seer of the Victorian age, the Scotsman was a volcanic compound of opposites: a student of the past celebrated for prophetic insights, a hero of the pen who honored the way of the sword, a stonemason's son who translated poets from the German, a hateful scourge of the city who made his home on the banks of the Thames. Even his body seemed to convey a powerful paradox: Carlyle was tall, spare, and rugged, but his hands seemed thin and even sensitive; he walked like a ploughman, it was said, and yet his eyes bore a mournful and other-worldly gleam.

Carlyle had disappointed his strictly Calvinist parents by refusing to serve the church. Still, he wrote in the language of the King James Bible, denouncing the rise of the mechanical age and the triumph of gold over spirit. A worshipper of work, he had married his way into wealth; a celebrator of the heroic, he complained of the pains of indigestion with a persistence more craven than unyielding. Scornful of modernity's tumult, Carlyle himself raved with a furious, repetitive, and unrelenting anger that could be heard even over the babble of the town.

But although tortured by contradiction, Carlyle was also driven by its troubling force. Across a series of remarkable works, the child of rural Dumfriesshire astounded his readers from the 1830s with a new way of writing— charged with symbolism, energy, and invention—a peerless sincerity, and an apparently miraculous foresight. In *The French Revolution*, Carlyle brought his readers into the maelstrom of aristocratic folly and convulsive, popular power; in *Chartism*, he shook polite society until it was understood that their world, too, tottered on the brink. *Past and Present* looked backward to find another way of life. *On Heroes and Hero-Worship* contained a terrible promise of how the world might be wrenched into another form. Although almost unknown until the beginning of his fifth decade, Carlyle was justly famous by the beginning of his sixth. And then, as if to confirm his visionary gifts, Europe blazed with the revolutionary fires of 1848.[30]

What would Carlyle say now? For the Scottish seer, the sound of the revolution and the new voice of "Democracy" were one great cacophony: "monstrous, loud, blatant, inarticulate as the voice of chaos." It seemed but a "species of delirium," yet this was also an important augury. The Age of Chivalry had already passed, and the Age of Hunger come. Now, "universal Democracy" had "declared itself" as an "inevitable fact of the days in which we live."[31]

Carlyle seemed at first silenced by the vindication of his earlier warnings, as if paralyzed by the crash that he had been so quick to foresee. Perhaps the crisis was also personal: his mother lingered at death's door, a close friend passed away, middle-aged recognition brought with it a sense of passing, and fiery ardor and matchless facility were extinguished alike. Carlyle's capacity for empathy—the historian's greatest gift—seemed also to have gone: "All the old tremulous affection lies in me, but it is frozen."

It was a malaise deepened by travel. Departing for Ireland in 1849, the critic complained that he was "very sick in body, perhaps still more in soul." Shocked by the "savagery" of the great famine, and the "ragged coat" of the country, he remained strangely unmoved by the suffering endured by the people—"brawling" and "unreasonable," "misbred" and "gone to waste"—or so they seemed to him.[32]

Returned to his cottage in Chelsea, the famed scribe abandoned an initial plan to write a grand volume upon "Democracy"; Carlyle regarded his own constitution as too "sick" and "dispirited" to begin. He pondered a work on Ireland itself, but this went no further. Finally, the critic knuckled down to a new kind of writing: a monthly series of pamphlets, dedicated to the problems of the present age. Twelve were planned, although only eight would eventually appear. Collectively, they were known as the *Latter-Day Pamphlets*, and they arrived from the beginning of 1850. Their difficult passage was itself a warning of their tumultuous reception.[33]

The pamphlets announced the presence of a central actor in modern history: *The Stump Orator*. The eponymous subject of Carlyle's fifth installment, this creature lurked across the pages of the entire series. Conscious of its apparently American origins, the Scotch historian deferred to "our adoring Yankee friends" to pinpoint a definition. The stump orator, Carlyle explained in his typically elaborate way, was a particular kind of public speaker:

> He who in any occurrent set of circumstances can start forth, mount upon his "stump," his rostrum, tribune, place in parliament, or other ready elevation, and pour forth from his appropriate "excellent speech," his interpretation of the said circumstances, in such a manner as poor windy mortals round him shall cry bravo.[34]

Voluble, fluent, masculine, and commanding, the stump orator was an expression of the democratic age: Carlyle described the new historical figure as a would-be hero, "mounted on the shoulders of universal suffrage." First sighted as a "public haranguer" spouting from a barrelhead and later witnessed perorating on a platform, the emergent species was also glimpsed on "Kentucky stumps" and at "tavern dinners." Parliament, according to Carlyle, was the "highest stump" of all.[35]

Democracy's new child had a complex ancestry. Although the notion that a "Convocation of all the Stump Orators" should be at the center of government was very new ("not seen in the earth till recently"), Carlyle discerned the rise of the stump orator in truly seismic changes in the substratum of public life. First, a "general insincerity of mind" had gripped the people over several troubled generations. In consequence, the "sham-excellent" had come to be worshipped, while the truly excellent had disappeared. The stump orator was a public talker in an age of artifice and deceit, both the product and the beneficiary of a society that had lost touch with the fundamental truths of the spirit.

Second, the principles of education had been transformed. In the "Old Ages," practical apprenticeship had encompassed the slow acquisition of something "weighty" and "valuable": "The thing to utter, here was the grand point!" But this had now been succeeded by an insubstantial elevation of verbal facility itself. The great professions had come to adjudge excellence as nothing more than a faculty of the tongue. "Premiership, woolsack, mitre, and quasi-crown: all is attainable if you can talk with due ability."[36] The emergence of stump oratory was therefore a public expression of a more complete collapse in the means and matter of learning itself.

Still, the deep roots of the new practice did not lessen the danger of its weedlike profusion. From the empty words of the eloquent, Carlyle identified many of the problems of the present age. The stump orator was an "ugly" and "perilous" new species: a proclaimer of "pseudo-virtues"; a "mouthpiece of chaos"; someone "envious," "cowardly," and "vain."[37] Satisfied with appearances, the stump speaker forfeited a "moral life." Offering words "beautifully fit for the market," he stoked the "incendiary madness" of popular rebellion. Propagating the "noxious habit" of talk, he ensured "less and less performance"; for Carlyle, no "grand Doer" could also be a "copious speaker about his doings." In short, stump oratory confirmed democracy as the kingdom of the tongue. If its presence was made possible only by generations of moral failure, its success promised utter ruination. As the falsely exalted talked, so did "destruction and annihilation" loom. Aye, averred Carlyle with an almost grim satisfaction, "the crisis, too, comes rapidly on."

The shock of Carlyle's dark prescience was heightened by his characteristic failure to proffer any real solution. In one melodramatic passage, he pondered hacking the tongues of an entire generation away, hoping that wisdom might sprout in the sudden silence of the butchered society. More sympathetically, but hardly more hopefully, he advised an imagined "young genius" to refuse the rewards of easy eloquence and to find a deeper, harder path to a genuine eminence:

> Be not a Public Orator; thou brave young British man, thou that art now growing to be something: not a Stump-Orator, if thou canst help it. Appeal not to the vulgar. . . . Hate the profane vulgar, and bid it begone. Appeal by silent work, by silent suffering if there be no work, to the gods, who have nobler seats in the Cabinet for thee![38]

The prophet's warning was agitated, insistent, even furious: a perpetual vehemence. As Carlyle's closest students would later acknowledge, the mode and the substance of the *Latter-Day Pamphlets* owed much to the singular extremity of their author's origins and biography. James Carlyle, a stonemason of Dumfriesshire, had built the home in which his son Thomas was born. Although this offspring would later become famous for the confusing thickets of his complicated prose, he aspired to the simple brevity of the patriarch's terse wisdom. Thomas admired his father's practical capacities. He remembered James as a "man of Action," whose "clear" words were like "sharp arrows" of justice. This was the paradigm for all the younger man's later judgments: a craftsman's bluff impatience for the fluencies of idle chatter.

Reflecting his paternal model, the historian's *Past and Present* privileged the "done Work" over the "spoken Word," and his meditation *On Heroes* considered Napoléon Bonaparte and Oliver Cromwell to be the outstanding figures of the preceding centuries. Carlyle despised Samuel Taylor Coleridge for his endless "tawlk" (almost as much as for his gross corpulence); he praised the fearsome Protector Cromwell precisely because his labored and "painful" speech indicated a sincere search for a genuine truth.[39]

Carlyle's fundamental values were deepened by his experiences of the late 1840s. Solicited for donations by the Irish of Kildare, he upbraided the hungry to fight rather than to beg. Frustrated at the use of his reputation by social reformers ("from Swedenborgians to Jesuits"), he longed to affirm his intellectual independence from the patrons of the "good cause." Increasingly courted by the powerful, Carlyle developed an admiring correspondence with the conservative leader Robert Peel. Perhaps tantalized by his new closeness to executive authority, the historian began to regret his earlier decision to follow a literary path.[40]

Certainly, readers identified the caustic extremity of the writing with the dark, unfathomable spirits of their author; most reviewers appraised the man as much as they did his works. Genuinely shocked by the tone of the pamphlets, many of Carlyle's former admirers worried that his heart had "got upon the wrong side" or that his brain was "cracked or softening." Fiercer critics likened the historian to a raven ("forever croaking of evil and predicting rain") or to a "sublime grumbler." The suggestion that Carlyle's analysis might be turned against himself was also relatively common: was not the scribbler himself "anything but a man of practical ability"? And were not his own words a more striking "exemplification of humbug" than any of the objects of his attack?[41]

Less-personal criticisms spared the man yet savaged his arguments more deeply still. Countering Carlyle's stark binaries, the *North British Review* argued that speech was as much an "intellectual production" as it was an "intellectual presentation." The *Eclectic Review* disputed that "doing" and "speaking" were always and necessarily antonymic: "Your hard-worker is often a brisk talker, and silence is quite as often the proof of an empty or stupid mind." In any case, the replication of stump oratory was not just a multiplication of foolishness; many "wise and pleasant things" were said from public platforms, even in mid-century England. Elizur Wright's *Perforations in the "Latter-Day Pamphlets"* denied the apparent "deterioration" of government in recent generations and the supposed agency of "democratic tendencies" in any alleged decline. Wright insisted (ironically begging Carlyle's "pardon") that "Universal suffrage" had ceased to be the object of any meaningful debate; it was simply a "necessity," given the social conditions of the New World.[42]

The notices were almost uniformly bad, and historians have since identified the *Latter-Day Pamphlets* as a watershed in the reception of Carlyle's work. *Punch* imagined the author as a petty criminal, brought before the courts for the offense of being "unable to take care of his literary reputation." Leading reviewers thought the pamphlets were "truthlessly eccentric," "incoherent," and an "unfortunate turn" in a previously glittering career. The Scotsman's status would never fully recover.[43] But if the quality of argument and exposition was by no means endorsed, then the impact of Carlyle's intervention is somewhat harder to refute. The debate provoked by the *Latter-Day Pamphlets* was a major episode in the intellectual life of modern Britain: the scandal of the season, in the eyes of some.

Critics lamented their unmerited "notoriety." Carlyle noted that his controversial words were not just "beautifully abused" but also "extensively read": such a "howl of astonishment" and "condemnation" had "seldom rose around a poor man before." He had his defenders as well as his critics. The pamphlets were reprinted on both sides of the Atlantic and even enjoyed, says one biographer, "something of a vogue" in later years. Journalists subsequently attributed their use of the term "stump orator" to the "illustrious" Carlyle, cited him in their designation of particular individuals as stump orators, and sometimes directly quoted from the great man's writings. If the increasing prominence of the term cannot be definitively attributed to the Scotsman's writings, then the historical coincidence of his pamphlets with its increasing currency is certainly suggestive. So great is the connection that one prominent historian has even mistakenly claimed that Carlyle "coined" the term.[44]

Carlyle's strange pamphlets helped elevate the stump orator into a commonly recognized figure of British political life. They also radicalized and greatly enlarged the accepted meaning of the term. In the critic's hands, stump oratory was a symptom of modernity's wrongs and a contributor to incipient crisis. The stump speaker was no longer primarily an American electioneer but rather any orator capable of artful, misleading, or provocative appeal. Only after Carlyle's interventions did the stump speech emerge as a subject of vigorous British debate. And, as we shall see, this political discussion bore the imprint of the Scotsman's influence and concerns.

Beginning in the second decade of the nineteenth century, Britain's radicals began to speak more frequently to large groups of working-class men assembled in fields and parks. Historians have dubbed the practice the birth of the "mass platform." Its leading practitioners were at first nobly born gentlemen. They orated only rarely in election campaigns or at celebratory dinners, more often speaking as part of an independent agitation for democratic rights. Henry Hunt is widely identified as the pioneer of this style of politics, Feargus O'Connor as his successor of the 1830s (his actions memorably, if misleadingly, described by one historian as "inventing stump oratory"), and John Bright as the last representative of this great dynasty in the 1860s and afterward.[45]

But although the charisma of notable speakers propelled the method, this development transcended the individual career. There was an enormous increase in the number of public gatherings in Britain as meetings went from an elite privilege to a commonly exercised political right. "Open air" meetings became a routine feature of political campaigns, as did "itinerant orators" and political camp meetings. Radicals claimed the platform as a "privilege due to us by the constitution" and asserted a right to meet together in "their own park."[46]

This trend was a challenge to earlier customs, and it elicited widespread opprobrium and alarm. Governments developed new legislation to constrain what they considered to be seditious meetings; cavalry massacred working-class auditors in St. Peter's Field, Manchester, in 1819; and metropolitan police frequently restricted access to parklands in later years. Public parks were "meant for recreation of [a] united and happy people," thundered the *Times*, "not for the discussion of painful questions."[47]

The orators who braved this storm were crowned with a variety of epithets: "demagogue," "mob orator," "waggon-orator," "travelling orator." Sometimes they were described as "agitators" or "professional agitators"; occasionally, their place of speech became a point of identification: "Hyde Park Orators" of London, "Eastern Market Orators" of colonial Melbourne, "tap-room orators" of city pubs. Increasingly, however, a distinctive label began to be applied: the radicals who spoke to the working class were designated as orators of the stump.[48]

Although Hyde Park was traditionally a pleasure ground for the aristocracy, and even a venue for horse racing, it was increasingly claimed by London's poor as the primary arena for mass political discussion over the second half of the nineteenth century. The stump orator was apparently active in the park by the middle 1850s, with speakers even reported to address great crowds "from the stump of a tree." Ever the sly observer, Sam Slick even noted this distinctive feature of London life in *The Attaché*, advising that in "the park," one might "see what's a goin' on" with "those pretty critters, the rads," doubtless "holdin' a prime minister 'parsonally responsible'" for all social ills. It was an apparently faithful depiction. One London daily confirmed the presence of a dozen or so orators in Hyde Park on an unremarkable autumnal Sunday, holding forth to crowds numbering up to one thousand souls.[49]

More rarely, campaigners for democratic change sometimes sought to use Hyde Park as a staging ground for assembly and procession, and an alarmed government attempted over the 1860s to prevent or regulate these much larger gatherings. But such restrictions merely provoked organized and successful defiance; the peacefulness and order of subsequent assemblies won commendation from even conservative commentators. Emboldened, radicals celebrated the "firmness and determination of the working men" and reaffirmed their intention to brave any future controls.[50]

London's *Graphic* lamented that "ill-judged" prohibitions had "unfortunately" granted Hyde Park "a new consecration as a spot for holding brawling assemblies." Gatherings organized by reformers typically clustered around a group of trees facing Marble Arch. One served as the chief speaking place and was therefore dubbed the "Reformers' Tree." Although the tree was leveled by the woodman's axe in the late 1860s, the site was nonetheless recognized in radical mythology. Later campaigners also assembled at this place, which was increasingly celebrated as a "spot sacred to the meetings," a "fallen relic" of the turbulent past, and a "customary" site of assembly. The "broken stump of the Reformers' Tree" was especially recognized in later attempts to defend the privileges of free speech and assembly. In one notable protest, agitators even climbed atop the stump and plunged flag poles into its rotten pith, unfurling a placard: "freedom of speech is the bulwark of our liberty." Historians have emphasized the relative freedom of London's parklands for political activity.[51] This was a freedom won by the stump orator and for the stump orator, too.

As the references to "Chartist" and "working men" in these events indicate (both references were common), and as the orators' attention to the franchise and economic inequality further suggest, the image of the stump orator was explicitly traced out in the language of class.[52] For Britons, stump oratory was overwhelming working-class political speech. When the gentleman ascended to the stump, this movement was the cause of controversy and even consternation; agonized responses clearly demonstrated the violation of political custom.

William Cowper, the president of the Board of Works and the son-in-law of Prime Minister Lord Palmerston, was widely thought to possess this dubious honor of oratorical pioneer. In the lingering days of a London summer in 1860, Cowper was enjoying a perambulation in the pleasure grounds of Hyde

Park when he was startled to hear the sound of his own name. The voice belonged to Samuel Owen, a red-bearded ex-Chartist who made his living as a political speaker. He charged Cowper with all the vices of the aristocracy: lassitude, exploitation, disregard of public opinion. Owen criticized Cowper especially for his reshaping of large parts of Kensington Gardens into a "ride" for the horses and carriages of the city's elite. For the minister of the Crown, this assertion was apparently too much to bear:

> He thought it most manly, when the orator had concluded, that he should jump on the bench and answer, to the best of his ability, the accusation against himself.[53]

Hitting his stride, Cowper apparently continued to vindicate the "equity and freedom" of England and to digress into the subjects of socialism and Chartism; reportedly, he "astonished the crowd" with a peroration that damned "professional grievance mongers" as a pestilential force. The whole incident seemed to Cowper to be a "proper and manly course," and he did win credit from some observers for his "English manliness" and "pluck." But the minister was mocked in the House of Commons for his "harangue," and his self-exonerations were met with laughter. *Reynolds's Newspaper* titled one account of these events "A Minister on the Stump," and another claimed, perhaps ironically, that a kind of historical significance was evident in these unusual events:

> A red mark in the calendar is surely due to that day which witnessed the public and unquestionable inauguration of aristocratic stump-oratory in England. . . . [N]ot, that we are aware of, until the above-mentioned day, was a truly liberal and undeniable "stump" mounted by a genuine and unimpeachable sprig of Great British nobility.[54]

One correspondent for the American press was equally impressed with the originality of Cowper's conduct. It was, said the *Daily National Intelligencer*, a "new feature of the times" for a "member of the Government" to be found "playing the part of a stump orator to a crowd in Hyde Park." The spontaneous ebullitions of the minister implied that, as in America, stump oratory would not always remain the sole preserve of the humbly born. But the outraged reaction of many chastened Cowper and elicited an apology: "If he had committed an impudence[,] he was sorry for it."[55] For the moment, at least, stump oratory was most strongly associated with the dangerous, untutored eloquence of an excluded and questing working class.

Britain's Australian colonies shared in the influence of Slick, Downing, and minstrelsy; they differed from the motherland in the absence of estab-

lished hierarchies, the capacity for rapid social elevation, and the relative open-
ness of the electoral franchise. The major colonies in the Southeast of the
continent won responsible government from Britain over the 1850s; their colonial constitutions or reforms soon afterward abolished property qualifications
for voting and representation and pioneered the secret ballot. One historian
has likened them to the frontiers of a Greater Britain: spaces of indigenous
expropriation, economic speculation, dizzying expansion, and popular self-
government.[56]

Contemporaries also noted the American resemblances. As early as the
1840s, London's dailies had already prophesied that the colonies of the New
World were "American" in character and "not English" in "modes of thought
and action." Locals admitted that their society was marked by an "effervescent
state." The portrait seemed especially to fit the colony of Victoria: formally
separated from its older sibling of New South Wales in 1851, overwhelmed by
a gold rush soon afterward, and shocked by a political conflict in 1854—the
Eureka rebellion—that left scores of disaffected miners dead or wounded. To
foreign visitors of the mid-1850s, Victoria seemed bound to "take the lead"
in any future "courageous experiment." The British radical Sir Charles Dilke
would later dub it "the leader in the democratic and State-socialistic movements." For the *Times* of London, it constituted "a sort of experimentum in
corpore vili" for "testing the precise value" of "manhood suffrage": "where," it
asked, "has that principle had freer scope or fairer play"?[57]

Given these conditions, it is perhaps unsurprising that local newssheets
rapidly took up the language of "bunkum" and "soft sawder," that elected
representatives liberally quoted Sam Slick, or that the gold seekers who struggled for popular rights admitted that they spoke "from the stump" when
planning their rebellious deeds. Victoria's governor, for his part, mourned the
influence of "professional Agitators" and "promoters of sedition."[58]

For many years, the label of "stump orator" maintained a close association in Australian minds with "universal suffrage" and "the diggings."[59] Still,
campaigners for reform to the land laws were soon more frequently described
in these dismissive terms. The Chartists of England and the radicals of Ireland had championed the cause of land reform in the British Isles, and the
apparent security of a small family plot continued to charm in the new country. But much of the most arable and accessible land had been seized from
indigenous people, claimed by squatters, or granted by government. A new
land law that guaranteed "free selection" to the enterprising migrant therefore
became a wildly popular claim.

In the "Eastern Market," on the hill that led up to the Victorian Parliament in Melbourne, orators first gathered to prosecute the agrarian cause.
The market was a kind of urban emporium: purveyors of fruits, vegetables,

fish, poultry, and meat were surrounded by vendors equally anxious to provide cutlery, puzzles, newspapers, ironmongery, and soft goods. In the late 1850s, Melbourne's press began to record "clamorous proceedings" as stump orators gathered there to address the demands of the unemployed. Within only a few years, it had become the central arena of a large and threatening campaign for land.[60]

Public meetings were held almost nightly at the peak of the agitation. The "very name" of "Eastern Market" seemed to summon up the image of the "stump." One satire from *Melbourne Punch* advertised "Good useful claptrap for the Eastern Market" and "Full flavoured stump oration, rich in quality," courtesy of the "General Speech, Address and Letter Composing Company." Another expressed pity for the masses who gathered:

> *When other Eastern-market dons are blustering,*
> *Braying like donkeys till their throats are sore,*
> *We've only pity for the crowd they're flustering*
> *With bosh and nonsense, "voice and nothing more."*

A third advised radicals, somewhat impatiently, to abandon the practice:

> *Burn your stump to ashes,*
> *And let no more be said.*[61]

Melbourne's *Argus* had supported the earlier demands of the diggers but took fright at the clamor. The "prophets of the stump" it now dismissed as "evil soothsayers and lazy malcontents"; nearly all who took part in the land movement were crowned with the scornful epithet. Intercolonial observers apparently agreed. Correspondents to Brisbane's *Courier* lamented the rise of "the inflated oratory of the Eastern Market and the 'stump.'" The *Sydney Morning Herald* could not "help being struck" by the "troublesome and dangerous element" that the "stump orator fraternity constitutes in a young community such as ours."[62]

As pained commentaries noted, the practice of stump speaking was widely shared. Nonetheless, one man especially symbolized the dangers of the radical technique. Charles Jardine Don was a stonemason hailing originally from Perthshire, Scotland, and an exponent of Chartist principles. His five feet and three inches belied his immense lung power; his unorthodox dress (a "turn-down collar," "thrown-off hair," and "jerked-back frock"), said the *Argus*, suggested a "cross between the poet and the pirate"—the dangerous poet, Byron, and a "marauder," with the latter, perhaps, "slightly predominating." A "dark visage" and a reportedly "egotistical" manner doubtless contributed to the powerful unorthodoxy. The *Argus* called him "our magniloquent stump orator," and the *Melbourne Punch* referred to him as a "stump Demosthenes." For the *South Australian Register*, he was the "incarnation of our democracy."[63]

Rising to prominence in the Eastern Market, he won election to the Victorian Legislative Assembly in 1859. There, he addressed the House as "one of a class hitherto unrepresented in any legislature within the British Empire." Hostile scribes detected an unfitting demeanor for the parliamentary chamber, as the habit of the stump orator predominated over the established conventions of legislative deliberation:

> In a little while Mr. Don was, imaginatively, on the democratic stump; his voice rose, his speed increased, and soon he shouted, screamed, bellowed, bullied, always talking with some point and ability, but with such a chaos of confused sentences, and with such abominable boisterousness and savagery of manner, that the House and galleries stopped their ears, shuddered, and shrank away from the tornado of the people's man. It was the fury and frenzy of Feargus O'Connorism, of the most exaggerated kind, revived.[64]

The *Melbourne Punch* excoriated his infection with "class prejudices" and absence of the "discipline" and "self-control" that the acquisition of knowledge legated to the more "educated" man. It mocked his low origins in one satire that imagined the stonemason upraised to the Peerage: "Baron Chippinstone and Tavernhouse, of the 'Stump,' in the County of Bedlam." Another rhyme drew attention to the democrat's dangerous flirtation with the passions of the mob:

> *A mob's sweet cheer will buy your voice*
> *At once from outraged common sense,*
> *To be declared the people's choice,*
> *You'd hesitate at no offence.*[65]

Don's fellow parliamentarians shared in the disdain, sometimes directly recalling Carlyle's favored epithet, "stump orator." Significantly, however, the proud artisan did not seem to cower before the slur. In one parliamentary debate, he rejected his accuser as "utterly ignorant of the nature of the term 'stump orator' . . . as he is of everything else." Don went on to advise "the honoured gentlemen," doubtless with a grin, that before speaking of stump oratory again, "it would be well for him to read the works of Sam Slick"; these would impart "more philosophy and sound sense" than "all the law he had learned in his life." The stonemason concluded the exchange by disclaiming the identity: "He was no stump orator: he was no orator at all."[66] In other situations, however, Don seemed quite happy to embrace the term.

Addressing perhaps the largest meeting that had ever assembled in Melbourne, at the Eastern Market in early June 1860, Don assured his audiences that "the star of the stump was rising, whilst the star of the *Argus* [newspaper] was setting (*loud cheering*)." His language, he admitted, "might not be parliamentary," but "he was in the Eastern Market now. (*Cheers and laughter.*) But if he was in the House, he would repeat it again and again." In a communication with Melbourne's unionists, he reaffirmed that "he would not be bound by the antiquated notions of the old country," and neither would he change his "dress," "phraseology," or "principles"; he would "continue to agitate questions favourable to the class to which he belonged." In Parliament in April 1860, Don went further still. When an opponent looked forward to the extinguishment of stump oratory, the Chartist of Perthshire rose to his feet. Don claimed he knew "perfectly well" what the honorable member meant by "the expression"; unashamedly, he seemed to embrace the term:

> Every member of the advanced portion of the working classes who spent his leisure in the Public Library, or in reading at home, and thereby making himself acquainted with the great political principles of the day, whenever he went and talked to his fellow-workmen was called a "stump orator."[67]

For Don, these were the shapers of public opinion in a democracy: "the very men who laid the foundation of laws which this House carried into effect." Although they exhibited an admitted "roughness," this did not impair the "common sense" and "sterling thoughts" that served as a "strong foundation of truth." These were men "more unselfish" and in some senses more able than other politicians: those who "cast their sneers" had not "brain enough" to become stump orators; they "had not sufficient intelligence to win the respect that a stump orator must command." Inverting his illustrious countrymen, the Scotland native therefore directly contradicted the strictures that Carlyle had first introduced, saying that the people should not stop their ears against the babbling of stump orators; on the contrary, he said:

> Just as far as the people observed these thoughts were they wise and intelligent; and just as they attended to other things were they ignorant.[68]

The utterance received great and merited attention in Melbourne's press. *Punch* ridiculed the stonemason's defense of "his darling 'stump,' the honored

institution, that had raised him from the obscurity of his native manure heap."
The *Argus* similarly mocked the Scottish artisan's tendency to set "The Stump"
above "all our altars" as the "shrine of wisdom" and "home of political virtue."[69]
Significantly, however, the radical's unblushing and spirited defense
prompted a surprising concession that stump oratory did not merit complete
and unreserved dismissal. For the first time, the Melbourne daily admitted that "the stump" could be found "among all the peoples" of the world
marked by "freedom of speech" and "activity of character." This was a relatively permanent feature of democracy, and its presence was not necessarily
to be mourned:

> Among ourselves, if the Stump has declined in dignity and in useful-
> ness, it is still liable to fits of activity, which render it a power in the
> state. And we should be sorry to see it altogether abolished in this
> colony. We are content to accept it as one of the fixed stage properties
> in that eccentric drama which is implied in popular government.[70]

It was a judgment often contradicted by colonial conservatives in later
years. Nonetheless, it marked a more general recognition that the identity
of "stump orator" need not be a source of political shame. Alongside Don,
one colonial radical declared to a crowd of two thousand that "he was not
ashamed of being called a stump orator whilst he addressed such an assemblage as that before him." Another shared this view:

> He was no professed stump orator, except when it was necessary to be
> so. Stump oratory was working its way up every day in this colony,
> and had done wonders for them already.[71]

The growing acceptance of radical stump oratory of this kind was an important historical development. It also revealed a continuing divergence from
the original home of stump oratory, the United States of America. As noted
in previous chapters, the stump had first been identified in the United States
as a space of vulgar electoral appeal to the uneducated but enfranchised. In
the British world, by contrast, the stump was initially understood as the platform of the demagogue and the agitator, and it was identified in these terms
long before it was commonly linked to electioneering speech.

Not surprisingly, this inversion of the layers of meaning altered the
context in which political actors deployed the "stump speech." As the years
passed, British and Australian politicians did increasingly make more exten-
sive oratorical appeals. But the radical meaning of "the stump" as a space of

contention and working-class mobilization continued to adhere to those candidates who directly sought electors' votes. When they made stump speeches for elections, they seemed to many Britons to be flirting with dangerous and unruly techniques. As a result, the stump speech remained a more controversial intervention than in the United States. This intertwining of cultural understandings and political practice is the subject of Chapters 4 and 5.

Despite the commonalities between Britain and Australia, there were also important differences between colony and metropole that merit equally close attention. As will become clear, Australian politicians were much quicker to experiment with stumping for electoral success than were their metropolitan counterparts. The history of the first electioneering tours of the Australian colonies, and their implications, form the subject of the next chapter.

4

ROUSING THE PEOPLE

The Stumping Tour in Colonial Australia

"Stump speaking" emerged in the United States as a useful instrument in the quest for elective office. By contrast, "stump speaking" was initially identified within the British Empire as a form of radical speech—a synonym for agitation out-of-doors. It would not be commonly deployed as a tool of electioneering until several decades had passed.

The use of stump speaking in elections within the Empire was first widely evident in the Australian colonies. Conceptualized by one influential historian as a kind of "frontier" of a "Greater Britain," its similarities to the American Southwest are striking. Land was seized from indigenous peoples; settlement was sporadic and often frenetic; periods of speculative boom drove rapid if uneven growth. Observers emphasized the spread of "social equality" and the absence of institutional barriers to participation in public life. Elites worried that "democratic feeling" was "much stronger" than in "any other English speaking community," excepting perhaps the "western states" of the American Union.[1]

The major Australian colonies won legislative independence from Britain in the mid-1850s under a system known as "responsible government." In the fresh colonial constitutions and in revisions of electoral law soon afterward, the structure of political representation was rapidly democratized: the suffrage was broadened to include nearly all white adult males, property qualifications were removed for aspirant members of Parliament (MPs), relatively equal electorates were designed, and the secret ballot was introduced. Of course, the democratic principle was still restricted in important ways.

Women were denied the vote. Aboriginal people were excluded in practice, even if this omission was at first made explicit only in the northeastern colony of Queensland. In bicameral parliaments, upper chambers acted as houses of review; elected on a more restricted franchise or constituted by nominees, they provided a bulwark against popular power. Governors, appointed in London and still answerable to the Colonial Office, acted as vice-regal heads of state. Imperial governments retained a right of review, although it was rarely exercised.[2]

If this was a system of parliamentary government modeled on British practice, then democratic political rights were much more developed in the new Britannia than in the imperial center. Members of the legislature were "suddenly constructed out of surprising materials," to cite one alarmed journal of record. Gentlemanly expectations were soon disappointed. One historian has even diagnosed a "catastrophic collapse" in the reputation of Australian politicians as early as the 1850s. Here, one might assume, the aspiring officeholder would soon take to the stump in the manner of a Davy Crockett, a Henry Clay, or a Sam Slick.[3]

In fact, Australian elections at first strongly adhered to British conventions. The struggle for office was typically initiated with the formation of an election committee, usually meeting in a public hotel. This meeting was succeeded by the publication of a "requisition," a formal invitation to a member of the community to stand for office. The requisition was designed to impress undecided voters and to frighten prospective opponents; the maximum number of influential signatories was sought. Reflecting the local and personal character of colonial politics, a "canvas" of the electorate was generally identified as the most effective campaign technique. Radicals, it was widely agreed, excelled in the labor of visiting electors in their homes. Wealthy, often conservative, candidates tended to rely on paid agents to undertake the task on their behalf.[4]

Other common methods of electioneering included the display of placards and posters, the deliberate cultivation of rumors, the circulation of public letters of support, the deployment of governmental patronage, and the "treating" of electors, especially with gifts of alcohol. The newspaper was the chief source of information and instruction. Successful politicians were often proprietors of newspapers or enjoyed their strong support.[5]

Political speech making nevertheless played an important role in the struggle for office. The election meeting was described in one mid-century pamphlet as "the most effective means of fairly and honourably carrying an election." In an election address, the candidate would lay out his principles, review his achievements, and brave his opponents. It was widely believed that such a "face to face" encounter with electors was a "duty" of all aspirants. Generally reported in the local newspapers, it could reach far beyond the immediate audience. Not surprisingly, nervous candidates sometimes relied upon "the pen of a ready writer" to get them through the ordeal.[6]

Writing in 1858, Henry Parkes, soon to become the leading colonial statesman in New South Wales, argued that a "talent for public speaking" was "generally considered the most attractive quality in a candidate." Several decades later, right at the end of a long political career, he was asked to specify the single element most conducive to success in public life; Parkes's declamatory reply expressed an unvarying judgment, if a more alliterative and compressed choice of words: "Manner—Manner—Manner." Daniel Deniehy's *The Attorney-General of New Barataria* (1860), the first acclaimed satire of colonial democracy, likewise evinced a cynical faith in the priority of performance:

If a man is called into public life, let him talk well, if he can, and mind what he's about—that's politics.[7]

Still, if loquacity was an undoubted virtue in the politics of the antipodes, then it would be a considerable exaggeration to equate the speech making of mid-century Australians with the much more developed practices of America's democratic stump. In Australia, as in Britain, the status of the member of Parliament as the representative of a bounded constituency greatly limited his range of operations. To speak outside one's constituency was to challenge the principles of the constitution. Even at the end of the 1860s, the stumping tour was widely condemned. "You shall have no stumping," one wirepuller assured the candidate under his management in 1871.[8] Nearly always contained within a single electorate, the office seeker's speech making was generally restricted to a handful of ritualized occasions.

Even if Parkes considered the art of political oratory to be highly important, his 1858 pamphlet, anonymously published, still ranked "speaking ability" below five other qualities that an ideal candidate should rightfully possess: personal integrity, independent judgment, stability of purpose, reasoning power, and observation of public affairs. Newspaper advertisements warned electors against the charms of "bombastic oration." Candidates emphasized their possession of "plain spoken" and "practical" forms of "common sense." "Many might raise the objection that other gentlemen of greater eloquence could be chosen," admitted one candidate in the 1859 New South Wales elections, but, he asked, "Was the man with larger powers of speech likely to be a more honest man?"[9]

The development of the stumping tour within Australia was therefore not a simple reflex of a more generous suffrage, for it followed the enfranchisement of working-class men by nearly two decades. Neither was it a direct reflection of unprincipled ambition: the aspiring candidate had long employed a great number of equally effective electioneering tools and had little motive to extend the domain of public speech; constitutional proprieties and cultural prohibitions made the adoption of a stumping tour a very hazardous course.

The pioneer of the first electioneering tour in Australia bore a greater resemblance to the liberal statesmen than to the ruthless parvenu, and his political experiments reflected much more than a lust for power. This was a quest to defend and to enlarge the scope of colonial self-government. Its initiator was an Irish-born radical, a former member of the House of Commons, and a friend of Thomas Carlyle. The story of his Australian career is also a chapter in the transnational history of the democratic stump.

Charles Gavan Duffy (1816–1903) at first sight appeared unlikely to be a pioneer of stump politics. Born in Monaghan, Ireland, he won prominence as a journalist and as a founder of *The Nation*, an important contributor to Irish literary revival and to the efflorescence of mid-century nationalism. Active in the movement for home rule and for tenants' rights, he served in the House of Commons from 1852 to 1855. An inveterate name-dropper, he cultivated relationships with John Bright and John Stuart Mill. A genuine intimate of Carlyle, he came to know the Scottish historian and scourge of "stump oratory" as a "considerate," "habitually serene," and loyal friend.[10]

Duffy aspired to the career of the statesman, and his opinions on "stump oratory" would appear to accord with those of the great critic. Like Carlyle, he thought of principles as the "fixed stars" of public life and saw education as the "greatest" of all the "revolutionary forces." In October 1849, Duffy even anticipated Carlyle in a notable article—"Wanted, a Few Workmen!"— wherein the Irishman mourned a national talent for "spouting," "speeching," and "writing" that was much greater than a capacity for "practical genius" or activity. The younger man at first avoided the platform and showed no overt ambition to become a recognized leader of the Irish people. The way of the demagogue was "odious" to him, and the "hysterics" of popular speech making repugnant.[11]

In any case, he lacked the physical gifts of the popular tribune. Standing no more than medium height, Duffy had something of a horse face: a "dome-like brow," riven by a large throbbing vein, and his visage commonly compared with that of a fragile ascetic or a "sphinx." The eyes were "cold" and "calculating," the voice "weak," "harsh," "thin," and "squeaky." Duffy himself described his voice as "incurably bad." He confessed to a "radical unfitness" for success in the public meeting.[12]

Although even the London press acknowledged the Irishman's "spotless integrity," "high character," and potential contribution to the Empire, Duffy's metropolitan career was ultimately unrewarded. Frustrated by the meddling of the clergy, the backbiting of his countrymen, and the moral fallibilities of his fellow parliamentarians, he decided eventually to withdraw and emigrate. Upon resigning from the British Parliament, Duffy departed for Australia on the good ship *Ocean Chief* in 1855, settling in colonial Melbourne. It did not seem the most obvious preparation for a demagogue of the stump.[13]

The resources of popular leadership were nonetheless present, if momentarily obscured. Duffy had entered Irish politics in the campaign to Repeal the Act of Union. That campaign's unquestioned leader was "the Liberator," Daniel O'Connell. From the battle for Catholic Emancipation in the 1820s, O'Connell had initiated and refined the tools of mass, democratic politics. By the time of the famous "monster meetings" of the early 1840s, he routinely combined outdoor processions, platform oratory, and evening banquets with telling effect.[14] Fergus O'Ferrall has suggested that Irish campaigns led by the Liberator were the "prototype" for the "extra-parliamentary" movements of later years, among them the Chartist agitation and the Anti-Corn Law League.[15] They also exerted a profound influence on the future migrant to Australia.

Duffy recalled O'Connell's energy in the Repeal campaign as "a marvel" and noted the growing "intensity" of his platform speeches. Doubtless inspired by his charismatic precursor, Duffy would help organize "public banquets" and "county meetings" as the leader of the Tenant Right League of Ireland (the so-called League of North and South). Later, in colonial Australia, he would advise opponents of dominant landholders (the "squatters") to call a popular convention, on the Irish model. On the floor of Parliament, he would defend the "right" of the "citizens of Melbourne" to hold "public meetings" in "public parks" and the "open air."[16]

If Duffy lacked the gifts of the tribune, then his prominence in Irish politics nonetheless granted him a kind of celebrity. Imprisoned on several occasions as a leader of the Hibernian struggle and intimate with the heroes of national self-assertion, his arrival in the antipodes was anticipated by ingenious advertising in the colonial press. Two Gavan-Duffy hotels and a Gavan-Duffy omnibus appeared in Sydney in tribute. Banquets greeted the Irish champion in Melbourne as well as in Sydney. Melbourne—"the capital of Australia; here the popular element is strong and triumphant," he thought—won his allegiance. Duffy's Victorian supporters collected some £5,000 to support his political career.[17]

In the two decades that followed, Duffy would hold several ministerial offices, sit as speaker of the House, and attain even the great prize of chief minister and premier. He moved the bill to abolish the property qualification for members and designed the first major legislation to encourage the settlement of the "industrious classes" on public lands (promoted, and then reviled, as the Duffy Land Act). Returning to Europe on two extended visits, he also challenged the "offensive superiority" of English observers of Australian democracy, defending governments elected under universal male suffrage as preservers of order, public credit, and prosperity.[18]

But a reputation for scheming ("thoroughly unscrupulous," a "sleek and stealthy mole," said critics), a previous commitment to free-trade principles (advanced Victorian liberals increasingly embraced protectionism), and persistent sectarianism (Duffy was a Roman Catholic) all undermined his prospects. Only in June 1871 was Duffy able to lead a parliamentary coalition powerful enough to topple a reigning government. His success on the floor of the legislature prompted an opportunity to form his own ministry, and Duffy seized his chance.[19]

Condemned as a "stop-gap Administration," Duffy's ministry rested upon the parliamentary support of the colony's leading protectionist, the part-owner of the influential *Geelong Advertiser*, and the new treasurer, Graham Berry. The Irishman's colleagues in cabinet did not include a single banker, merchant, squatter, or representative of Melbourne. The ministry represented, Berry said, "the country constituencies." It was radical in spirit and provincial in membership. Its first major act was to pass a clearly protectionist tariff; its second was to seek the extension of railways to those regional bastions that offered the government the strongest support.[20]

These and other measures drew swift rebuke. Duffy was assailed for his Catholicism and his Irish past. Parliament was soon increasingly hostile, and the fire of opposition journals "fierce and incessant" (one sympathetic newspaper even described it as a "virulent opposition"). Parliamentary majorities in the Upper and Lower Houses overturned the ministry's plans for mining, railways, and the post office. What would the new government do?[21]

Duffy believed that a government remained "strong" only while "the tramp of the people is heard on the same highway, marching to the same goal." His experiences in Ireland and Australia had confirmed the power of oratory, delivered from public platforms. His major supporters mostly dwelled outside Melbourne, in the major inland centers. Recognizing the threat to Duffy's ministry and anxious to express their support, messages from what Duffy called "the great towns of the colony" were quickly dispatched, inviting the premier and his cabinet to banquets and popular demonstrations. Although conscious that acceptance would signal a break with British traditions, Duffy was also convinced that he "could not allow the authority of the Government to be undermined by slander."[22] Principle, personal history, and political threat all pushed the Irishman toward a daring political experiment. Thus, Australia's first stumping tour was launched.

Within four months, the ministry visited Ballarat, Creswick, Stawell, Ararat, Beaufort, Castlemaine, Sale, Clunes, Kilmore, Maryborough, and Carisbrook, among other mining and agricultural centers. Although marked by important differences, all of these excursions shared a common repertoire of organization and performance: formal invitation, public processions, local consultation, banqueting, speechifying.

First, the ministerial visit was initiated by the dispatch of a formal invitation. As in Great Britain, at this time, the "gentleman" still served as the paradigm of the nineteenth-century leader: unacquainted with self-promotion, dedicated to public service, disinterested. To openly seek personal popularity was therefore to court suspicion; to appeal to the people directly was to risk censure. The presence of a prior request therefore served to legitimate the campaign and to dispel mistrust. It signaled, moreover, the presence of "popular sympathy" for the government.[23]

Political friends openly sponsored these occasions. The Ballarat Liberal Association requested attendance at the first banquet of the tour. Later events were also described as "complimentary" gatherings, organized by "friends" of the ministry. Official bodies appear to have been established for these purposes, and there is reference in the press to banquet committees and sometimes to demonstration committees; the *Argus* claimed that the invitation to Castlemaine had "emanated" from a "public meeting" especially convened for the purpose.[24]

The membership of these committees is nowhere specified, although the chair and vice-chairmen of the banquets perhaps provide clues. These were members of the provincial elite: invariably mayors, ex-mayors, town councilors, or directors of significant public institutions (such as the local Mining Board or Water Commission). Sympathetic local MPs sometimes accompanied the ministry; occasionally, they welcomed them as guests.[25]

The visits themselves were designedly imposing and elaborate events. A special train from Melbourne conventionally delivered and returned the cabinet and the urban press. Upon arrival, the ministers were publicly received by an official party and then conveyed through the township's most prominent streets. Local preparations were sometimes flamboyant. In Maryborough, members of the town enjoyed a holiday, and the borough council used local funds to erect "three triumphal arches." Flags and banners waved from the housetops, and a welcoming escort of some two hundred horsemen greeted and then fell behind the ministerial carriages. At Stawell, there were also triumphal arches, flags, and evergreens suspended across the road. Oddfellows, Rechabites, and the fire brigade displayed their banners and regalia; guns were fired, and a band played. Other towns arranged similar carnivals.[26] Clunes was bedecked by two "arches of greenery" and a profusion of "gay-coloured flags." The borough band "burst into triumphant strains" when the ministry arrived at Castlemaine, as "See the Conquering Hero Comes" filled the air. And flags and evergreens were prominent in Ararat and in Carisbrook, too.[27]

Ministers were not simply entertained. Typically, they were required to exercise some ceremonial function, to undertake a local survey, or to take part in some kind of consultation. The foundation stone of a new town hall was laid in Clunes; the opening of the northeastern railway was officially recognized in Kilmore and in Maryborough. In Ballarat, the Waterworks were inspected. In Ararat, local needs for clean water and a refurbished "Lunatic Asylum" were assessed. Ministers in Sale saw selectors and listened to their grievances, and the official party in Stawell also discharged equivalent business.[28]

A grand banquet was the apotheosis of proceedings. These were ticketed affairs. The prices charged, the lavishness of the entertainment, and the scale of the celebration differed across the colony. Four hundred and fifty sat down in Maryborough, three hundred in Ballarat, and only half that number at the Apollo Hall in Clunes. The norms governing the participation of women were similarly variable: in Ballarat, "ladies" were charged one-fifth of the male fee merely for "looking on"; in Maryborough, they were "thrown in, or 'invited,'" with every male guest (or so one disparaging commentary would claim). At Carisbrook, women were "allowed to enter the hall in order to hear the speeches"; in Castlemaine, they "crowded" into the gallery above the feasting men.[29] Always subordinate, never granted a formal role, the presence of women was notable, if inconsistent.

The excellence of the gastronomy remained a universal preoccupation, the merits of the local cuisine being prominently assessed in the leading journals. A scarcity of "edibles and drinkables" provoked outrage in Ballarat; a postponement in Maryborough threatened the supply of turkeys, geese, and ducks. Creswick's residents were reassured of the quality of the local cookery; Beaufort's luncheon was thought a "credit" to even a "Melbourne caterer of the modern time."[30]

With the plates cleared and the glasses filled, the speeches began. These were organized as a long series of toasts and responses; indeed, a pride of worthies seemed anxious to rise to their feet. Duffy usually spoke for the ministry. His oration was typically the longest, most artful and fully reported speech.[31]

A noted writer, Duffy's speeches displayed great literary panache. They were not extemporized but relied instead upon "adequate preparation" for success: Duffy "prepared in the closet for delivery" or "duly weighed in some guarded solitude," his critics would allege. Although his weak voice sometimes drew disapprobation, even hostile reporters nonetheless commended the premier for his eloquence. The speeches apparently made for "very pleas-ant reading." They were "of a totally different order" than "the general run of after dinner orations": "graceful," "exceeding able," "lucid," "luminous," "admirable," "elegant," "magnificent," and "charming."[32]

Reading from his Chelsea study, Carlyle was even more complimentary. In December 1871, the great critic of stump oratory wrote to Duffy, declaring "real pleasure" at the latter's elevation to the premiership of Victoria. Duffy's ideas for reform, outlined in widely reported speeches, he thought "good," "sound," and "deserved" of "success." In May of the next year, the Scottish sage was even more impressed. Carlyle declared his friend's latest speech "a real image of your best self." Duffy was "modelling" the first elements of a "mighty nation," even "scattering beneficent seeds" for a great Australian future. "Nothing in your list of projects raises any scruple in me," Carlyle assured the colonial statesman; Duffy needed only to stand to his work, "hero-like, the utmost that you can."[33]

But if Carlyle certainly endorsed his friend's speech making, colonial crit-ics just as vigorously deployed the Scotsman's favored epithet for corrupting democratic speech. Duffy was attempting to "saddle the colony with class legislation," backed up with "all the bunkum of Collingwood stump oratory," alleged one colonial newspaper, referencing the Melbourne suburb of Colling-wood, most closely associated with working-class radicalism. Ministerial speakers offered nothing but "stump, stump, stump," agreed a second journal. Duffy's "selected beef eaters" were nothing more than "stump orators" and "democratic fire eaters," claimed a third. The *Daily Telegraph* explicitly ac-cused the premier of "stumping the country" and mounting the stump ("that is what all this banqueting comes to"). To the average newspaper writer, one more-sympathetic journal advised, Duffy "is merely a superior kind of stump orator, and his utterances are buncombe."[34]

Across the colony, critics of the banquets damned the tour as a divergence from British custom. This was an "unconstitutional and revolutionary at-tack" waged by a "Ministerial Supper Party," warned one correspondent from the *Daily Telegraph*. The *Argus* agreed that the procedure would be unthink-able in the nursery of parliamentary democracy; in the United Kingdom, the idea of a minister "rushing" from "one town to another" to declaim policy "would constitute a spectacle as novel as it would be ridiculous." Most "un-favourable criticism" of the premier tended to focus on his "enunciation of a policy" outside Parliament as the primary source of outrage. This was widely thought "not in accordance" with "that conduct which should characterise a Minister of the Crown."[35]

How was the stumping tour a challenge to accustomed methods? First, it displaced the process of election. Duffy claimed to discern the state of public opinion through his visits. According to the *Daily Telegraph*, this was a "thoroughly unconstitutional" means of "taking the opinion of the constituencies." The "ballot-box" served as the only "legitimate" measure of the popular will. In surveying the colony, the premier had therefore claimed too much.[36]

Second, this was a diminution of the "local member." Parliamentary representatives served a constituency; they therefore acted as the precise "constitutional agent[s]" designed to provide "local information." But in elevating the ministry, the stumping tour overshadowed this "unit of our political system" and threatened to put them "into the shade." The local member was conceivably reduced to a "nonentity" under this arrangement. There was "nothing to be gained" by such a distraction, prominent Melbourne dailies warned.[37]

Third, and most alarmingly, the banquet tour was thought to threaten the preeminence of the legislature itself. The English Constitution mandated that ministers were responsible to Parliament rather than to the country. The House served as a "people's committee"—a body formed to "investigate, discuss and deliberate" in a way beyond the "populace" as a whole. Outside Parliament, the minister was released from "the consciousness of an opposition," argued the *Australasian*, and could hold forth "like the preacher in his pulpit." Inside, however, the minister required "more than cleverness in tongue-fence" to prevail. Indeed, as the *Argus* suggested, business in Parliament could not be determined by a "pleasant after-dinner speech" alone.[38]

But Duffy's actions were thought to "disturb" this imposing edifice, to reduce the House to "a mere convention of delegates" that acted only to "ratify" decrees a minister had already developed "in direct communication with the people." The premier's appeal to the country was designed to overawe Parliament. It formed part of a "plan" for Duffy to become "a power outside and above the Parliament." "So far[,] we have been governed by Parliamentary Ministers," summarized the *Daily Telegraph*, but through Duffy's actions, the Victorian people were now "asked to set them aside," exchanging the order of responsible government for the dangerous turbulence of "public Tribunes." In essence, "constitutional government by true representation is coming to an end," argued the *Riverine Herald*. This was an "experiment" in "direct government by the people"; the "disastrous" fates of revolutionary France and of Athens loomed in terrible warning.[39]

The depth of the outrage reflected the principles under contest. For Duffy's most impassioned critics, the stumping tour was much more than a method of political campaigning: it was a violation of British conventions and a dangerous invocation of popular power. Democracy itself was the issue. Duffy's defenders, likewise, understood the banqueting tour as part of a struggle for genuine self-government in Victoria.

Not surprisingly, the ministry itself was quickest to defend the novel procedure, although parts of the colony's provincial press also supported these new methods and the democratic theory that underpinned them. According to its proponents, the banqueting tour should be understood as a contribution to a vigorous democracy. Duffy's stumping made a democratic contribution in two ways: first, it demonstrated the people's views, and second, it elevated the people to a more central role in the activity of self-government.

First, Duffy sedulously presented the banquets as evaluative and demonstrative bodies. In Ballarat, he declared it his "duty" to "review" the ministry's "transactions" before those assembled and then to "ask whether or not we have done our duty with respect to them." Likewise, the premier addressed banqueters at Castlemaine as "this great assembly," announced his government's policies, and even anticipated that his "countrymen" would then "be able to clearly understand and definitely test" the use he proposed "to make of political power."[40]

In this conception, the people possessed an adjudicative capacity at least as important as the legislature. At the Creswick banquet, Duffy identified "the confidence of the people" as the basis of his ministry's survival, warning parliamentary opponents that "it cannot be legitimately displaced" one "moment" before it "loses" popular confidence. In Maryborough, he basked in demotic adulation ("I am not acquainted with any case in which the public feeling of a country has more spontaneously or significantly displayed itself"). Further, he suggested that the obvious "goodwill" toward the government was important for the coming legislative session, enabling "us" to "return to parliament fortified by the frank and unequivocal sympathy of the people. (*Cheers.*)"[41]

Likewise, the colony's provincial press identified the "heartiness of the reception[s]," the size of the welcoming escorts, and the clamorous scale of the meals as signifiers of the popular will.[42] According to this view, the banquet was a form of "demonstration" (a term used by the *Ballarat Courier*, the *Bendigo Independent*, the Melbourne *Age*, and the *Mount Alexander Mail*).[43] And the meaning of this demonstration was thought unambiguous: the *Ballarat Post* described the ministry's progress across the colony as "not so much a victory as a conquest"; the *Bendigo Advertiser* referred also to "triumphal progress," and the *Kyneton Guardian* to a "triumphant procession." The nature of the reception was not just "gratifying" to the government, according to Geelong's *Advertiser*, but a symbol of the "confidence" it had "inspired" and the "satisfaction" it had given. It followed that Parliament needed to register the results of the tour and to respect the popular will. Parliament must "accept the verdict of the country," argued the *Advertiser*—"stamping out all faction" and assisting the ministry to "give effect to its policy."[44]

But the stumping tour involved communication as well as demonstration. One toast to the ministry at Creswick praised the administration for its "democratic practice of frequent consultation with the people." Duffy was also commended by rural newspapers because he had "gone to the fountainhead"—

"the electors." The government and the people had joined together, according to this view, a union that required ministers to see "with their own eyes," hear complaints and wants, and "frankly" exchange ideas. The result was a "mutual recognition," suggested the provincial press: "Ministers have recognised a democratic people," and "the people have recognised a democratic Ministry."[45]

For the *Geelong Advertiser*, the newspaper partly owned by Graham Berry and the most outspoken supporter of the tour, the episode confirmed the new government's commitment to the "genius of democratic institutions." Realizing that their policy required "the country at their back," Duffy's government had "boldly" gone "to the country," seeking "their approval and assistance." Their actions therefore reflected the status of the people as "the grand jury of the country," a body capable of expressing directly "what they wish, and mean, and hope."[46] This tour was clearly a more robust and participatory version of self-government than the conventions laid down in Westminster. To the advocates of Duffy's stumping tour, the actions of the ministry helped elevate the people to a more central role in political life.

The radicalism of this doctrine clearly spooked colonial elites. If the people's will had been invoked and harnessed, then this action far from secured the ministry's future. Many parliamentarians resented Duffy's apparent attempt to diminish their political centrality. In the act of administration, further dangers loomed. The premier was charged with neglecting the urgent need for a new education policy. Duffy's appointment of Irishmen and fellow Catholics to official positions drew condemnation, a personal scandal engulfed the treasurer (allegations of immoral conduct and corruption), and the ministry was accused of the bestowal of patronage. In a conflict over the propriety of an appointment to the agent-general's office in London, the government was defeated on the floor of the House.[47]

Duffy immediately sought an election, and even the hostile London *Times* anticipated a victory. The Irishman's appeal to the governor for a dissolution was rejected, however, and a new ministry was constituted out of skillful factional maneuvering.[48] If the people supported Duffy, then no occasion existed to formally register that support. Believing elite conspirators were trying to keep him from office, the disappointed radical withdrew to lick his wounds.

Although it had galvanized popular passion and disrupted conventional understandings of self-government, Duffy's stumping tour had not afforded his ministry genuine longevity: his government lasted less than a year. Nonetheless, the Irishman's political experiments confirmed the capacity of colonial party leaders to break with British traditions as much as it did the potential appeal of stumping techniques. Largely forgotten by historians, Duffy's pioneering tour helped remake colonial democracy.[49]

It was Duffy's treasurer, Graham Berry, who perfected the stumping tour, deploying the technique only a few years later to win the most substantial majority in Australian political history. Son of a Chelsea tradesman and apprenticed to a linendraper at the age of eleven, Berry was an antipodean counterpart of those self-made men that had so successfully prosecuted stumping tours across the United States in the early nineteenth century. Berry emigrated to Victoria as a somewhat mature thirty-year-old, winning prosperity and some local prominence as a small shopkeeper, newspaper proprietor, and member of Parliament. A devotion to self-improvement was evident in his reading habits (Edward Gibbon's *Rome* was a youthful enthusiasm) and in a growing mastery of chess. While conceding his oratorical fluency, critics drew attention to Berry's scattered aspirates and imperfect knowledge of English grammar. *Melbourne Punch* mocked the ambition of a "persevering grocer . . . working up *Knowles' Elocutionist* in the back parlour."[50]

Berry's political ascendancy drew a straight line between the agitators' stump and the stump of the electioneer. His political career began in the agitational gatherings of the Eastern Market (discussed at length in Chapter 3), where he invoked the name of Giuseppe Garibaldi and excoriated the conservative press. In October 1860, Berry was caricatured in the pages of Melbourne's *Argus* as "an Eastern Market demagogue of a very objectionable class," possessing, nevertheless, a "smooth and pliable tongue." Standing for election in that same month, he declared his "favour" for the gathering of the people "where they liked, when they liked, in as great numbers as they liked." Heckled with cries of "Eastern Market," he defended the political worthiness of Victoria's radical stump:

He was proud of those meetings in the Eastern Market. . . . [M]ore respectable and intelligent meetings had never assembled in any part of the world. (*Laughter*.)[51]

The epithet of "stump orator" haunted this and later election campaigns. He was "a burning and shining light on the Eastern stump," said the *Ballarat Star*, a "specimen of the genus stump." The *Argus* castigated him as "long allied with the stump" and a "dangerous propagandist of political error." The *Telegraph* thought him "a far greater man on the stump than in the Senate," while *Melbourne Punch* called Berry an "empty-headed wind-bag."[52]

In fact, Berry's skills as a platform advocate helped him win election and shape government policy. The former grocer was one of the first within the colony to reject the liberal nostrum of free trade and to champion the principle of protection for native industry. He promoted the policy with fellow veterans of the Eastern Market from the early 1860s (*Melbourne Punch* would allege that he took up the cause merely because it "was a good cry for the stump"). Whatever the motive, Berry's oratorical industry cannot be doubted. Although he confessed as early as 1861 that "he had so often addressed meetings on the subject" that "he feared he had exhausted it," the dauntless propagandist ranged widely in the prosecution of the measure over succeeding years. In combination with David Syme, the editor of Melbourne's *Age*, he would eventually be canonized as the "father of protection."[53]

If the parliamentary representative could not conventionally trespass beyond one's own constituency in open electioneering, then Berry's pursuit of industrial protection provided a kind of political license to transgress such curtailment. At the invitation of protection leagues and committees, he traveled to the major inland towns to deliver "lectures" on the subject throughout the 1860s. As one newspaper noted, Berry's performances at such events did not constitute a "lecture" in "the received sense of the word." Instead, these were political speeches he had been "in the habit of delivering" at "public meetings" across metropolitan Melbourne for many years. Welcomed as the "great gun" of countless such gatherings, Berry helped promote himself and his preferred policy.[54] Therefore, when Duffy launched a banqueting tour in 1871, the junior politician was already a practiced and well-known platform advocate. It also helped Berry recognize the great electoral potential of the Irishman's then unconventional course.

Like Duffy, Berry's first premiership was brief and controversial. A leading opponent of the free-trade ministry of G. B. Kerferd, the fierce protectionist took the initiative in the defeat of that government's proposals on the floor of the assembly in August 1875. Although he lacked a stable majority, Berry nonetheless accepted a commission to form his own administration. Welcomed by the Melbourne *Age* as the first government leader "to have any strong sympathy with protection," the new premier promised to maintain and selectively increase protective duties, reform the civil service, reduce the costs of railway transport, and levy a tax on the wealthiest landowners within the colony ("we will begin at the top of the tree"). Berry prophesied that "a new era has dawned" and threatened to "speak from one end of Victoria to another," addressing "assembled thousands on every platform he could mount." Opponents decried his policy as "crude" and "ill considered." Observers guessed that Victoria was entering a period of renewed political crisis.[55]

Alarmed by the radicalism of these new proposals, Berry's opponents coalesced in the House to eject the ministry from office in October 1875. The first Berry government was "short and sweet, like a donkey's gallop," noted one mocking obituary.[56] Resembling his former chief, the defeated premier now sought an election; like Duffy, Berry's requests were refused. But whereas the Irishman had quickly withdrawn from battle upon the governor's denial of a dissolution, the radical from Chelsea instead renewed his devotion to political warfare. Drawing upon the political weapons that had sustained his rise, Berry fashioned a great platform campaign.

As the numbers in Parliament lined up against his ministry, Berry and his supporters revived the public meeting and the stump speech. Opponents in the press discerned his efforts "to get up an agitation" and "resort to out-of-door agitation." *Melbourne Punch* imagined a desperate Berry in the guise of "Jerry Braham," surreptitiously writing to allies in the country centers:

In a Democratic country there is nothing like demonstrations, and I will take it as a great favour if you will kindly get up a mass meeting.[57]

Whether by nefarious design or unprompted anger, it is difficult to tell, but the facts of public assembly are beyond dispute: nearly one hundred public meetings were organized across the colony, "petitioning the Governor" for a dissolution. Even Berry's formidable opponent, the Melbourne *Argus*, admitted that "scarcely a district" went untouched. Ministerial supporters from perhaps fifty localities also joined a delegation to the colony's capital. It was the beginning of one of the "fiercest" partisan campaigns ever waged within "the Empire."[58]

One might have expected the popular energy to dissipate with time, but the defeated premier and his allies acted to prolong the sense of crisis. In what he admitted was an "unusual course," Berry actively campaigned against his successor as premier, Sir James McCulloch. Unlike present-day parliamentary democracies, in the nineteenth century, new ministers faced a fresh constituency election when they agreed to join a government. Berry was not an elector or a candidate in McCulloch's seat of Warrnambool, but he nonetheless broke with convention and accepted an invitation to address the voters. Justifying his behavior as a necessary response to an "exceptional" circumstance, Berry argued that "the people" had been "refused their ordinary constitutional rights," that his late government had been misrepresented, and that "important policies" required urgent public debate.[59] Although McCulloch returned to Parliament, the broiling political atmosphere was not permitted to cool.

Challenging British tradition within Parliament as much as without, Berry and his supporters now organized a disciplined obstruction of parliamentary business they dubbed "the stonewall." Shocking even radical liberals,[60] and anticipating Charles Stewart Parnell's better-remembered tactics by some years, Berryites aimed, quite openly, to make Parliament unworkable and thereby to precipitate an election. But the battles within the House were also directed outward. Berry promised "he would not allow the public attention to sleep." The "stonewall section of the Assembly," he told auditors in Geelong, hoped to "succeed in rousing every elector from a feeling of apathy into one of intense interest."[61]

It was an aspiration advanced partly through organizational maneuvering. At Berry's initiative, two previously separate institutions—the Reform League and the Protective League—were amalgamated to form a new body, with Berry serving as its president. The impassioned orator urged league members to recall "the importance of organisation" and spearheaded the formation of local branches across the colony. An expanded organizational base helped simplify the selection of candidates, limiting contests between liberal protectionists. It also acted as a network for promoting lectures and circulating pamphlets. Berry unashamedly declared that the league "desired to see public opinion focused" by the use of "platform speeches" and "other legitimate means."[62]

As the league's president, Berry now occupied a formal position that might justify further public speech making outside his own constituency. He personally visited and addressed almost every branch of this rapidly expanding organization. The party leader claimed in early 1877 that "he had never refused an invitation to visit any part of the colony." As historian Joy Parnaby has perceptively noted, Berry was able to appeal to electors in "the manner popularized by Charles G. Duffy" some years before.[63] But Berry's untiring efforts were now extended over many more months and linked to an increasingly powerful machine of electoral mobilization. Consequently, the immediate outcomes were much more successful, and their significance much more sustained.

Like Duffy's earlier efforts, this political campaign was maligned for its challenge to traditions. On the hustings, Sir James McCulloch predicted that voters would "resent" his opponent's "outside interference" in elections beyond his own constituency: "It was not right for Mr. Berry to try to persuade the electors" and "scarcely consistent" with his earlier occupation of high office. One correspondent from the *Argus* alleged that Berry had "undignified himself" by accepting the leadership of an organization outside Parliament. Major G. P. Smith, a member for Hawthorn, argued that it was "the first time . . . within his knowledge" that a "leading politician" had become the "chief actor" in an outside organization: "This parading about in the country" in such an "improper fashion" was "simply calculated to degrade politics and political men."[64]

The language of the stump and the politics of the United States loomed large in many of these attacks. Berry had been "stumping the country," it was argued in Parliament and in the press: he had hopped from "stump to stump," had undertaken a "stumping expedition," and had "done duty all over the colony on many a stump." He was "our chief stump orator," a "mouthpiece of chaos" (the latter a direct citation of Carlyle). One satire in *Melbourne Punch* imagined Berry as a brooding malcontent, stung into oratorical action by his lust for office and hatred of the wealthy:

> I will stump the country. I will rouse creation. I will give the propertied, the mercantile, the educated classes particular fits.[65]

Another burlesque, originally published in the *Freeman's Journal*, depicted stump speaking as the cause of Berry's unseemly elevation and his political threat:

> *Graham Berry started stumping—stumping in a rural town;*
> *Did a little pulpit thumping—brought a little thunder down!*
> *He who might have shone at tillage in a certain sort of way*
> *Grew the "big man of his village"—lost his head and went astray.*[66]

Comparing Berry and his colleagues with the corrupt political machines of New York, *Melbourne Punch* likened the Berryites to a "Tammany ring." In another satire, the radical stumper was equated with a mammoth bug— "an American importation." A third imagined the visit of a well-connected American agent, impressed with the prospect of exhibiting the Berryites in the home of stump oratory itself:

> Run 'em as a travelling company—Grand Burlesque and Farce combination. Berry on the stump would take immensely.[67]

The bitterness of the satire was a measure of conservative antipathy, but at first it was only a feeble weapon of political combat. Berry—veteran of the Eastern Market, understudy to Premier Duffy, president of a national league for "Reform and Protection," great exponent of platform oratory— could not be resisted. In a storming victory at a general election in 1877, the Berryites swept to power, with the league winning fifty-five seats of the seventy-one contested. It was a "complete rout," announced one astonished correspondent, and a "national calamity" thought another. Addressing one thousand electors at the Mechanics' Institute in Geelong, the premier-elect put it somewhat differently: "The people," he said, "have come to power."[68]

For the historian of colonial politics, Berry's triumph has usually been understood as a formative moment in the rise of the mass party. For the historian of the stump speech, it was also a threshold, marking the general acceptance of the modern electioneering tour. Holding power for the next few years, Berry and his ministers would continue to stump the colony in the pursuit of financial and constitutional reform. Conscious of their self-admittedly "bungling" campaign efforts, Berry's opponents followed suit: increasingly speaking out beyond their own constituencies, developing what one historian has called a "curiously conservative version of the stump tour."[69]

Beyond Victoria's borders, the success of apparently radical and American methods of winning votes also inspired emulation. Henry Parkes, now the premier of New South Wales, traveled to the western region of the colony at the end of 1880 to attend banquets in Cudal and Orange, performing ceremonial duties but also vindicating his government's performance in stirring after-dinner orations. Parkes's address in Orange, the *Sydney Morning Herald* observed, was a kind of "political manifesto," "just that sort of speech which he might make to his own constituents." One scribe suggested that he was "stumping the colony à la Graham Berry." Other newssheets also used the language of the stump to describe his novel activities. Reports of stump speaking in Queensland and South Australia also emerged around this time.[70] The stumping tour, it seemed, was now a fixture of Australian political life.

Viewed from the distance of nearly a century and a half, the passage of these events can take on the misleading shape of an inevitable forward march: the American modern supplanting the antique Briton. In fact, as this chapter has shown, the adaptation of stump speaking to the Australian colonies was a slow, contested, and conflictual process. It took several decades for the agitational methods of the Eastern Market to be successfully deployed in the quest for ministerial office. Experiments with stump speaking incited opprobrium and alarm. Charles Gavan Duffy, its first major exponent, failed to secure his aims.

The pioneers of Australia's electioneering tours were neither ruthless Machiavellis nor would-be Sam Slicks. Veterans of mass campaigns in Ireland and Australia, they turned to the stump speech as a means of exciting public interest, manufacturing public opinion, and pressuring Parliament and governors. Criticized as violators of British tradition, they broke with convention in the name of popular self-government. Their purpose was to rouse the people, not simply to win votes. Unquestionably, their efforts changed the ways in which colonial elections were fought. But their willingness to mount the stump altered the culture and the meaning of Australian democracy, too.

5

TO MIDLOTHIAN AND BEYOND

Gladstonian Stumping,
Performed and Remembered

At the end of the 1870s, Britain was transfixed by perhaps the most influential stumping tour of all time. William Gladstone's campaign for the Scottish seat of Midlothian, waged from 1879 to 1880, has been widely identified as a transformative event in modern political history. Emerging from retirement to challenge the foreign policy of then prime minister Lord Beaconsfield, the Grand Old Man of British politics delivered more than a score of speeches to a rapturous audience of electors and voteless Scots. Gladstone confided his best estimate in a diary entry: 15.5 hours of speeches to 86,930 souls.[1]

But the campaign far transcended the local, and the great orator exploited the modern technologies of rail and the telegraph to command the national stage. His labors helped deliver the Liberal Party a substantial majority, defined the major themes of future political debate, confirmed his status as a popular idol, and secured him enormous power in a renewed prime ministerial term. Seemingly in the space of only a few months, Britain was vaulted from oratorical laggard to arguably the most outstanding example of the power of "the stump." The Gladstone tour would be reported across Europe and the Americas. It would even become the touchstone of political theories of "charismatic" leadership in action.

"I should like to write about these marvellous events but how can I?" Gladstone asked his most prominent host and colleague, Archibald Primrose, the fifth Earl of Rosebery. "I was stunned at the end of the first night: and I am still out of breath from the endeavour to keep up with the rapidity of events." His diary entries were still more extravagant: the oratory tour was the culmination of a "political experience which I believe is without example in our Parliamentary history"; my "retroactive" involvement in politics "appears to me to carry the marks of the will of God."[2]

Participants often overestimate the historical significance of the labors they strive to complete. Still, Gladstone's was an assessment apparently shared by foe as well as friend. Admirers immediately extolled the Liberal Party leader's tour as "historic," "a great event in the political history of the nation," and "one of the foremost events of English history." Even critics thought it an "extraordinary phenomenon" and "a campaign of no ordinary magnitude."[3] Historians have largely echoed these views.

Authoritative studies have described Gladstone as "the first major states-man to stump the country," the initiator of a "new method of electioneering," and the director of political scenes "as yet unknown on the eastern shores of the Atlantic." The 1880 election is conventionally described as "unprecedent-ed": the "first modern election," the herald of a "new age," a "new departure," and a "new era." Before Gladstone, the *Oxford History of England* recorded, "it had never been etiquette for leading British statesman to 'stump the coun-try'"; after Midlothian, stump speaking was soon a "matter of course."[4]

Certainly, contemporaries turned to the language of the stump to describe these amazing events. The *Edinburgh Courant* called Gladstone's campaign a "stump tour" and an "electioneering raid." Conservative rivals spoke bitterly of "Mr. Gladstone on the stump." Queen Victoria likened one of her least-favorite ministers to "an American stump orator," "going about Scotland" and "making the most violent speeches." One satire depicted a "Wandering Willie" (in thick Scottish brogue) as willing to "Stump the haill country frae cottage to hall." A second mocked the statesman's apparent oratorical garrulity:

> *Surely, since the first roving Statesman stumped,*
> *The public ear was never so bethumped*
> *With words—words—words.*[5]

A third burlesque equated Gladstone with the minstrel show protagonist "Bones—Stump Orator." Reworking Byron Christy's famous comic address "Any Other Man," it pictured the learned Liberal on the stump as a blackface illiterate, flirting with anti-Semitism, claiming affiliation with Scotland, and projecting a hypocritical friendship to all:

> We are de great conglomerative party. For what am we here for? To upset de great Beaconsfield or any odder man. . . . Beaconsfield am a Jew; I am an Englishman and a Scotchman, but I lub all countries.[6]

Clearly, this was a feat of platform eloquence that summoned up the ubiquitous and disreputable precedent of the American stump. But how was it enacted with such towering and charismatic force? And why did Britons seem finally to embrace the "American" stump at this late stage? As a number of careful historians have already argued, the Midlothian campaign was not an immediate improvisation, and neither was it a purely individual achievement. Gladstone's great performance rested upon long-term developments in electoral law, public communications, and the oratorical repertoire.

The Midlothian stumping expedition reflected as well as extended the process of democratization. As the celebrated leader ventured to the Scottish capital, he contemplated an electorate greatly expanded by an enlargement of the franchise in 1832 and again in 1867. A Ballot Act in 1872 had also extended the protection of a secret vote, thereby reducing the scope for traditional forms of bribery or intimidation.[7] Of course, the extent of these changes should not be exaggerated. Women could not vote. It has been estimated that in the county of Midlothian in 1880, only one man in seven had the right to vote.[8] Allegations of fraud and manipulation swirled.[9] But while voting remained a definite privilege, it was now more widely shared. And with an expanded electorate, so came the need for mass persuasion.

British advocates of a broader franchise understood this challenge in particular ways. Writing in *Essays on Reform* (1867), R. H. Hutton suggested that working-class voters lacked "intellectual range," a deficit partly remedied by their possession of a "sure instinct" for "great political ideas," and a more "unwavering fidelity" to these than Britain's privileged orders.[10] This was a diagnosis perhaps based on the long commitment of British workers to the cause of democratic reform, sustained over several decades. It implied that successful appeals to an enlarged electorate might best be carried by bold statements of fundamental belief. From this perspective, enfranchisement seemed to signal the need for a new combination of persuasion and principle. In the forceful articulation of great ideas, one might help win popular sympathy and electoral support.

The infrastructure of the modern public sphere aided such appeals. The capacity of newspapers to publish British parliamentary proceedings—formally accepted only from the early nineteenth century—had helped stimulate interest in political oratory. An expanding provincial press in later decades offered new support to the Liberal Party and to political agitation. The establishment of central news agencies simplified the transcription and distribution of platform speeches; the extension of the telegraph enabled their much more rapid diffusion. These developments bequeathed a national audience eager for political oratory as well as the technical means to carry it.[11] If Gladstone's rhetoric rang out across Britain, it was not through the power of his great voice alone.

The sweep and drama of the campaign also owed much to other forms of technological advance. The Liberal icon was borne northward to Edinburgh on a rail network that symbolized modern industrial progress. Gladstone was transported in an American-style Pullman carriage, specially hired, and train stations en route staged moments of vivid encounter between leader and people. One *Punch* satire ("Electioneering á la Mode") imagined the orator's conveyance as stopping at "Muddleton" and "Longwyndham," before Gladstone eventually addressed the passengers of dozens of trains from atop a junction signal box; he arrived at an Edinburgh terminus some five hours late. Burlesque and reality here converged: Midlothian was a "whistle-stop" campaign, and it relied on the methods of mass transit.[12]

Changes in technology and in the electorate were matched by no less radical developments in the activity of speech making itself. By the inauguration of the Midlothian tour, the American Republic had a continuous history of stump speaking that went back more than half a century; earlier chapters have established its profound influence on British political debate. As we have seen, most British observers were at first repulsed by the emergence of the stump orator. However, the extension of the franchise and the beginnings of a substantial party machine in Britain eventually encouraged a more applied interest in American electoral affairs. By the early 1870s, British visitors now looked on the customs of Brother Jonathan with a more disciplined and less moralistic eye.

In an 1873 tour of the United States, Lord Rosebery, an aspiring Liberal politician and laird of Dalmeny House and Barnbougle Castle, closely observed the Democratic Party of New York. At the Manhattan Club, he appraised the spontaneous and voluble eloquence of the gathered party notables (speaking without the aid of a lectern): "Speaking very much above the average . . . it would have been impossible for an Englishman without anything to hide his legs to speak at all." Looking down at the Democratic National Convention and the party's procession from Madison Square Garden, he was still more impressed:

> There appeared a moving column of lights, clustering and silent. . . . There was cavalry indeed, but it was unarmed[;] there were banners[,] but they bore the names of peaceful citizens or the shibboleth of political principles[;] there were cannon[s,] but they were loaded only with ballot balls. All was silence, earnestness and decorum. It was a monster

procession of American citizens on its way to salute a political chief.
. . . This was both a great moral spectacle and a great political lesson.[13]

The lesson was quickly learned. It was Rosebery who worked together with
Liberal Party Whip W. P. Adam to convince Gladstone to stand for a Scottish
parliamentary seat. Before the Liberal icon had even accepted, the laird of
Dalmeny was already plotting a major public event: "If he accepts," Rosebery
wrote to John J. Reid, the local party chieftain, in late December 1878, "our
best plan would be to organize a great Liberal banquet to him in the Corn Exchange." Rosebery and Reid stayed in regular contact as the plan for a series of
public meetings was refined. The earl sent Gladstone a proposal for six major
public engagements more than a month before the prospective candidate set
out on his first electioneering raid. Rosebery substantially funded the Liberal
campaign and took what Gladstone called "great care and consideration" in
the supervision of arrangements over late 1879. The Midlothian meetings
would be marked by the visual drama that Rosebery had witnessed in New
York: the mass gathering of enthusiasts, the display of flags and banners, the
discharge of fireworks, the insistence on moral and upright deportment, and
the unified salutation to a great political chief.[14]

In the aftermath of victory, in April 1880, Gladstone made it obvious that
the overall imagination and planning of the campaign had been Rosebery's:

The great merit of it I apprehend lay in the original conception, which
I take to have been yours, and to overshadow even your operations
towards the direct production of the result.[15]

Gladstone's prose is here characteristically circumlocutory. But it seems a
clear concession that the Midlothian campaign owed much to the house of
Dalmeny, and thereby something to America, too.

Rosebery's American interests were well known, and his centrality to the
unfolding of the Midlothian miracle was widely conceded. By contrast, the
evidence that Australian stumping influenced British experiments is perhaps
less compelling.

Unquestionably, the electioneering tours led by Charles Gavan Duffy and
Graham Berry were widely reported in the metropolitan press. Something of
a big-noter, Duffy even claimed that the published commentary on his banquets in Britain and Australia would "fill a volume." Berry's storming victory
in May 1877 had also inspired British press coverage, and the subsequent history of his administration brought antipodean politics even greater notoriety.[16]

A conflict between Berry's ministry and the Upper House (the nominal
issue was payment of parliamentary representatives) provoked a constitutional

crisis that raged from 1877 until the early 1880s. Berry visited London in a special "Embassy" over the first half of 1879 in an effort to win imperial intervention and support for constitutional reform. Here, the apprenticed linendraper, former grocer, and colonial stumper met with members of the Conservative administration as well as leading Liberals. His return to the family bosom in the borough of Chelsea was marked by a meeting of the local Liberal Association, chaired by the future radical minister Sir Charles Dilke (one doubts that Thomas Carlyle, also a resident of Chelsea, received an invitation). A speech delivered at the close of that public meeting even drew a parallel between the tradesman's son and Britain's most revered statesman, suggesting that Graham Berry "exercised almost the same influence over the people of Victoria that Mr. Gladstone exercised over the people of England."[17]

Accompanying the Victorian premier as fellow ambassador was Charles Henry Pearson, a former president of the Oxford Union and a professor of modern history at King's College, London. Emigrating to the colonies from a sense of professional disappointment and in an effort to master persistent health problems, he had come, via sheep farming, serving as a school headmaster, and working in journalism, to a significant position in Victorian Liberal politics. Elected to Parliament in June 1878, Pearson was included in the Berry Embassy as a guide to London's political society (*Melbourne Punch* pictured him advising on etiquette, without much success) as well as a skillful publicist. Already, in a prominent chapter in *Essays on Reform*—"On the Working of Australian Institutions"—he had vindicated the liberal institutions of his adopted home as well as the qualities of its statesmen. Now returned to the metropole, Pearson's contribution to the *Fortnightly Review* in July 1879 reasserted confidence in the Victorian Lower House (composed, he said, of "practical, sensible, and fluent men") and identified the central role of "public meetings and political union" in the winning of reforms within Britain itself. The old Oxonian openly declared that the platform should take precedence over Westminster: "The genesis of great changes must be and ought to be outside Parliament." His conclusion was an expression of faith in the capacity of "electors" to adjudge the "merits" and "demerits" of major public measures.[18]

Nonetheless, if colonial liberals confirmed the possibilities of democratic persuasion, then there is little suggestion that Australian perspectives carried much weight with British party leaders. Duffy's claims of metropolitan interest were mostly inflated posturing. Pearson's status as the clear junior to an apprenticed linendraper attracted more attention than his thoughtful reflections on the relationship of Parliament and platform. Berry's social class also likely restricted his capacity to influence Britain's parliamentary elite. Indeed, Dilke's musings on closer contact with Premier Berry related less to the methods of that politician's remarkable rise than they did to the persistence of his cockney diction: "My interviews convinced me that the letter H was likely to disappear in the democracies of the future."[19] The Victorian premier's only contact with the Grand Old Man appeared to leave no more notable impression. When Berry tried to claim Gladstone's support for his efforts of political reform, the eminent Briton cut him down in a letter to the *Times*: "No conversation of a practical nature has been held by me with him, but he may have formed his own opinion as to the bearings of my mind."[20] If Berry stumped with success long before Gladstone, then it seems unlikely indeed that the former grocer's conduct served to inspire the labors of the great statesman of Britain.

From where, then, did Gladstone draw his rhetorical inspiration for the Midlothian speeches? Earlier studies have suggested the special influence of religious oratory and of recent developments in the extra-parliamentary speech of British MPs.

The first influence was religion. For the Liberal leader, political life was only a subordinate part of a deeper religious life. Gladstone had trained himself in the art of speech through the close study of Christian sermons and then his private attempts to deliver them anew. A sophisticated consumer of religious oratory throughout his life, he had been impressed by the preaching of visiting American evangelists Dwight L. Moody and Ira D. Sankey in the mid-1870s. Several historians have suggested that oratory of this kind may have shaped Gladstone's Midlothian appeals.[21]

Certainly, religious language was prominent in Gladstone's self-exculpation. His decision to contest the seat was justified as a "duty" rather than an opportunity, a judgment that reflected an inner call. He called the gatherings he addressed "moral demonstration[s]." He described his tour as a "pilgrimage." He appealed, explicitly, to the "inner conscience" of his listeners. His aim, he said, was to "bring home" to them the great questions of foreign policy, so that these would be felt in "the conscience of the community at large." The language of "duty," "shame," and "honour" was frequently deployed. Later historians have compared the orator with revivalist preachers and even with an Old Testament prophet.[22] As in the United States, the oratory of the pulpit also helped shape the rhetoric of the British election campaign.

Likewise, the brawling world of British party politics exerted an independent influence. As established in Chapter 3, Britain possessed a long tradition of hustings speech making, especially in the larger urban constituencies, such as Westminster and the City. Political banquets also provided an opportunity for electioneering oratory, while radical reformers extended the scope of speech making in more daring and adventurous acts.[23]

British popular movements of the early nineteenth century had organized around a "radical mass platform," linking outdoor oratory with determined political assembly. Its leading exponents were often well-born and charismatic speakers: Henry "Orator" Hunt and Feargus O'Connor loomed especially large. In later years, John Bright deployed these techniques in more sober and disciplined campaigns against the Corn Laws and for electoral reform. Radical oratory of this kind helped demonstrate the power of public speech and establish conventions and structures that regulated its use. In trespassing beyond the customs of traditional electioneering, Britain's radicals created precedents that more established politicians would later exploit.[24]

From the first half of the nineteenth century, there are several examples of parliamentary leaders taking more brazenly to the public platform. Conservative prime minister Robert Peel responded to the challenge of an enlarged franchise by issuing the famous Tamworth Manifesto of 1834, a declaration of willingness to carefully review "civil" and "ecclesiastical" institutions, redress "real grievances," and contemplate future reform. He supported this publication with a major speech in the Mansion House only a few days later, and he made further public addresses outside his electorate toward the end of the decade. Liberal prime minister Lord Russell was also an active extra-parliamentary speaker, as was another of Gladstone's precursors as Liberal chief and national leader, Lord Palmerston.[25]

Gladstone's greatest rival, Benjamin Disraeli, the Earl of Beaconsfield, also preceded him into the field. Disraeli was renowned as a phrasemonger of uncommon pungency and wit. His address at the Manchester Free Trade Hall in April 1872—wherein he likened Gladstone's government to a "row of exhausted volcanoes"—helped win the ascendancy that would bring him to the top of the greasy pole in 1874. Disraeli was also featured as the guest of honor in political banquets in earlier years, and these would become an object of emulation (Lord Rosebery called them "the model") for Gladstone's key supporters as they contemplated the Midlothian campaign. Certainly, when the Grand Old Man of politics took to the hustings in 1879, he was keen to emphasize that it was Disraeli's party that had driven earlier changes, with Liberals merely endeavoring to learn their lessons:

> Let me tell you, gentlemen, that our opponents in electioneering matters are frequently very shrewd indeed. We have much to learn from them in that respect; and, ladies and gentlemen, I trust we shall learn from them many useful and valuable lessons, not as to the ends exactly that they have in view, but as to the judicious and careful use they make of the means of obtaining those ends.[26]

In truth, the growing willingness of the parliamentary representative to speak beyond Westminster was no product of a single party. If mid-century politicians had rarely spoken beyond the hustings at election time, then the 1860s and 1870s witnessed the beginnings of definite change. The then-long recess of parliament offered an opportunity for what were first called "vacation" or "recess" speeches. Here, the MP might survey major events, explain his conduct in the chamber, and anticipate future policies. The seasonal nature of the practice was registered in newspaper commentary: the speeches came "after the grouse" and coincided with the slaughter of red deer, it was said, falling "like autumnal leaves."[27]

Critics scorned these occasions as little more than "a vent for spare oratory" and a "tepid *rechauffe* of the session." The orations were also explicitly identified as versions of the stump speech, designed for an "electioneering purpose." Nonetheless, MPs increasingly embraced the custom. In the early 1860s, the *Times* adopted the new and somewhat sensational label of "extra parliamentary utterances" to describe the proliferating practice. Members of Parliament also began to defend these vacation speeches more confidently ("right and good things"), and some newspapers agreed ("well worth the space they occupy"). By the early 1870s, one newssheet thought recess orations "the rule among the vast majority of constituencies." Under the heading "The Extra Parliamentary Campaign," another outlet even feigned distress at the ubiquity of the practice: "Are we to have no peace?"[28]

The lion of British Liberalism was an important pioneer in many of these changes. Invited to Manchester to unveil a monument to Robert Peel in 1853, Gladstone here spoke to what he called a "great assemblage" that included, for perhaps the first time, large numbers of "working men." Over the following days, he delivered several impromptu addresses. In notable tours of Tyneside and Lancashire in the early 1860s, he spoke at town halls and free-trade halls. Gladstone was by now conscious of a growing personal magnetism. His diary disclosed something of an internal debate over the novel and turbulent nature of events:

So ended, in peace, an exhausting, flattering, I hope not intoxicating circuit. God knows I have not courted them. I hope I do not rest on them. I pray I may turn them to account for good. It is, however, impossible not to love the people from whom such manifestations come, as meet me in every quarter . . . [s]omewhat troubled by dreams of hall, and lines of people, and great assemblies.[29]

The growing closeness between the people and their leader also troubled the more privileged electors of Oxford University. Gladstone lost his seat in that constituency in 1865. The defeated politician's subsequent candidacy for the very large seat of South Lancashire was propelled by a dramatic address to the Manchester Free Trade Hall: "At last my friends, I am come amongst you. And I am come . . . unmuzzled." His labors continued. Before the 1868 election, the aspirant for the prime ministership gave platform speeches in fourteen separate towns. In 1871, Gladstone even thought he had "over-stumped."[30]

The events of the mid-1870s provided a further impetus for oratorical experiment. Supplanting Gladstone as prime minister in 1874, Disraeli almost immediately struck out with a new foreign policy. Disraeli's willingness to form alliances with the Ottoman Empire brought stability to Europe but also sacrificed the Bulgarian people to the depredations of the Turkish government. As R. T. Shannon has documented, the so-called Bulgarian atrocities that followed in 1876 prompted a widespread campaign of speeches and meetings in Britain, especially among nonconformist Christians.[31] The intensity of this dispute gave electoral politics an added moral dimension and also drew Gladstone back to active participation in public life, justifying his interventions as a response to what he called a "crisis of an extraordinary character."[32]

In late 1876, Gladstone published a pamphlet on the issue: *The Bulgarian Horrors and the Question of the East.* On September 9, he returned to the public platform, speaking to a crowd of ten thousand souls on Blackheath in his then constituency of Greenwich. George Holyoake, a prominent radical and later author of a guide to oratory, wrote to his leader in the aftermath of the powerful event:

It was a great & generous thing to come & speak to us in the rain, & mist, and & wind. Voices in the streets speak only of gratitude and gladness. Horror-stricken, indignant, articulate, but aimless, the nation craved direction it could trust. It seems now as though the Humanity of the world had spoken in your voice.[33]

Gladstone's response is unknown. But there is no question that the act of public advocacy bound him more strongly to the issue and renewed his commitment to the electoral struggle, too. Writing to his successor as Liberal leader, the Second Earl Granville, in August 1879, Gladstone made his new resolution clear: the future member for Midlothian advocated vigorous "autumn work" by party members, with the hope that this might "join on the proceedings of 1876–9 by a continuous process to the dissolution." By these means, Gladstone believed, the controversies around foreign policy could be kept "alive and warm."[34]

Considered in these terms, the Midlothian campaign was an extension of earlier performances much more than an entirely independent creation. The new candidate for the Scottish constituency was heir to decades of oratorical change in the American, Australian, and British polities. He was a student of religious oratory, and he was the beneficiary of important developments in electoral law, transport, and communications. In the absence of these broader transformations, the miracle of Midlothian would not have been possible. Gladstone's greatest hour was prefaced by rehearsals spanning many years.

To understand the prehistory of this tremendous event is not, of course, to deny its forbidding and alchemical power. This owed something to the context, but perhaps more to Gladstone's qualities as a public performer.

Gladstone was an orator of uncommon talents. He did not write out an address in advance but rather jotted down the main intended points of a speech just before his appearance. A close study of literature and history provided an authority for judgments and a reservoir of words, phrases, and symbols. Attentiveness to the audience ("watch them all along," Gladstone advised) granted him what one admirer called a "spontaneity of expression." The union of speaker and listeners that resulted was described in one of Gladstone's own works, *Homer and the Homeric Age*:

His [the orator's] work . . . is an influence principally received from his audience (so to speak) in vapour, which he pours back upon them in a flood.[35]

As the metaphor of the flood implied, Gladstone's words never failed. Indeed, the problem was rather a prolixity and qualification that did not translate so well to the printed page.[36] The Grand Old Man was better experienced than read.

Physical gifts overwhelmed any rhetorical failings. Although standing less than six feet tall, Gladstone's spare and wiry form—disciplined by the pastime of tree felling—granted the speaker an erect carriage and a superb physical vigor, even into his seventies. He wielded gestures with actorly command and bold sweep: the sledgehammer fist, the smiting of the open palm with the blow of the right, the fine movement of unusually long fingers.[37]

The voice was probably a tenor, blessed with the depth and harmonics of a baritone, and Gladstone spoke with a northern burr. Although capable of carrying great distance, his voice never forfeited a "clearness" and "melody." It was "silver" and "bell-like," listeners said, and its tone could vary wonderfully: enunciating a single syllable with a withering emphasis, now pausing, and resuming with a rolling and relentless fluency.[38]

The face was malleable and expressive, reputedly in "perpetual motion." A broad forehead loomed above dark and prominent eyebrows and was crowned with thinning hair, pushed back from the face. The eyes were his greatest resource: intensely bright and animal, likened to a falcon's, with their "strange imperious flash." Gladstone's remarkable magnetic quality, a mystery often pondered, rested partly on that fierce and powerful gaze.[39]

The overwhelming impression was one of earnestness: the orator believed what he said and aimed to impress his convictions upon the gathered crowds. It was as though Gladstone's soul "seemed to go out of him," wrote one observer; his "exaltation lifted his hearers out of themselves," claimed another. The Irish journalist and parliamentarian T. P. O'Connor thought the voice and body of the speaker were but the "outward signs" of an "inward glow." The religious overtones are obvious: in a fusion of self and cause, the person was transmuted into the embodiment of a moral principle. This is perhaps why Gladstone's contemporaries understood his victories on the platform as triumphs of "moral force" as much as achievements of an "eloquent tongue."[40]

A kind of "cult" of Gladstone, discernible from the later 1860s, amplified the presence and authority of the man wrought in flesh and bone. The Liberal leader's name was reconfigured in multiple tributes: "Gladstone and Reform," "Gladstone for ever," the "People's William." Popular gatherings offered still more varied greetings: "Champion of Finance," "An Honest Man the noblest work of God!" Portraits of the Liberal leader were painted and pottery decorated with that worthy, gloomy visage; Gladstone's speeches were collected, bound, and published. The orator's home of Hawarden Castle even became a place of pilgrimage, with the woodchips from a tree felled by the master a prize souvenir, often carried off. From the time of Gladstone's first retreat from politics, in the mid-1870s, a succession of biographies was also rapidly composed. Coming out almost every year, these volumes included a "Life of Gladstone" in pamphlet form, purchased in a bulk order of three thousand copies for distribution within Midlothian and surrounds.[41]

The growing celebrity of the Liberal lion was paralleled by the adulation of Victorian sporting stars, like W. G. Grace. It coincided with the queen's withdrawal from visible participation in public life. The cult was never national and gripped the North and West of Britain much more than the home counties. In some senses, it was based on a misunderstanding of the statesman and an inflation of his popular sympathies. But the folk myth was no less powerful for its confusions: Gladstone appeared to many to be a sort of "Galahad of Virtue" and "Demosthenes of Eloquence."[42] When he came before the people of Midlothian, even grim-faced Scots recognized the arrival of no ordinary man.

In 1879, Gladstone had not appeared in Edinburgh for nearly twenty years,[43] while his withdrawal from politics over the late 1870s had further burnished his reputation. The preceding years of agitation over the "Bulgarian atrocities" had enhanced the prevailing political excitement, and Gladstone's growing participation in that campaign magnified the impression that his efforts in Midlothian were more than a purely parliamentary affair. The choreography and setting of the tour exploited the incipient enthusiasm. Rather than a single address at an appointed time, Gladstone elected to deliver a series of major speeches over more than a week. Each contemplated a particular topic or theme. None possessed "completeness" or "comprehensiveness," Gladstone admitted to Rosebery, and yet this allowed for a deeper and more complete coverage "in the operation as a whole." Gladstone further believed that once on his "political circuit," he needed to "keep the anvil hot": a series of speeches delivered on "successive days" was a "more telling plan" than a more extended and physically less arduous tour. Such an arrangement granted Midlothian events a rapid tempo (from day to day), an internal momentum (a passage from triumph to triumph), and an overall unity of purpose. Moreover, Gladstone's ability to endure these labors also provoked admiration: "wonderful," "astounding," a "positively hideous amount of toil." By mid-December even *Punch* was moved to celebrate what it called "The Colossus of Words": an "old man eloquent," who managed to bear

> *Blithely the burden of his seventy years*
> *A true Colossus, firmly poised and bold*
> *The light of principles to hoist and hold.*[44]

Scottish Liberals perfected arrangements further. Local organizer John J. Reid intervened to help set a railway route to Edinburgh that increased opportunities for Gladstone's admirers to pay homage on the way. Lord Rosebery matched Gladstone's topical speeches to their most appropriate venues. He also anticipated situations when Gladstone might address what he called "the multitude" unable to gain admission to oversubscribed meetings. And he set the time of Gladstone's evening meetings somewhat earlier than convention, to enable "crowds to see you by daylight."[45]

Meeting places were decorated with flags and lanterns, portraits, evergreen, draperies, and messages of support: "Come awa', Willie and sweep clean"; "Glorious Welcome to Gladstone, Liberator of his country, Guardian of Britain's honour, peace and prosperity" (this calico flag must have been rather long). String bands and parties of vocalists kept the crowds entertained.[46] The dramatic force of the setting was registered in one notable satire, "The Bearding of the Buccleuch," wherein a gallant Gladstone challenged the Earl of Dalkeith:

> *I come with banner, band and bow,*
> *As strong man seeks strong man, for foe.*

THE COLOSSUS OF WORDS.

"The Colossus of Words," illustration for *Punch*, 13 December 1879.
(Courtesy of Look and Learn/George Collection.)

Not surprisingly, the union of man and moment produced an enormous outpouring of enthusiasm. It was a kind of "Gladstone mania," bemoaned one contributor to the conservative journal the *Edinburgh Courant*. Railway platforms overflowed, farmers lit bonfires, and cottagers placed candles on window ledges as he passed. The *Scotsman* claimed that not one-tenth of applicants garnered tickets for Gladstone's major events. Crowds surged, coachmen were trampled, and hats and handkerchiefs were waved. "All Scotland is panting for a look at him," recorded Gladstone's daughter, Mary. The People's William was gifted with rugs and table covers, albums, caskets, rugs, tweed suits, and much else besides.[47]

Importantly, however, Gladstone's own speeches framed and interpreted his excited reception in quite particular ways. The orator certainly received the "vapour" of enraptured attention (to use his preferred term), but he also returned it as a "flood."

Gladstone told the people of Scotland that he journeyed northward on a "very grave errand." The circumstances of British politics were, he asserted, "far from being ordinary": the "whole system of Government" was at issue, and the "most important crisis" in fifty years had reached a crucial testing time. To vindicate his opposition, "a detailed exposition of a difficult and complicated case" was required. In consequence, the orator made his case "on the highest grounds of principle," laying out his fundamental beliefs regarding foreign policy at some length. He also urged his listeners to "look to my proofs and my arguments." And he spoke plainly and clearly and earnestly: "I will endeavour to be intelligible to the end."[48]

In essence, it was an appeal of high seriousness. Never playing down to his audiences, Gladstone instead paid them the compliment of assuming an aptitude for reasoned, tempered, moral judgment. He professed to detect this competence in the "stillness" and "evident interest" of auditors. He explicitly rejected the pursuit of "uninformed cheers." When thousands gathered in the Waverley Market, he responded with a tribute to the rationality of the masses. This was, he claimed, a "festival of freedom." Not an expression of popular license, however, it was dedicated to "that rational freedom . . . which is essentially allied with order and with loyalty."[49] The people were ordered, loyal, reasoning beings. In freely gathering to hear him speak, they exercised a capacity for citizenship by no means yet formally guaranteed.

What was the effect of this tremendous demonstration? In the immediate aftermath of the statesman's peregrinations, several conservative journals publicly doubted his oratorical efficacy. The tour, it was said, had "failed in getting up . . . steam." London journals were especially skeptical, while Disraeli's chancellor of the exchequer likened events to a "great discharge of musketry," arresting attention but wounding only a "very few." In a letter to the Rugby and Dunchurch Conservative Association, Lord Dalkeith argued that Gladstone "has done himself no good by the speeches but rather the contrary." Many journals carried hostile commentary alongside the Liberal lion's words: "fervid harangues," "wildness of utterance," and "general overstatement and overstrain." The *Times* drew an unflattering contrast between the vaunted leaders of Britain's past and the unconventional oratory of the candidate for Midlothian:

We have only to imagine, if we can, a Pitt or a Castlereagh stumping the provinces, and taking into his confidence, not merely a handful of electors, but any crowd he could collect in any part of this island.[50]

This was a distaste overwhelmed by the heady progress of events, however. All the major newspapers covered Gladstone's speech making in great detail, and the *Times* itself published more than eighty-five thousand of his words during the first week of the tour alone. Pictorials, sometimes a full page in length, adorned the *London Illustrated News.* Two editions of Gladstone's speeches—one a large octavo volume, the other a smaller pamphlet—appeared in mid-December.[51]

The dominant response was approbation. Contributors to the leading journals described Gladstone's efforts as "astounding," "extraordinary," and "the most wonderful speeches ever made by any statesman." *Blackwood's Edinburgh Magazine* was confident that "the views of Mr. Gladstone are in the ascendant." Gladstone himself had no doubt that his labors presaged success: the "overall effect," he wrote to Rosebery, "has I think surpassed all our hopes." Other Liberals adjudged the stumping "admirably effective," a "conquest," and even a "series of well-ordered triumphs."[52]

The Liberal victory in the general election of April 1880 strengthened this interpretation. Conservative losses of more than one hundred seats were matched by massive Liberal gains; from a position of weakness, the Liberal Party secured a very firm grip on the House of Commons. Chastened, Robert Gascoyne-Cecil, the third Marquess of Salisbury—Disraeli's supplanted foreign secretary—likened the episode to a "hurricane that has swept us away," "so strange and new a phenomenon that we shall not for some time understand its real meaning."[53]

Robbed of confidence, Conservative critics of Gladstone's unconventional course now fell comparatively silent. It was the Liberal icon, said *Macmillan's Magazine*, who had instead attained a further "proof" of his "unrivalled insight into the popular temper." The *Manchester Guardian* thought Gladstone's personal triumph "at least as grand" as that of the party: "In contesting a county he really has been challenging the suffrages of a nation. . . . It is Mr. Gladstone who has been winning." The *Daily News* agreed, describing Gladstone's success as a "kind of epitome" of the Liberal victory "all through the country."[54]

Even those who most detested the outcome of the elections tended eventually to admit that it was in some sense Gladstone's personal majority. Queen Victoria conceded as much when she commissioned him to form a new government. The *Times* admitted that Gladstone had roused electors "by the very dregs of electioneering rhetoric." *Punch*, for its part, greeted the results of the poll with a portrait of the Liberal champion as "the Bagpiper of Midlothian," leading the electors as if helpless children:

> But the voters flocked from east, west, south
> And the Midlands, witched by that magical mouth;

Voters from counties, and cities and boroughs,
From toil at the furnace, from work at the furrows;
Voters of all sorts and sizes, in fine,
Rushing and crushing, ran eagerly after
That wonderful music, and shouting and laughter
. . .

A mighty flood whose resistless roll
Swept the Piper's foes from their place at the Poll.[55]

Whether this popular judgment was well founded is quite another matter. Several clear-eyed historians have questioned the direct influence of the Midlothian campaign on national political fortunes. The British economy had entered a downturn, and Disraeli's conservative government bore the blame. The Liberal Party greatly improved its internal organization, and a National Liberal Federation, founded by the Birmingham radical Joseph Chamberlain, was prominent in some sixty constituency victories. Even in the seat of Midlothian, Gladstonian oratory was only one of several forces that contributed to success. The Grand Old Man's election victory cost the party some £2,567. Electioneering agents were employed in eight separate districts. Handbills and posters were pasted up in city streets, pamphlets and postcards were dispatched to electors, and the Earl of Rosebery exerted his power as landowner to counter the interventions of Gladstone's conservative rival, the Duke of Buccleuch. And although the labors were great, the margin of Midlothian victory was narrow enough to incite commentary. In January 1879, local Liberal organizers estimated that Gladstone would command some 1,569 votes in any future poll. After the great campaign, the celebrated oratory, and the national attention, William Ewart Gladstone's final tally was no more than 1,579.[56]

These were facts at first obscured by the entrancing loquacity of the Liberal icon, however. Gladstone had stumped, and Gladstone had conquered. With its air of American modernity and its unambiguously successful resolution, Midlothian appeared as a model for subsequent British electioneering.[57] As the Birmingham radical Joseph Chamberlain wrote to Gladstone in 1885, platform oratory now seemed a necessity even to the governing party:

The Platform has become one of the most powerful and indispensable instruments of Government, and any Ministry which neglected the opportunities offered by it would speedily lose the confidence of the People.[58]

Chamberlain himself was a stump orator of undoubted competence and unflagging industry. Perhaps more surprisingly, however, Britain's conservative politicians also took up the technique in the aftermath of Gladstone's entrancing tour.

Lord Salisbury (who supplanted Gladstone as prime minister in mid-1885) complained to Queen Victoria that the "duty" of "making political speeches" was an "aggravation" that "Your Majesty's servants . . . owe entirely to Mr. Gladstone." Nonetheless, as Gladstone's own secretary noted, Salisbury apparently lost "no opportunity of haranguing the mob at railway stations and from his railway carriage." Likewise, Sir Stafford Northcote, the leader of the Conservative Party in the House of Commons, also took to the platform ("'Staffy' on the Stump!" wrote London's *Fun*), while Randolph Churchill emerged as a major political force principally through his facility for popular speech.[59]

Scion of the House of Marlborough, short, vigorous, and bold, Churchill was, said the *County Gentleman*, a "stump-orator born." His voice was resonant (although not musical), his gestures theatrical and even melodramatic, with the twirling of a long moustache and the extravagant waving of arms. His talents as a phrasemaker were widely acknowledged (perhaps an echo of his hero, Disraeli?), and his recourse to invective and ridicule notorious. The Gladstone ministry, he said, comprised "children of the revolution . . . robbers of churches . . . destroyers of property"; the Grand Old Man was the "Moloch of Midlothian." Although critics were perplexed by the "almost burlesque exaggeration" and "errors of taste," they were also forced to concede the "pluck" of a "very effective speaker for a Tory platform."[60]

Over the first half of the 1880s, Churchill kept up a continuous and telling platform attack on Gladstone's newest government. One admiring publication presented him as "St. Randolph," come to meet the challenge of "St. William the Woodcutter." Only Churchill, it seemed, was something of a match for the Liberal champion. By the end of 1885, his speeches had been collected under the title *Politics for the Working Classes*, and he was secretary of state for India in a new Conservative government.[61] By 1886, he was the chancellor of the exchequer and the leader of the House.

Churchill's fall from the pinnacle was as rapid as his ascension. He resigned amid rumor and political miscalculation in December 1886, never to regain such lofty heights. But as what one historian has called "the first Conservative to set up as a hustings orator in Gladstone's style," Churchill nevertheless helped inaugurate a great change in the ways and means of British politics. If Conservative tradition had been against stump oratory, Churchill put an end to such false modesty.[62] And throughout the 1880s, Britain's leading journals also came to recognize, and to accept, the permanent presence of the politics of the stump.

"On the Stump."

Randolph Churchill "On the Stump,"
illustration for *Judy*, 12 September 1883.
(Courtesy of the HathiTrust and ProQuest LLC.)

The *Morning Post* was among the first to acknowledge "a considerable change" in public life at this time: "the inordinate increase of what the Americans have called stump oratory." London's *Graphic* also suggested that "the platform is rapidly superseding Westminster Palace as a means of direct popular communication." The *Pall Mall Gazette* welcomed a new situation in which the "statesman of the stump" (an unaccustomed and revealing combination) "is moulding a public opinion which in Parliament he is merely endeavouring to learn." Other papers described extra-parliamentary speech as "the order of the day" and "less the exception than the rule." One provincial newspaper, the *Ipswich Journal*, summed up the passage of events with perhaps the greatest acuity:

The remarkable feature in all this flood of talk is the gradual alteration in our political manners, which has made it a matter of course for the leaders of parties to stump the country. . . . The Grand Old Man himself set the fashion, and it appears to be followed pretty readily by the chieftains on both sides.[63]

The first draft of history, contemporary journalism clearly anticipated the main lines of subsequent interpretation. As the years passed, the legend of the great transformation of Midlothian grew to substantial dimensions. Gladstone's labors came increasingly to be seen as a major episode in modern political history.

The carriers of Midlothian into historical memory were diverse: partisan, educative, cultural. First and perhaps most remarkably, the Conservative Party returned often to Gladstone's Scottish orations in the years immediately following the 1880 poll. For the Tories, the Midlothian speeches were a textbook of heresies: the inciter of disturbances in Ireland and of foreign wars, the poisoner of relations with the German Empire. They were "rabid orations," and, it was argued, they were the means by which Gladstone had "floated into power." A thinly veiled version of the Midlothian campaign was imagined in H. D. Traill's fictional composition, *The New Lucian* (1884):

> The English people laid themselves a few years ago . . . at the feet of one man—for no better reason that any impartial observer could perceive than that he passionately entreated them to do so—and there they have remained ever since.[64]

Although the perspective was critical, the emphasis on Gladstone's alchemical power was significant. In their repeated attacks on the supremacy and the evil of the Midlothian orations, British Conservatives contributed to their continuing prominence, and thereby to their enduring historical reputation.

The Liberal Party, of course, held tightly to events as a great and treasured victory. The notion that Gladstone was solely responsible for the triumph of 1880 became a defining feature of party mythology. The table on which Gladstone composed the notes for his Midlothian speeches was donated to the Scottish Liberal Club in Edinburgh. Party publications came to include extracts from his glowing words, as do present-day websites. Later party leaders have quite explicitly drawn inspiration from Gladstone's great deeds when framing their own election tours.[65]

Biographies of Gladstone amplified the theme. These appeared almost annually over the late nineteenth century, sometimes in anonymous and popular forms. John Morley's *Life of Gladstone* was the apotheosis of the genre. When Macmillan published the book in 1903, crowds besieged the publisher's offices, such was the expectation. Morley promoted the idea that the Midlothian campaign was central to Disraeli's defeat: "Mr. Gladstone's tremendous projectiles had pounded the ministerial citadel to the ground."

A celebration rather than an analysis, it became the classic account of these increasingly mythical events.[66] Major works of history have shared these emphases. In 1892, Henry Jephson published *The Platform: Its Rise and Progress*, since acknowledged as a monument to the utility of platform oratory and still the only major historical work to consider the subject in some depth. Like Morley, Jephson was convinced of Gladstone's import. He treated the 1879 speeches as a major episode in the career of his historical subject—the "principle feature" of the "Platform campaign" of the period and a marker of a new moment in a developing political practice:

> Never had a more striking tribute been paid to the status and dignity of the Platform, never had its position been so fully recognised and acknowledged, not merely in word, but in act, as the superior, and ultimate arbiter of Parliament.[67]

Subsequent memoir and history echoed Jephson and Morley. Studies of Midlothian have remained relatively common, as have biographical studies of Gladstone that have paid close attention to his oratorical achievements. Plays and radio and television documentaries have considered the topic. The contest between Gladstone and Disraeli has been described as a "hardy perennial" of upper-level high school history in Britain, which has helped sustain a sophisticated textbook market, too. "Gladstone's Midlothian Campaign" is included as a standard topic in the school curriculum that covers British history from 1865 to 1915.[68]

In consequence, the "time of Midlothian" and a "Midlothian type campaign" have become shorthand in British political culture. Not just Liberals but Labour and Conservative Party leaders have invoked Midlothian in major public interventions. The custom has been shared by several political commentators in Britain and the United States.[69]

Outside Britain the reputation of the speeches has also long glittered brightly. Contemporary newssheets in the United States greeted Midlothian as a "campaign in the American sense" and a "democratic triumph" accomplished by "popular methods." Gladstone's victory, it was said, "brought a long stride of advancement for democracy in England," and his capacity for platform speech was even favorably compared with that of American presidential candidates.[70]

Likewise, in the Australian colony of Victoria, the *Argus* suggested that Midlothian was "as famous" as America's most venerated stumping battles, further arguing that the campaign "led to the adoption of the stump" as a "familiar institution" in British politics.[71] In the neighboring colony of New Zealand, the *Wanganui Herald* ventured a parallel view, noting the performance of stumping in Britain "from the Prime Minister down" in the early 1880s and reasoning, on this basis, that "the 'stump'" was no longer a "dishonoured or dishonourable institution" but rather had become "highly respectable and altogether constitutional."[72]

European observers were also fascinated by Gladstone's efforts.[73] Perhaps most famously of all, Max Weber's 1919 lecture, "Politics as a Vocation," drew attention to the political efficacy of Gladstone's "'grand' demagogy" as a device through which he became "the dictator of the battlefield of elections." Weber's interpretation treated Gladstone as the archetype of the "charismatic personality" in democratic politics, powerful enough even to direct the party machine.[74] Embedded in this justly celebrated analysis, the Midlothian speeches were therefore subject to much more than historical narration: they were also imprinted upon the very intellectual foundations of modern political sociology.

The transformative power of political events rests not simply upon their enactment but also upon the lessons they are thought to carry. Gladstone's Midlothian tour not only brought a new government to power but also attracted immediate and enduring political attention. Although Gladstone's speeches were undoubtedly important, their place in historical memory came to be elevated more highly still. Remembrances of the events of 1879 tended to focus most fully on the individual achievements of the Grand Old Man on the stump. If other forces helped secure the Liberal Party's victory, then these were downplayed in historical memory. If some were unmoved by Gladstone's stump oratory, then this response was largely forgotten, too. The label "Midlothian" came to signify a great orator winning a triumph against the odds in the exercise of dauntless moral eloquence. The reception and the framing of the event helped secure its importance perhaps almost as effectively as the labors of the great Liberal himself.

The familiar perspectives of biography and national history typically treat the Midlothian campaign as a great individual achievement and a pivotal moment in the struggle for British parliamentary power; it was certainly both of these. But viewed from the less familiar vantage of transnational history, the campaign was also a major episode in the Anglo-American practice of the politics of the stump.

Stump speaking had been named on the American frontier and had long been identified with the Republic. Most Britons rejected stumping as a symbol of the rough democracy and vulgar self-seeking that prevailed across the Atlantic. The few British radicals who spoke outdoors for democratic rights from the 1830s confirmed the apparent danger and radicalism of the technique. Widespread stumping in the turbulent and democratic Australian colony of Victoria further entrenched these associations.

Therefore, when a former prime minister of Britain attracted mass enthusiasm through a series of thrilling speeches, this appeared as much more than the adoption of a particular technique of vote winning. To Britons and to others, it was understood as a moment in the passage of "American" and "colonial" methods to the home of parliamentary government. It was a contributor to a more open, vigorous, and radical political culture. It was an expression of the rise of the platform, as compared with the formal halls of Parliament. And it was thereby an agent of democratic change.

A transnational perspective allows one to better comprehend the import of events in Scotland in 1879 and 1880. Likewise, the historical processes identified in earlier chapters also help explain the full acceptance of the British stump. Just as in the United States and Australia, stump speaking in Britain grew out of earlier experiments in political and religious oratory (including experiments in these other English-speaking lands). It reflected the emergence of mass political parties, and it exploited the opportunities of modern transport and communications. As in the earlier Australian case, the tools of electioneering owed something to more radical struggles. And as in other examples, the successful deployment of the technique by an effective orator created a precedent that opponents and admirers quickly followed. Individual performances were encompassed by repeated political interactions.

Yet the story of the British stump also departs from the other cases considered in this book. Gladstone was a more accomplished politician than any of the earlier pioneers of stump speaking active in Australia or the United States. At the time he joined the first Midlothian struggle, he had served as chancellor of the exchequer for more than seven years and as prime minister for more than five. He was renowned as a Christian and a classicist. He was widely understood as a disinterested statesman rather than a ruthless seeker after personal reward. He came to the platform to challenge apparent violations of human rights. He spoke in the language of "sin" and "conscience." He claimed that his auditors were rational and moral beings.

This background undoubtedly contributed to his political successes. It also meant that his oratorical performances carried even greater cultural significance. When the Grand Old Man took to the stump in the manner that he did, it became much harder for critics to present the method as a disreputable act or an immoral intervention. If stumping helped Gladstone become the people's idol, then Gladstone also helped stumping win a final acceptance as an ethical and rational practice in a modern, liberal democracy. For the bulk of the nineteenth century, Britain was a laggard in the deployment of stump oratory. Through the enactment of memory of Gladstone's performances, it was transformed into an example of what stump oratory might achieve as well as a model of what the stump orator might aspire to be.

CONCLUSION

POLITICS, THE MODERN WAY

Going "on the stump" is now a routine feature of democratic politics. Leading campaigners conventionally undertake often long and grueling tours, and media outlets report the daily round of campaign addresses and replies. Conventional, uncontroversial, apparently unremarkable, the stump speech is now so fully accepted that its ubiquity passes almost without comment.

The history of this performance has never before been traced in a detailed and disciplined study. Nonetheless, the fact of this earlier history is sometimes registered in public memory and debate. The "stump speaking" of the nineteenth century is mostly recalled as a kind of golden age: a more elevated and noble era, when the giants of oratory spoke out in bold phrases and when citizens listened with concentrated and eager attention.

In Britain, William Gladstone's Midlothian tour remains a touchstone of democratic vigor. With some reverence, it is consistently cited as a moment when oratory mattered, when speakers demanded the best of their auditors, and when a moral case might be prosecuted through elaborate and sophisticated rhetoric. British politicians wearied with the hegemony of "soundbite politics" reference the Midlothian campaign as a model for contemporary debate. Roy Jenkins, Gladstone's biographer and a major figure in Labour and then Liberal-Democratic politics, has put the case most fully:

> No-one would expect a Gladstone speech of two and a half hours, redolent with many Latin quotations, to be persuasive [today]. . . .

But nonetheless I think one does regret the almost complete decline in politics, in the last twenty-five years or so, I think, of the sustained arguing of a case, with the careful use of language and phraseology which helps to advance it. But there we are.[1]

Neither is this a purely British preoccupation, for as in so many stump-related matters, here the Americans were pioneers. The lamentation for a lost age of political rhetoric was evident in the United States as long ago as the last quarter of the nineteenth century. Stump speaking had deteriorated, leading American journals claimed from the 1880s: it was now a "lost art." As America had developed beyond a "pioneer condition," the oratory "adapted" to this society had also been left behind. The "old-fashioned political campaign orator" had "gone out," said the *Los Angeles Times* in 1887, and he was most likely "never to return."[2]

American lamentation for a passing age was linked to a growing veneration of its most influential stump speakers. Abraham Lincoln, America's sixteenth president, had emerged as a major national figure in a series of Illinois stump debates with Stephen Douglas ("the Little Giant") in 1858 as these rivals competed for election to the U.S. Senate. A child of Kentucky and a youth in Indiana, Lincoln had been exposed to stump speaking at its rawest; one friend recalled that Lincoln had "made quite good stump speeches when between the age of 15 & 20" for the "amusement" of neighbors and friends. Occasionally, so the stories go, he would test himself against visiting electioneers.[3] Then, in the late 1820s, he reportedly "turned Whig" and embraced the example of Henry Clay (his "beau ideal" of a statesman). In the years before 1858, he worked hard to propel the Whigs and then the Republicans into a dominant position in national affairs.[4]

The 1858 contest between Lincoln and Douglass was therefore a vigorous partisan battle waged without restraint and regulated by little decorum. Observers criticized an apparently bitter atmosphere of "sophistry" and "personal vituperation." The protagonists interrupted each other, repeated false charges, exploited race prejudice, and argued with reporters. But if these features of the Illinois contest were once widely known, then little of their detail survived the worshipful attentions of later years. Increasingly, the hard edges were smoothed away. Over the passage of several decades, the 1858 debates were reimagined as the noble jousting of principled advocates, symbols of a more rational and moral age.

Lincoln and Douglas were men of "deep" and "profound" convictions, it was said, "brave," "fearless," and "indomitable." The "glorious" clashes were "sacred" events in American memory, claimed one president; his successor affirmed their greatness. Chief Magistrate William McKinley thought them a trial in the "forum of reason" that inspired "love of liberty" and "devotion to free institutions." Theodore Roosevelt paid tribute to "winged words" that "will fly through that portion of eternity recorded in the history of our race," making the nation "united" and "free."[5] Increasingly, it was as though the antagonists had shared a common platform for ceremonial or religious oratory, not a tooth-and-nail conflict for office and favor.

The higher status of the debates was built up in new constructions and traced out in ceremonial spaces. A commemorative bronze tablet was unveiled at the site of one encounter, and an immense boulder was used to mark a second, and then a third. The cottage in which the debates were planned was handed over to the state of Illinois. The debates were reenacted at popular pageants and revisited in stage plays, anniversary addresses, and television productions. They became, by common consent, the most famous debates that the country had known.[6]

Acknowledged as the most distinguished and worthy exemplar of democratic electioneering—the "high point of stump oratory," said the *New York Times*—the debates understandably became a tool of evaluation.[7] The contest of 1858 thereby became a weapon of political criticism, too. This was a practice that upraised the status of Lincoln's contributions higher still: the more rational and principled the antagonists of 1858, the more attentive and respectful the people of the prairies, the more forcefully one might censure the politics of the contemporary Republic.

American political critics fixed upon Lincoln's debates with Douglas in this way only a few decades after his passing. Evident throughout the twentieth century, the practice became increasingly prevalent with the coming of television. The first televised debates between presidential contenders encouraged the practice. The clash of Lincoln and Douglas was invoked as a model for the 1960 contest between John F. Kennedy and Richard Nixon and then, swiftly, as the basis for disaffection. Debates between the latter duumvirate, it was said, lacked the moral seriousness of their illustrious forebears as well as a philosophical depth, rough directness, sufficient time, and genuine adherence to the debate form.[8]

Politicians of later decades figured little better in comparisons of these kinds. Lincoln and Douglas did not use ghostwriters, it was observed, nor did they take "cheap shots" to "score points." Their conflict concerned "fundamental disagreement," their debate was "unfettered," and their speeches were witty and eloquent.[9]

Dissatisfied politicians also commended the 1858 debates as an alternative to contemporary electioneering. So did leading journalists, pundits, political scientists, and venerable historians. A series of prestigious volumes considered the debates. Although some perceptive observers acknowledged

Lincoln and Douglas debate at Galesburg, Illinois, 7 October 1858.
(Getty Images/Kean Collection.)

that Lincoln's most famous campaign had become a "mythic standard," this reflection was seldom shared.[10] Dejected with the politics of the present, critics only rarely considered the stumping of the past with steady and unromantic eyes. Once imagined as an arena of coarseness, danger, and self-aggrandizement, the nineteenth-century stump came, ironically, to figure as a symbol of a more heroic and elevated age.

This is the first full study of stump speaking from origins to acceptance. Rejecting the nostalgia of American and British myth, it offers a very different perspective on the performance, reception, and significance of this fascinating political form. There is not much indication of a "golden age," in the sense of a purely principled and rational period of deliberative exchange. But there is ample evidence that stump speaking made an important, little understood contribution to the making of modern democratic politics. Briefly, this book has advanced seven distinctive arguments.

First, "stump oratory" was identified, named, and developed in a very specific environment: the southwestern states of the early American Republic. These polities were among the first to extend the right to vote and to stand for office to white men without property. For their chosen inhabitants, they offered an unprecedented opportunity for advancement and an absence of traditional social authority. Stump speaking reflected a rough, masculine, and unequal democracy. It also expressed and extended a demotic oral culture of rich inventiveness and voluble power.

Second, the orators of the southwestern stump were not simply candidates for office; they were also challengers to social deference. In the stump speeches of the most prominent frontier candidates, a distinctive mode of political appeal was starkly expressed: the profession of a humble birth (indeed, sometimes the pretense of a poverty not fully experienced), the assertion of a masculine power through speech, and the preference to speak in a plain and unadorned way. Leading stump speakers reimagined the place of oratory in the life of the Republic. Their performances won them public positions but also helped fashion a world of values and actions that would come to define modern mass democracy in the years that followed.

Third, as an undoubted challenge to convention, "stump oratory" inspired great public interest. Widely reported in a growing press, it was also the subject of (often parodic) treatment in fiction, plays, minstrelsy, painting, and much else besides. The character of these representations tended often to exaggerate the novelty, vulgarity, and radicalism of the stump speech. It magnified the influence of stumping on public culture, as the "stump orator" became a kind of lightning rod for anxieties around democracy. And it thereby shaped the context in which the method was more widely taken up, influencing the reception of stump speeches in America's North and in other countries, too.

Fourth, the diffusion of stump speaking across the continent was relatively slow and controversial. The performance of "stump oratory" was still considered a novelty in the northeastern states of America some two or three decades after its identification in the Southwest. It was propelled northward by the growing intensity and sophistication of a mass partisan struggle. This transformed as well as transported the performance, so that the stump oratory that came eventually to define the American Republic was shaped by party networks and resources—delivered by party champions, reported by party journals, contained within party-sponsored spectacles, directed toward the incitement of existing party supporters as much as the persuasion of uncommitted electors. Partisan stump oratory, not the original frontier form, became a national American custom.

Fifth, although acknowledged as an American creation, stump oratory had an equally significant international career. The system of parliamentary government in Britain and its colonies traditionally granted electioneering oratory only a very circumscribed role. The hustings possessed a venerable lineage, and hustings speeches could be unruly and colorful affairs. Nonetheless, American-style stumping seemed different for several reasons. First, it savored of democracy, and in Britain the franchise was greatly restricted. Second, it involved movement across the land (the "stumping tour"), whereas a British member of Parliament (MP) was understood to be the representative of a single constituency. Third, it implied promise giving and deference to the electors' wishes; British political tradition elevated the autonomy and deliberative capacities of those enclosed within the parliamentary chamber, deprecating the relative import of public opinion.

Sixth, stumping migrated from the United States through complex and varied labors. Newspaper reports, fictional composition, minstrel performance, and pamphleteering conveyed something of the method, although they sometimes misled more than illuminated. Meanwhile, over several decades, British radicals took to the platform in the quest for political and social justice. Their willingness to speak outdoors, their habit of traveling beyond a single constituency, and their declaration of a democratic faith all resembled reported American practice. British rebels were therefore increasingly dubbed (and frequently scorned) as "stump orators." Their experiments heightened the sense that this was a dangerous and contentious act, and their capacity to incite mass enthusiasm established a model for the more established politician in the years that followed.

The first major stump electioneering campaign waged outside the United States was ventured in the Australian colony of Victoria. The principal Australian colonies had won new constitutions in the 1850s; property qualifications were dismantled for male electors, and a secret ballot was soon introduced. In these new circumstances, radical and liberal politicians began to appeal to the newly enfranchised; they increasingly campaigned for office within their own electorates and outside them, too.

These departures from convention drew swift condemnation as "American" and unconstitutional forms of "stump oratory." They were not direct imitations of partisan American vote winning, however. The first British and Australian politicians to be labeled as "stump orators" were convinced of the moral failure of elites and of the virtues of the people. They adopted stump oratory as a means of invoking the moral power of the masses and of reshaping public culture. This was not merely a means of winning elections; it was a challenge to the meaning and practice of parliamentary government.

In Victoria, Charles Gavan Duffy, the former Irish radical and later the premier of the colony, turned to stump speaking in the early 1870s to galvanize popular enthusiasm and to pressure the Upper House of the legislature to let his most radical measures pass into law. Graham Berry, Duffy's treasurer and later his successor as the leader of Victorian radicalism, rose to prominence in a long series of platform orations delivered in urban parks, city electorates, and regional halls. Ejected from office by factional intrigue, Berry deployed the technique in the late 1870s to coerce his usurpers to accede to an election. Agitation therefore blended with electioneering and movement campaigning with partisan appeals. When Berry won a great majority in the 1877 election, the method was widely vindicated, and it was soon embraced across the continent.

Events moved more slowly in Britain. A habit of "vacation" or "recess" oratory developed from the second half of the nineteenth century as a response to changes in electoral arrangements and to the new technologies of telegraph and rail. William Gladstone was among the first British politicians to understand and exploit these opportunities. Like Duffy and Berry, he ascended to the stump to prosecute a moral and democratic cause, not simply to find a new way to personal power. His famous Midlothian tours, beginning in 1879, came to symbolize high principle and righteous passion at least as much as practical advancement in the methods of winning votes.

Seventh, the consideration of three national cases not only establishes patterns of temporal succession and influence but also clarifies the broader forces that drove the adoption of the stump speech. This was a modern and democratic form of oratory, and it clearly reflected the extension of the franchise. The United States was the first polity to grant a mass franchise and was also the midwife of stump speaking. Australia followed as a democratic and oratorical pioneer; Britain was a comparative laggard in broadening the suffrage and embracing the stump speech. Contemporary journalists sometimes identified a direct connection between changes in franchise and in oratory, as did sophisticated observers, among them Max Weber. Distinguished historians have since reinforced this view.

Yet the historical relationship between these developments was somewhat more contingent than is often assumed. A vast majority of white men possessed the vote in the aftermath of the American Revolution, yet the practice of stump speaking spread across the continent only from the 1820s. Nearly all white males could vote in the Australian colonies in the second half of the 1850s, yet Charles Gavan Duffy did not undertake the first major stumping tour until a decade and a half later. William Gladstone, by contrast, waged the Midlothian campaign when the British franchise was still a relatively exclusive possession. Despite electoral reform in 1832 and again in 1867, it has been estimated that in the Midlothian electorate of 1879, only one man in seven had the right to vote. Across Britain, only one in three men possessed the privilege at this time.

The time lag between the extension of the suffrage and the adoption of stump speaking in the United States and Australia makes it clear that a full male franchise, in and of itself, was insufficient to guarantee the immediate embrace of the stump. On the other hand, the British case establishes that democratic campaign speeches could predate the establishment of a democratic franchise for all men. Here, a mass electorate rather than universal male suffrage served as a sufficient precondition for the adoption of the stump speech.[11] Other factors, beyond the franchise, clearly played some role.

A number of additional forces seem to be common across the three cases of oratorical invention. In all three cases, the adoption of the stump speech was associated with episodes of intense political conflict. American politicians desperately struggled for partisan advantage from the middle 1820s. Australian radicals of the 1870s fought to pass legislation and drive apparent violators from office. In Midlothian, Gladstone waged a battle for Britain's soul that was also a quest to conquer a great political foe. In these febrile political episodes, antagonists were willing to brave odium in the resort to radical and proscribed means of winning votes. And in periods of close and continuous competition, the isolated performance of the stump speech, if successful, could promote emulation so that it eventually passed into common political usage. Competitive dynamics were therefore central to the rise of the stump.

But if competition helped drive leaders to create new forms of campaign oratory, then earlier forms of public action also appeared to serve as direct inspirations. As the early chapters of this volume established, the stump speech of the American Southwest followed earlier performances of peripatetic and demotic oratory in the cause of religion and the practice of the law. The tours of Henry Clay that promoted the stump speech rested upon a well-known tradition of political banqueting. And the success of presidential tours (that at first lacked persistent speech making) established a precedent for the roving stump tour by the aspirant for national power. Likewise, the first Britons and Australians who stumped for office could look back on a consistent practice of platform oratory among radicals striving for major reform. Radical orators of the British world helped demonstrate the power of public speech and establish conventions that regulated its performance and reception. Without these experiences, it is difficult to foresee its successful deployment by such parliamentary leaders as Duffy, Berry, and Gladstone.

Finally, the compelling character of oratorical originators was also a common factor in the three different polities. Whether American, British, or Australian, the pioneers of the stump speech were all distinguished by undoubted oratorical capacity and by appreciable personal magnetism. Their physical presence galvanized attention and inspired enthusiasm; their commanding personalities justified departure from political convention. It is surely no coincidence that adored and compelling popular leaders piloted the first stump tours of national consequence. If their noted oratorical travels helped confirm a general admiration, then their reputations also helped attract auditors and thereby win stumping expeditions great success. The adoption of the stump speech was therefore not the automatic reflex of a more democratic electorate. The capacities of a great popular champion also contributed to the successful enactment of this novel political form.

The transformations I have sought to chronicle and explain unfolded more than one hundred years ago. Can they offer insights into the campaign oratory and political culture of contemporary democracies? Or is the stumping of the twenty-first century simply too different for lessons or processes to be easily transposed?

Certainly, the divergences are immediately striking. In the electronic age, radio, television, and now online audiences vastly outstrip the number of electors directly assembling for any candidate's speech. Moreover, it is widely believed that it is the nature of the electronic media to impose distinctive pressures and constraints on speech making: elevating the import of images over text; limiting the time granted to a candidate's message (so that the synoptic moment has supplanted the developed discussion); creating new forums for political speech, such as talk shows, and televised debates; and crossing the threshold that once separated the public and intimate spheres.

These changes have not eliminated the activity of public speaking, and the words of the candidate remain highly important to the electoral contest. But close observers now depict the political eloquence of the electronic era as quite changed from earlier generations. Persuasion, it is said, rests less on the articulation of compelling argument than on the projection of an appealing personality. Political speech is more conversational, and the coining or delivery of memorable phrases is more highly prized. The successful candidate is more likely to be at ease in apparent self-disclosure and in the cultivation of a simulated intimacy. Celebrity and scandal form routine elements of the struggle for power. Media professionals with expertise in advertising and market research now help craft messages and candidates. And the infrastructure of a mass party is thought to have become less significant.

These notable developments have been charted and analyzed in many distinguished contributions to social science and contemporary history; I do not seek to challenge the major findings of such scholarship.[12] Nonetheless, placed in the fuller historical context that this book provides, the character of contemporary political talk emerges as more continuous with the past than is typically recognized. The stump orators surveyed in this book spoke in a plain and conversational language in performances imprinted with passionate desire. They sought to project personality as much as argument, and their efforts were supported by political professionals and party enthusiasts. The setting of the stump speech was often framed or manipulated to aid electoral appeals. The words of the orator were carried to many electors through the agency of (print) media; their best-known phrases became widely known.

Certainly, the differences between the nineteenth-century campaign and the vote winning of the present should not be overlooked. But the eloquence of the electronic age is not of a completely different character from what has come before, nor is it simply a debasement of an earlier purity.

If the findings of this volume are a reliable guide, then future versions of democratic persuasion are also likely to preserve many elements of past practice, even as they take on new forms and emphases. They are likely to draw upon changes in public performance and communication outside politics and to put them to work in the cause of vote winning. And they are likely to emerge from the experiments and improvisations of charismatic campaigners, straining for any advantage in close and unyielding political contests.

In documenting a past marked by controversy, I have sought to remind democrats of the significance of contentious and sometimes divisive speech. In charting consistent transformations, I have confirmed that democracy is always an unfinished journey, never a perfected state. And in the restoration of a relatively unexplored aspect of political history, I have attempted to provide resources that might support a political future that is as yet unknown and unsaid.

As previous pages have disclosed, the stump is a sometimes disruptive and ignoble tool. Yet it is partly through stump controversies that today's imperfect and contentious polities have been formed. It is in the capacity for oratorical contention—on the stump, and beyond—that they might yet be called to follow a better and a truer path.

ACKNOWLEDGMENTS

The research for this book was aided by an Australian Research Council (ARC) grant, held jointly with Professor Murray Goot, Macquarie University, Sydney, Australia. These funds supported the employment of research assistants Cam Binger and Jackie Dickenson. I thank Murray for his guidance and encouragement and both Cam and Jackie for their initiative, effectiveness, and many insights. All three helped shape the manuscript. Working with them has been a great pleasure. My thanks also go to the ARC.

I researched and wrote this book over a number of years, including a sabbatical from my teaching post at the University of Melbourne. While I was on sabbatical, I served as a visiting fellow in the History Department at Columbia University and as a visiting senior fellow at the Australian Studies Centre at King's College, University of London. I am very grateful to these institutions.

This book's transnational and comparative scope required and enabled me to extend my reach as a historian. Ira Katznelson, Gil Troy, and Richard Bensel provided valuable assistance with American history. Jon Lawrence and Neville Kirk helped with Britain. Fellow members of the history discipline at the University of Melbourne were also extremely generous with their expertise and their time. In particular, I thank Roland Burke, Trevor Burnard, Joy Damousi, David Goodman, Pat Grimshaw, Marilyn Lake, and Peter McPhee. Stuart Macintyre has been an indispensable source of wisdom and support for many years. Having leaned on him particularly heavily in the drafting of this book, I offer him special thanks.

In my search for a publisher, I appreciated the advice and good wishes of Ira Katznelson, Trevor Burnard, Fitzhugh Brundage, and Joyce Seltzer. Temple University Press provided a very welcome home for the manuscript. I am extraordinarily grateful to members of its staff—particularly Aaron Javsicas, Nikki Miller, Joan S. P. Vidal, and copyeditor Heather Wilcox—for their interest, enthusiasm, professionalism, and fair dealing. Two anonymous referees appointed by the press provided advice that helped improve the final product.

My family and friends have graciously lived with this book project for a number of years. The support of Nathan Hollier, Georgie Arnott, Rosa Holman, Paul Jones, Kurt Iveson, Cam Logan, Paul Martin, and Gilly Dempsey has been a great help. The Riordan family and the Scalmers have aided with the stresses and have provided much more. My great love and special thanks go to Bridie, Vida, and Chloe; their forbearance helped make the book possible, while their love helped place its challenges in proper dimensions.

My interest in stump oratory doubtless springs from several sources, but personal history certainly played a role. Like the stump orators of the nineteenth century, my father and mother did not enjoy a long formal education, spending most of their working lives as a truck driver and a secretary, respectively. But they conveyed a passionate interest in politics and a hatred of class inequality. They also modeled forms of argument—based on experience, everyday language, name calling, and even sometimes fabricated "facts"—that helped me better understand and value the subject of this research. I am very grateful to them for so much, and I dedicate this book to them.

NOTES

ABBREVIATIONS

ANL: David Crockett, *A Narrative of the Life of David Crockett of the State of Tennessee* (Knoxville: University of Tennessee Press, 1973), a facsimile edition of the 1834 edition, published by E. L. Carey and A. Hart, Philadelphia

Bear: John W. Bear, *The Life and Travels of John W. Bear, "The Buckeye Blacksmith"* (Baltimore: Binswanger, 1879)

DCC: James R. Boylston and Allen J. Wiener, eds., *David Crockett in Congress: The Rise and Fall of the Poor Man's Friend, with Collected Correspondence, Selected Speeches and Circulars* (Houston, TX: Bright Sky Press, 2009)

GP: Gladstone Papers, British Library

JJR: J. J. Reid Papers, National Library of Scotland, MS 19623

LRB: Lord Rosebery Papers, National Library of Scotland, MS 10022

LRBB: Lord Rosebery Papers, National Library of Scotland, MS 10074

LRBC: Lord Rosebery Papers, National Library of Scotland, MS 10075

LRBD: Lord Rosebery Papers, National Library of Scotland, MS 10076

PC: Henry Parkes Correspondence, Mitchell Library, State Library of New South Wales

*PHC*1: James F. Hopkins, ed., *The Papers of Henry Clay*, vol. 1, *The Rising Statesman, 1797–1814* (Lexington: University of Kentucky Press, 1959)

*PHC*2: James F. Hopkins, ed., *The Papers of Henry Clay*, vol. 2, *The Rising Statesman, 1815–1820* (Lexington: University of Kentucky Press, 1961)

*PHC*3: James F. Hopkins, ed., *The Papers of Henry Clay*, vol. 3, *Presidential Candidate, 1821–1824* (Lexington: University of Kentucky Press, 1963)

*PHC*4: James F. Hopkins, ed., *The Papers of Henry Clay*, vol. 4, *Secretary of State, 1825* (Lexington: University Press of Kentucky, 1972)

*PHC*5: James F. Hopkins and Mary W. M. Hargreaves, eds., *The Papers of Henry Clay*, vol. 5, *Secretary of State, 1826* (Lexington: University Press of Kentucky, 1973)

*PHC*6: Mary W. M. Hargreaves and James F. Hopkins, eds., *The Papers of Henry Clay*, vol. 6, *Secretary of State, 1827* (Lexington: University Press of Kentucky, 1981)

*PHC*7: Robert Seager II, ed., *The Papers of Henry Clay*, vol. 7, *Secretary of State, January 1, 1828–March 4, 1829* (Lexington: University Press of Kentucky, 1982)

*PHC*8: Robert Seager II, ed., *The Papers of Henry Clay*, vol. 8, *Candidate, Compromiser, Whig, March 5, 1829–December 31, 1836* (Lexington: University Press of Kentucky, 1984)

*PHC*9: Robert Seager II, ed., *The Papers of Henry Clay*, vol. 9, *The Whig Leader, January 1, 1837–December 31, 1843* (Louisville: University Press of Kentucky, 1988).

*PHC*10: Melba Porter Hay, ed., *The Papers of Henry Clay*, vol. 10, *Candidate, Compromiser, Elder Statesman, January 1, 1844–June 29, 1852* (Lexington: University Press of Kentucky, 1991)

SE: *Sketches and Eccentricities of Col. David Crockett* (New York: J and J Harper, 1833)

Troy: Gil Troy, *See How They Ran: The Changing Role of the Presidential Candidate*, rev. ed. (Cambridge, MA: Harvard University Press, 1996)

PREFACE

1. "Political speeches": "stump" in *The Free Dictionary*, available at http://idioms.thefree dictionary.com/stump. "Candidate" or "cause": see definition 14b of "stump" (n.), in *The Oxford English Dictionary*, available at www.oed.com.ezp.lib.unimelb.edu.au/view/Entry/192144?rskey =EGN7ef&result=1#eid. "Campaign or canvass": "stump," in *Collins English Dictionary* (online), available at www.collinsdictionary.com/dictionary/english/stump?showCookiePolicy=true. "Speak informally": William Safire, *The New Language of Politics: A Dictionary of Catchwords, Slogans, and Political Usage*, rev. and enl. ed. (New York: Collier Books, 1972), 652. Verb: "stump" in *Online Etymology Dictionary*, available at www.etymonline.com/index.php? term=stump&allowed_in_frame=0. *The Oxford English Dictionary*: 14a of the noun "stump"

and the compound "stump orator" in *The Oxford English Dictionary* (online), available at www
.oed.com.ezp.lib.unimelb.edu.au/view/Entry/192144?rskey=EGN7ef&result=1#eid. One hun
dred years before: Safire, *The New Language of Politics*, 652, citing Ann Maury in her "Memoirs
of a Huguenot Family."

2. Frontier states (note the designation as being associated with western states): "Election-
eering Anecdote," *New England Palladium*, 23 October 1807. Southern and western: "Stump
Oratory," *Portland Gazette and Maine Advertiser*, 30 July 1816, and "Stump Speeches," *Public
Ledger*, 16 August 1836. Southwestern mode of electioneering: "The Stump," *Daily Herald
and Gazette*, 5 September 1837. Peculiarly American: "The Stump," *Fayetteville Observer*, 11
October 1860. Essentially American: "'The Stump' as an Educator," *Frank Leslie's Illustrated
Newspaper*, 19 July 1856. *Charleston Patriot*, reproduced in "Stump Speaking," *New-Orleans
Commercial Bulletin*, 17 August 1844. Lecturer: General John L. Swift, paraphrased in "City
and Vicinity," *Lowell Daily Citizen and News*, 30 January 1868.

3. Public harangue: Thomas Carlyle, ed., "The Present Time," in *Latter-Day Pamphlets*
(London: Chapman and Hall, 1887), 6. Stumps and taverns: Thomas Carlyle, ed., "Stump-
Orator," in *Latter-Day Pamphlets* (Boston: Phillips, Sampson, 1855), 223. Universal suffrage:
Thomas Carlyle, ed., "The New Downing Street," in *Latter-Day Pamphlets* (London: Chapman
and Hall, 1887), 113. Ugly and perilous: Thomas Carlyle, ed., "Model Prisons," in *Latter-Day
Pamphlets* (London: Chapman and Hall, 1887), 60. Destruction and annihilation: Carlyle,
"Stump-Orator," 265.

4. See *The Oxford English Dictionary*, "stump" (noun) definition 14(b).

5. Alternative versions of a cultural approach: e.g., Marvin Meyers, *The Jacksonian Per-
suasion: Politics and Belief* (New York: Vintage Books, 1960); Daniel Walker Howe, *The Politi-
cal Culture of the American Whigs* (Chicago: University of Chicago Press, 1979); Mary P. Ryan,
Civic Wars: Democracy and Public Life in the American City during the Nineteenth Century
(Berkeley: University of California Press, 1997). Dramaturgical approaches in history: Simon
Gunn, "Analysing Behaviour as Performance," in *Research Methods for History*, ed. Simon
Gunn and Lucy Faire (Edinburgh: University of Edinburgh Press, 2011), 184–200. Key
works: Erving Goffman, *Presentation of Self in Everyday Life* (New York: Doubleday, 1959);
Victor Turner, *Schism and Continuity in an African Society* (Manchester, UK: Manchester
University Press, 1957). Gender: Judith Butler, *Gender Trouble: Feminism and the Subver-
sion of Identity* (New York: Routledge, 1999). Terrorism: Robin Erica Wagner-Pacifici, *The
Moro Morality Play: Terrorism as Social Drama* (Chicago: University of Chicago Press, 1986).
Liberalism: Patrick Joyce, *The Rule of Freedom: Liberalism and the Modern City* (London:
Verso, 2003). Nonviolence: Sean Scalmer, *Gandhi in the West: The Mahatma and the Rise of
Radical Protest* (Cambridge, UK: Cambridge University Press, 2011). On performative turn:
Peter Burke, "Performing History: The Importance of Occasions," *Rethinking History* 9, no.
1 (2005): 35, 42. Nineteenth-century America: e.g., Jean H. Baker, *Affairs of Party: The
Political Culture of Northern Democrats in the Mid-nineteenth Century* (Ithaca, NY: Cornell
University Press, 1983). British elections as performance: Jon Lawrence, *Electing Our Mas-
ters: The Hustings in British Politics from Hogarth to Blair* (Oxford, UK: Oxford University
Press, 2009).

6. Australians as more "American" than "English": "Literature," *Daily News*, 9 February
1849. For further information on transnational and comparative approaches to history that
have influenced me, see, e.g., Ian Tyrrell, "Reflections on the Transnational Turn in United
States History: Theory and Practice," *Journal of Global History* 4, no. 3 (2009): 453–474;
Michael Werner and Bénédicte Zimmerman, "Beyond Comparison: *Histoire Croisée* and the
Challenge of Reflexivity," *History and Theory* 45, no. 1 (2006): 30–50; Stefan Berger, "Comparative History," in *Writing History: Theory and Practice*, ed. Stefan Berger, Heiko Feldner,

and Kevin Passmore (London: Bloomsbury, 2010), 187–208. My approach to transnational history and attempt to combine this method with comparison is evident in an earlier work: Scalmer, *Gandhi in the West*.

7. The method is analogous to Lucy Riall's study of Garibaldi: *Garibaldi: Invention of a Hero* (New Haven, CT: Yale University Press, 2007). Riall does not celebrate Garibaldi's status as a "Great Man"; rather, she explores how his performances and his reception helped him be seen as "Great" as well as how his "greatness" had important political consequences. For more on her method, see Lucy Riall, "The Shallow End of History? The Substance and Future of Political Biography," *Journal of Interdisciplinary History* 40, no. 3 (2010): 375–397.

8. Performance and fluidity: Gunn, "Analysing Behaviour," 190; Burke, "Performing History," 38–39. Performance, repetition, and remaking: Butler, *Gender Trouble*; Scalmer, *Gandhi in the West*; Peter Snow, "Performing Society," *Thesis Eleven* 103, no. 1 (2010): 83.

9. The best of this work on the United States includes Richard Bensel, *The American Ballot Box in the Mid-nineteenth Century* (Cambridge, UK: Cambridge University Press, 2004); Gil Troy, *See How They Ran: The Changing Role of the Presidential Candidate*, rev. ed. (Cambridge, MA: Harvard University Press, 1996); Kathleen Hall Jamieson and David S. Birdsell, *Presidential Debates: The Challenge of Creating an Informed Electorate* (New York: Oxford University Press, 1988); Michael E. McGerr, *The Decline of Popular Politics: The American North, 1865–1928* (New York: Oxford University Press, 1986); Alexander Keyssar, *The Right to Vote: The Contested History of Democracy in the United States* (New York: Basic Books, 2000); Tracy Campbell, *Deliver the Vote: A History of Election Fraud, an American Political Tradition—1742–2004* (New York: Carrol and Graf, 2005). The relevant British literature includes the excellent Lawrence, *Electing Our Masters*, and, a little earlier, Frank Gorman, *Voters, Patrons and Parties: The Unreformed Electorate of Hanoverian England, 1734–1832* (Oxford, UK: Clarendon Press, 1989). On the platform: Henry Jephson, *The Platform: Its Rise and Progress* (New York: Macmillan, 1892). My debts to many excellent party histories and biographies are evident in subsequent chapters.

10. Oratory, colonialism, and revolution: Sandra M. Gustafson, *Eloquence Is Power: Oratory and Performance in Early America* (Chapel Hill: North Carolina Press, 2000). Conflicts over language: Thomas Gustafson, *Representative Words: Politics, Literature, and the American Language, 1776–1865* (New York: Cambridge University Press, 1992). Radical oratory: John Belchem, *Popular Radicalism and Nineteenth-Century Britain* (New York: St. Martin's Press, 1996), and *"Orator" Hunt: Henry Hunt and English Working-Class Radicalism* (Oxford, UK: Clarendon Press, 1985). Democratic eloquence: Kenneth Cmiel, *Democratic Eloquence: The Fight over Popular Speech in Nineteenth-Century America* (Berkeley: University of California Press, 1990). Public speech and public life: Carolyn Eastman, *A Nation of Speechifiers: Making an American Public after the Revolution* (Chicago: University of Chicago Press, 2009), and Joseph S. Meisel, *Public Speech and the Culture of Public Life in the Age of Gladstone* (New York: Columbia University Press, 2001). On the literary insignificance of election speeches, see Harry V. Jaffa, *Crisis of the House Divided: An Interpretation of the Issues in the Lincoln-Douglas Debates* (New York: Doubleday, 1959), 20.

11. For earlier works, see George D. Lillibridge, *Beacon of Freedom: The Impact of American Democracy upon Great Britain, 1830–1870* (Philadelphia: University of Pennsylvania Press, 1955); David P. Crook, *American Democracy in English Politics, 1815–1850* (Oxford, UK: Clarendon Press, 1965); Henry Pelling, *America and the British Left: From Bright to Bevan* (London: Adam and Charles Black, 1956); Frank Thistlethwait, *The Anglo-American Connection in the Early Nineteenth Century* (Philadelphia: University of Pennsylvania Press, 1959). More recent studies include Dror Wahrman, "The English Problem of Identity in the American Revolution," *American Historical Review* 1016 (2001): 1236–1262; Kathleen Burk,

Old World, New World: Great Britain and America from the Beginning (New York: Atlantic Monthly Press, 2007); Fred M. Leventhal and Roland Quinault, eds., *Anglo-American Attitudes: From Revolution to Partnership* (Aldershot, UK: Ashgate, 2000). P. J. Marshall, *Remaking the British Atlantic: The United States and the British Empire after American Independence* (Oxford, UK: Oxford University Press, 2012); Emma Macleod, *British Visions of America, 1775–1820: Republican Realities* (London: Pickering and Chatto, 2013). On the failure of much work to examine the period between the revolution and the Civil War, see Macleod, *British Visions,* 2.

INTRODUCTION

1. General challenge to deference: Gordon S. Wood, *Empire of Liberty: A History of the Early Republic, 1789–1815* (Oxford, UK: Oxford University Press, 2009), 16, 27, 221–222. Western states: "Electioneering Anecdote," *New England Palladium,* 23 October 1807. Southern and western: "Stump Oratory," *Portland Gazette and Maine Advertiser,* 30 July 1816, and "Stump Speeches," *Public Ledger,* 16 August 1836. Southwestern mode: "The Stump," *Daily Herald and Gazette,* 5 September 1837. Kentucky: "Stump Oratory," *Portland Gazette and Maine Advertiser,* 30 July 1816; John Reynolds, *My Own Times, Embracing Also the History of My Life* (Belleville, IL: B. H. Perryman and H. L. Davison, 1855), 294–295; "A New Mode," *Aurora and Franklin Gazette,* 2 May 1826. Kentucky's oratory as nationally noted: James A. Ramage and Andrea S. Watkins, *Kentucky Rising: Democracy, Slavery, and Culture from the Early Republic to the Civil War* (Lexington: University Press of Kentucky, 2011), 3. Spouting: Andrew W. Robertson, "Voting Rites and Voting Acts: Electioneering Ritual, 1790–1820," in *Beyond the Founders: New Approaches to the Political History of the Early American Republic,* ed. Jeffrey L. Pasley, Andrew W. Robertson and David Waldstreicher (Chapel Hill: University of North Carolina Press, 2004), 60. Stump oratory in Maryland: David Hackett Fischer, *Revolution of American Conservatism: The Federalist Party in the Era of Jeffersonian Democracy* (New York: Harper and Row, 1965), 101.

2. Free land, frontier, and westward movement: Frederick Jackson Turner, *The Frontier in American History* (New York: Holt, Rinehart and Winston, 1962), 1. Rhythms of migration: *Peck's New Guide to the West* (1837), cited in Turner, *The Frontier,* 19–21, and Malcolm J. Rohrbough, *Trans-Appalachian Frontier: People, Societies, and Institutions, 1775–1850,* 3rd ed. (Bloomington: Indiana University Press, 2008).

3. Individualism and practicality: Turner, *The Frontier,* 37. Hereditary station in America: J. G. A. Pocock, "The Classical Theory of Deference," *American Historical Review* 81, no. 3 (1976): 523. Networks and authority: Robert H. Wiebe, *The Opening of American Society: From the Adoption of the Constitution to the Eve of Disunion* (New York: Vintage Books, 1985), 131, 147. Social capital: Joyce Appleby, *Inheriting the Revolution: The First Generation of Americans* (Cambridge, MA: Belknap Press of Harvard University Press, 2000), 237. Social challenge to deference: Michael Zuckerman, "Tocqueville, Turner, and Turds: Four Stories of Manners in Early America," *Journal of American History* 85, no. 1 (1998): 13–42. Coarse familiarity: Frances Trollope, *Domestic Manners of the Americans* (1832; repr., London: Penguin Books, 1997), 95.

4. Illiteracy: Kenneth S. Greenberg, *Masters and Statesmen: The Political Culture of American Slavery* (Baltimore: John Hopkins University Press, 1985), 63. Newspapers: "Stump Oratory," *New Hampshire Gazette,* 22 January 1839. Postal system: Richard B. Kielbowicz, *News in the Mail: The Press, Post Office, and Public Information, 1700–1860s* (New York: Greenwood Press, 1989), 44. Speaking and news: Waldo W. Braden, *The Oral Tradition in the South* (Baton Rouge: Louisiana State University Press, 1983), 42–43. Militia and court: Rohrbough, *Trans-*

Appalachian Frontier, 35, 267. Peculiar modes of life: "The Miscellany," *Middlesex Gazette*, 12 September 1827. Wordy etc.: William D. Gallagher, ed., "Select Miscellany—Western Literature," in *Hesperian: A Monthly Miscellany of General Literature*, vol. 3 (Cincinnati: John D. Nichols, 1839), 461. Free invention etc.: Constance Rourke, *American Humor: A Study of the National Character* (1931; repr., Tallahassee: Florida State University Press, 1959), 61–62. Storytelling: Braden, *The Oral Tradition*, 26, 28. Vulgarity: Ralph Leslie Rusk, *The Literature of the Middle Western Frontier*, vol. 1 (New York: Columbia University Press, 1925), 209. On the political implications of the comparatively oral culture of the South, see Paul Bourke and Donald DeBats, *Washington County: Politics and Community in Antebellum America* (Baltimore: Johns Hopkins University Press, 1995), 12.

5. Original states: Robert J. Dinkin, *Voting in Revolutionary America: A Study of Elections in the Original Thirteen States, 1776–1789* (Westport, CT: Greenwood Press, 1982), 39. Kentucky: Thomas Perkins Abernethy, *Three Virginia Frontiers* (Baton Rouge: Louisiana State University Press, 1940), 77. Ohio Valley states and pressure: Turner, *The Frontier*, 172. Western counties: Charles S. Sydnor, *The Development of Southern Sectionalism 1819–1848* (Baton Rouge: Louisiana State University Press and the Littlefield Fund for Southern History of the University of Texas, 1984), 278. Changes to franchise (extension and restriction): Fletcher Melvin Green, "Democracy in the Old South," in *Democracy in the Old South and Other Essays by Fletcher Melvin Green*, ed. J. Isaac Copeland (Kingsport, TN: Vanderbilt University Press, 1969), 73–74, 75–76, 78–79.

6. Turner, cited in Richard Hofstadter, *The Progressive Historians* (New York: Knopf, 1968), 74. Turner's exclusions: William Cronon, "Revisiting the Vanishing Frontier," *Western Historical Quarterly* 18, no. 2 (1987): 159; Patricia Nelson Limerick, "Turnerians All," *American Historical Review* 100, no. 3 (1995): 714. Individual and state: Patricia Nelson Limerick, *The Legacy of Conquest: The Unbroken Past of the American West* (New York: Norton, 1987), 71, 82. Racist violence and state: Patrick Griffin, *American Leviathan: Empire, Nation, and Revolutionary Frontier* (New York: Hill and Wang, 2007), 14–15, 154, 166–167. Slavery: Robin L. Einhorn, *American Taxation, American Slavery* (Chicago: University of Chicago Press, 2006); Staughton Lynd, "On Turner, Beard and Slavery," *Journal of Negro History* 48, no. 4 (1963): 235–250. Narrow "democracy": Lacy K. Ford Jr., "The Turner Thesis Revisited," *Journal of the Early Republic* 13, no. 2 (1993): 147–148.

7. Seeking land: Rohrbough, *Trans-Appalachian Frontier*, 18. Courthouse and slave market: Ramage and Watkins, *Kentucky Rising*, 265. Self-made man and frontier: Richard Hofstadter, *The American Political Tradition and the Men Who Made It* (New York: Vintage Books, 1948), 48. Flint writes specifically of Missouri: Timothy Flint, *Recollections of the Last Ten Years, Passed in Occasional Residence and Journeyings in the Valley of the Mississippi* (Boston: Cummings, Hilliard, 1826), 207. Southwestern adventurers in public life contrasted with comparative statesmen of New England: Alexis de Tocqueville, *Democracy in America*, ed. J. P. Mayer (New York: Harper and Row, 1966), 200. Self-nomination: Noble E. Cunningham Jr., *The Jefferson Republicans in Power: Party Operations, 1801–1809* (Chapel Hill: University of North Carolina Press, 1963), 193, 281.

8. Tears, mercy: W. P. Strickland, ed., *Autobiography of Peter Cartwright, the Backwoods Preacher* (New York: Carlton and Porter, 1856), 30. Auditors: William Henry Milburn, *The Pioneers, Preachers and People of the Mississippi Valley* (New York: Derby and Jackson, 1860), 357–358.

9. Model: Appleby, *Inheriting the Revolution*, 198; Braden, *The Oral Tradition in the South*, 30. Altars and platforms: Trollope, *Domestic Manners*, 127. Sheds: Strickland, *Autobiography of Peter Cartwright*, 45. Festivals: Michael Chevalier, *Society, Manners, and Politics in the United States: Letters on North America* (New York: Anchor Books, 1961), 306. Friendship: Jo. C.

Guild, *Old Times in Tennessee, with Historical, Personal, and Political Scraps and Sketches* (Nashville: Tavel, Eastman and Howell, 1878), 41. Foods: "Winchester, Va," *New York Herald*, 27 August 1844; Strickland, *Autobiography of Peter Cartwright*, 361. Teams of preachers: Trollope, *Domestic Manners*, 127. Jerks etc.: Strickland, *Autobiography of Peter Cartwright*, 48, 51. Too bright: "A Modern Miracle," *Louisville Public Advertiser*, 11 September 1824. Final day: "The Camp Meeting," *Macon Telegraph*, 30 July 1827. Stedman: Frances L. S. Dugan and Jacqueline P. Bull, eds., *Bluegrass Craftsman: Being the Reminiscences of Ebenezer Hiram Stedman, Papermaker 1808–1885* (Lexington: University of Kentucky Press, 1959), 52.

10. Courting, depredations: "Winchester, Va," *New York Herald*, 27 August 1844. Insidious lips: Trollope, *Domestic Manners*, 131.

11. Democratization and untutored: Appleby, *Inheriting the Revolution*, 133, 145, 198. Ordinary language: Wiebe, *The Opening of American Society*, 157. Spitting: Anne Royall, *Letters from Alabama on Various Subjects* (Washington, DC: n.p., 1830), 123–124. Volume: Flint, *Recollections of the Last Ten Years*, 68. Unmemorized speeches and uneducated preachers: Strickland, *Autobiography of Peter Cartwright*, 80, 358. Gestures and feelings: "The Camp Meeting," *Macon Telegraph*, 30 July 1827. Doctrinal debates: Braden, *The Oral Tradition in the South*, 30. On and on: "The Rev. H. B. Bascom," *Supporter and Scioto Gazette*, 16 December 1824. For a fine study of the "democratization" of Christianity in America, including attention to the development of popular preaching, see Nathan O. Hatch, *The Democratization of American Christianity* (New Haven, CT: Yale University Press, 1989). Hatch emphasizes how the democratic sentiments associated with the Revolution helped change Christianity. In the pages that follow, I emphasize how changed forms of Christianity helped alter public performances in the new Republic.

12. Rowdies: Strickland, *Autobiography of Peter Cartwright*, 50, 236, 383. Revival and electioneering tension: Daniel Dupre, "Barbecues and Pledges: Electioneering and the Rise of Democratic Politics in Antebellum Alabama," *Journal of Southern History* 60, no. 3 (1994): 486. Camp meetings, hierarchy, etc.: ibid., 499. To electioneer: "A Camp Meeting," *Louisville Public Advertiser*, 14 November 1829. Place of gatherings: Edmund Kirke, *Among the Pines: Or, South in Secession Time*, 2nd ed. (New York: J. R. Gilmore, 1862), 239. Language of "Camp" (Camp Hickory): "The Great National Democratic Mass Convention at Nashville," *New York Herald*, 27 August 1844. Itinerant preachers: Appleby, *Inheriting the Revolution*, 198–199; F. Garvin Davenport, *Ante-bellum Kentucky: A Social History, 1800–1860* (Oxford, OH: Mississippi Valley Press, 1943), 132.

13. County court responsibilities: Robert M. Ireland, *The County in Kentucky History* (Lexington: University Press of Kentucky, 1976), 4, and J. R. Pole, "Historians and the Problem of Early American Democracy," *American Historical Review* 67, no. 3 (1962): 636. A legal circuit: Judge John H. Doyle, "Early Courts of Maumee Valley: An Historical Sketch," in *Bench and Bar of Ohio*, vol. 1, ed. George Irving Reed (Chicago: Century Publishing and Engraving, 1897), 49.

14. Few books brought: Doyle, "Early Courts of Maumee Valley," 49. Environment shapes bar: Joseph G. Baldwin, *The Flush Times of Alabama and Mississippi: A Series of Sketches* (New York: Sagamore Press, 1957), 176. Common sense: Ernest J. Wrage, "Henry Clay," in *A History and Criticism of American Public Address*, vol. 1, ed. William Norwood Brigance (New York: McGraw-Hill, 1943), 615. Popular to be democratic: Flint, *Recollections of the Last Ten Years*, 51. Quick tongue and clients: Braden, *The Oral Tradition in the South*, 31. Metaphors: W. W. Braden, "The Emergence of the Concept of Southern Oratory," *Southern Communication Journal* 26, no. 3 (1961): 175. Bombastic: Carl Holliday, cited in Braden, "The Emergence," 177–178. Florid images: J. Jeffrey Auer, "Tom Corwin: 'King of the Stump,'" *Quarterly Journal of Speech* 30, no. 1 (1944): 53. Gross inaccuracies: Gallagher, "Select Miscel-

lany—Western Literature," 461. Oral tradition: Braden, *The Oral Tradition in the South*, 30. Courtroom invective etc.: Auer, "Tom Corwin," 54.

15. Earlier title: George Caleb Bingham to James S. Rollins, 7 November 1853, in C. B. Rollins, ed., "Letters of George Caleb Bingham to James S. Rollins," *Missouri Historical Review* 32 (October 1937–July 1938): 166. To canvass: *The Oxford English Dictionary* (online). The rounds: Robert H. Grayson, cited in Cunningham, *The Jeffersonian Republicans in Power*, 279–280. Personal recommendation: James Madison, cited in Charles S. Sydnor, *Gentlemen Freeholders: Political Practices in Washington's Virginia* (Chapel Hill: University of North Carolina Press, 1952), 44. Treats: ibid., 51–53. Salutation: Cunningham, *The Jeffersonian Republicans in Power*, 276. Election meetings, speeches, debates: Noble E. Cunningham Jr., *The Jeffersonian Republicans: The Formation of Party Organization, 1789–1801* (Chapel Hill: University of North Carolina Press, 1957), 190. Robertson draws attention to the role of speech in late-eighteenth-century electioneering in Andrew W. Robertson, *The Language of Democracy: Political Rhetoric in the United States and Britain, 1790–1900* (Ithaca, NY: Cornell University Press, 1995), 22–23, although his book is a study of electioneering rhetoric in the press (xiii) that "largely" omits the Lower South before the Civil War (xiv).

16. Robert Mumford, *The Plays of Robert Mumford: The First Comic Plays Written in America. The Patriots—the Candidates* (Tucson, AZ: American Eagle Publications, 1992), 23.

17. Dominance of colonial elite: John B. Kirby, "Early American Politics—The Search for an Ideology: An Historiographical Analysis and Critique of the Concept of 'Deference,'" *Journal of Politics* 32, no. 4 (1970): 835. Superior status and culture: Pocock, "The Classical Theory of Deference," 516. Social obligation: Hofstadter, *The American Political Tradition*, 20. Courage and dedication are among qualities of character noted in Wiebe, *The Opening of American Society*, 12. Truth not favor: ibid., 39. Personal ambition: Greenberg, *Masters and Statesmen*, 5. Love of power: Harry L. Watson, *Jacksonian Politics and Community Conflict: The Emergence of the Second American Party System in Cumberland County North Carolina* (Baton Rouge: Louisiana State University Press, 1981), 73. Virtue and competence: Elijah Hayward to Azariah Flagg, 19 November 1832, in *Azariah Flagg Papers*, New York Public Library, Box 1, 104 J-1. For a sophisticated discussion of deference, rhetoric, and electioneering, see Robertson, *The Language of Democracy*, intro. and chap. 1.

18. Personal character and elections: Cunningham, *The Jeffersonian Republicans*, 250. Office-hungry: Watson, *Jacksonian Politics and Community Conflict*, 76–77; James Madison, cited in Dinkin, *Voting in Revolutionary America*, 75. Woud'be: Mumford, *The Plays*, 42.

19. Properest: Mumford, *The Plays*, 43. Pledged interests and newspapers: Dinkin, *Voting in Revolutionary America*, 59, 85. Private letters and Jeffersonians: Cunningham, *The Jeffersonian Republicans in Power*, 101, 110. Public meetings as electioneering strategy presented satirically in Letter 15, Downingville, 18 April 1830, Seba Smith (Major Jack Downing, pseud.), *My Thirty Years out of the Senate* (New York: Oaksmith, 1859), 88–91. Seriously: Fischer, *The Revolution of American Conservatism*, 97–98. Orations and speeches: Greenberg, *Masters and Statesman*, 12. On listening to election spouting as deference of voters: Andrew W. Robertson, "Voting Rites and Voting Acts: Electioneering Ritual, 1790–1820," in *Beyond the Founders: New Approaches to the Political History of the Early American Republic*, ed. Jeffrey L. Pasley, Andrew W. Robertson, and David Waldstreicher (Chapel Hill: University of North Carolina Press, 2004), 60.

20. Marc Bloch, *The Historian's Craft* (Manchester, UK: Manchester University Press, 1954), 168.

21. Contemporary history painting: Gail E. Husch, "George Caleb Bingham's 'The County Election': Whig Tribute to the Will of the People," *American Art Journal* 19, no. 4 (1987): 10. Green, Sappington, Rollins, and proof that no precise subject: Rollins, ed., "Letters of

George Caleb Bingham to James S. Rollins," 172n. Bingham and crowd: Paul C. Nagel, *George Caleb Bingham: Missouri's Famed Painter and Forgotten Politician* (Columbia: University of Missouri Press, 2005), 126. Benton as subject: George Caleb Bingham to James S. Rollins, 7 November 1853, in Rollins, ed., "Letters of George Caleb Bingham to James S. Rollins," 167–168. Bingham's account: George Caleb Bingham to James S. Rollins, 12 December 1853, in ibid., 171–172.

22. "Tradition" and "history": "Tom Corwin of Ohio," *Harper's New Monthly Magazine* 35 (June–November 1867): 80. On admission speeches not recorded, see "Stump Speaking," *Fayetteville Observer*, 4 October 1860; Dallas C. Dickey, "Were They Ephemeral and Florid?" *Quarterly Journal of Speech* 22 (1946): 17. On partisan accounts, see, e.g., "The Editor," *Philadelphia Inquirer*, 5 September 1833; *Albany Argus*, cited in "The Democracy of Mr. Clay," *Extra Globe*, 21 August 1839. Pressed upon: "We Publish," *Daily Commercial Bulletin and Missouri Literary Register*, 19 June 1837.

23. Fallen tree: "Electioneering Anecdote," *New England Palladium*, 23 October 1807. Top of stump and hogshead: "Mr. Quincy's Speech Concluded," *National Intelligencer and Washington Advertiser*, 20 January 1809. Stump orator and slang-whanger: Lieutenant Francis Hall, *Travels in Canada and the United States*, 2nd ed. (London: Longman, Hurst, Rees, Orme and Brown, 1819), 305. Spouting speeches: "Speaking before the People," *Daily National Intelligencer*, 24 September 1823. Note that Robertson identifies the presence of "spouting" somewhat earlier in Virginian history in "Voting Rites and Voting Acts," 60.

24. Paintings as symbol of American democracy: Glenn C. Altschuler and Stuart M. Blumin, *Rude Republic: Americans and Their Politics in the Nineteenth Century* (Princeton, NJ: Princeton University Press, 2000), 129. Bingham's painting and Eastern Markets: Nancy Rash, *The Painting and Politics of George Caleb Bingham* (New Haven, CT: Yale University Press, 1991), 40. Prints and national diffusion: ibid., 120. Changing canvas for engraving: ibid., 137–138; Rollins, cited in ibid., 136. Fortune: George Caleb Bingham to James S. Rollins, 23 November 1853, in Rollins, ed., "Letters of George Caleb Bingham to James S. Rollins," 170.

25. 1820s fashion: O. H. Smith, *Early Indiana Trials and Sketches* (Cincinnati, OH: Moore, Wilstach, Keys, 1858). Stumping it: Francis Johnson to Daniel Webster, 7 July 1826, in Charles M. Wiltse, ed., *The Papers of Daniel Webster, Correspondence*, vol. 2, *1825–1829* (Hanover, NH: University Press of New England, 1976), 121. Technical meaning: "Eastman's Wakefield Speechification," *Dover Gazette and Strafford Advertiser*, 5 March 1839. Political tactic: John Sloane to Henry Clay, 24 November 1840, in Robert Seager II, ed., *The Papers of Henry Clay*, vol. 9, *The Whig Leader, January 1, 1837–December 31, 1843* (Louisville: University Press of Kentucky, 1988), 454.

26. English newspapers define: "Texas," *London Times*, 12 June 1841. American dictionaries: John Russell Bartlett, *Dictionary of Americanism: A Glossary of Words and Phrases Usually Regarded as Peculiar to the United States*, 3rd ed. (Boston: Little, Brown, 1860), 459; "Inroads upon English," *Littel's Living Age*, 4th series, vol. 7 (Boston: Little and Gay, 1867), 227; "On Some Popular Americanisms," *The Broadway: A London Magazine*, new series, vol. 1 (September 1868–February 1869): 571. Stumping: "Cents and Nonsense," *Punch, or the London Charivari*, 6 October 1860, 139.

CHAPTER 1

1. Giant of the stump: "Texas," *Times* (London), 12 June 1841. Partisan press promotion: Richard Boyd Hauck, "The Man in the Buckskin Hunting Shirt: Fact and Fiction in the Crockett Story," in *Davy Crockett: The Man, the Legend, the Legacy 1786–1986*, ed. Michael A.

Lofaro (Knoxville: University of Tennessee Press, 1985), 10–11. Itinerant preachers: "Daniel Webster," *Dover Gazette and Strafford Advertiser*, 5 December 1837. Crockett line: see, e.g., "Log Cabin Meeting," *Cleveland Daily Herald*, 15 May 1840. Illustrations: see, e.g., *Life of David Crockett: The Original Humorist and Irrepressible Backwoodsman* (Philadelphia: John E. Potter, 1865).

2. On ranking as orator: see, e.g., Calvin Colton, *The Life of Henry Clay*, vol. 1 (New York: A. S. Barnes, 1855), 47. On Cicero: Carl Holliday, *A History of Southern Literature* (Port Washington, NY: Kennikat Press, 1969), 126. Demosthenes etc.: "Henry Clay," *Virginia Free Press*, 21 March 1839. British agreement: *London Quarterly Review*, cited in "American Orators," *Boston Courier*, 28 January 1841. Collecting speeches: Merrill D. Peterson, *The Great Triumvirate: Webster, Clay, and Calhoun* (New York: Oxford University Press, 1987), 148. Transcribing: Ernest J. Wrage, "Henry Clay," in *A History and Criticism of American Public Address*, vol. 1, ed. William Norwood Brigance (New York: McGraw-Hill, 1943), 625. Whole country: "Mr. Webster's Testimony in Favor of Mr. Clay," *Daily Atlas*, 28 November 1843. Handbills: "Mr. Clay's System of Electioneering for the Presidency," *Ohio Statesman*, 20 February 1844. Illustrated newspapers: "The Illustrated Weekly Herald," *New York Herald*, 3 August 1844. Pilgrim: "The President," *Richmond Enquirer*, 23 August 1839. Table: "The Table Orator," *Globe*, 8 August 1835. Traveling: "A Travelling Speech Maker," *Mississippi Free Trader and Natchez Gazette*, 9 March 1844. Itinerant: "The Democracy of Mr. Clay," *Extra Globe*, 21 August 1839. Hero: *Jeffersonian Republican*, cited in "Mr. Clay," *Louisville Public Advertiser*, 12 September 1829.

3. Lexington: Henry Clay to Francis Lieber, 15 September 1834, in *PHC*8, 747. Athens: Timothy Flint, *Recollections of the Last Ten Years, Passed in Occasional Residence and Journeyings in the Valley of the Mississippi* (Boston: Cummings, Hilliard, 1826), 67. Philadelphia: Richard C. Wade, *The Urban Frontier: The Rise of Western Cities, 1790–1830* (Urbana: University of Illinois Press, 1996), 18. Lexington described: ibid., 20–21. Talents: Henry Clay to Charles James Lanham, 28 October 1817, in *PHC*2, 392–393. Marriage and slaves: James A. Ramage and Andrea S. Watkins, *Kentucky Rising: Democracy, Slavery, and Culture from the Early Republic to the Civil War* (Lexington: University Press of Kentucky, 2011), 24, 39; Robert V. Remini, *Henry Clay: Statesman for the Union* (New York: Norton, 1993), 205. Lawyer aristocracy: Henry Clay to Francis Lieber, 15 September 1834, in *PHC*8, 747. Difficult to describe: The assessment of a nameless observer, cited in Epes Sargent, *The Life and Public Services of Henry Clay*, edited by Horace Greeley (Auburn: Miller, Orton, and Mulligan, 1854), 22. Laid the foundation: Colton, ed., *The Speeches of Henry Clay*, 7. Elections and popular will: "Scaevola," "To the Electors of Fayette County," 16 April 1798, in *PHC*1, 6–7. Power of truth: "Scaevola," "To the Citizens of Fayette County," February 1799, in ibid., 1:11. Open declaration: "Scaevola," "To Joseph Hamilton Daveiss," January 1803, in ibid., 1:93–94.

4. Ingenuous appeals: George D. Prentice, *Biography of Henry Clay* (Hartford: Samuel Hanmer Jr. and John Jay Phelps, 1831), 25–26. Frontier electioneer: Peterson, *The Great Triumvirate*, 13.

5. Election results: Results available at http://uselectionatlas.org/USPRESIDENT/GENERAL/pe1824.html. Kentucky legislature: "Barbecues," *Louisville Public Advertiser*, 31 August 1825.

6. Intrigue etc.: Andrew Jackson to W. B. Lewis, 29 January 1825, contained in *Letters of W. B. Lewis from A. Jackson and Others*, vol. 1, *1806–1827*, New York Public Library. Want of principle: Andrew Jackson to W. B. Lewis, 24 January 1825, contained in ibid. Self-aggrandizement: Andrew Jackson to William Berkeley Lewis, 20 February 1825, in Harold D. Moser and J. Clint Clifft, eds., *The Papers of Andrew Jackson*, vol. 6, *1825–1828* (Knoxville: University of Tennessee Press, 2002), 37. Traitor: Secretary of Navy John Branch to Andrew

NOTES TO CHAPTER 1 | *167*

Jackson, 14 August 1830, in John Spencer Bassett, ed., *Correspondence of Andrew Jackson*, vol. 6, *1829–1832* (Washington, DC: Carnegie Institution of Washington, 1929), 172. Devil: John Pemberton to Andrew Jackson, 15 February 1825, in Moser and Clifft, eds., *The Papers of Andrew Jackson*, 6:30. Barter: Andrew Jackson to William Berkeley Lewis, 20 February 1825, in ibid., 6:37. Horrible precedent: Andrew Jackson to Joseph Desha, 24 June 1825, in ibid., 6:86.

7. Enthusiasm: Marvin Meyers, *The Jacksonian Persuasion: Politics and Belief* (Stanford: Stanford University Press, 1960), 16. An idol: Nathan Sargent, *Public Men and Events in the United States* (1875; repr., New York, 1970), 346. Leaders' support: Robert H. Wiebe, *The Opening of American Society: From the Adoption of the Constitution to the Eve of Disunion* (New York: Vintage Books, 1985), 234. New organizations: William James Cooper, *The South and the Politics of Slavery, 1828–1856* (Baton Rouge: Louisiana State University Press, 1978), 9. Alliances: William B. Hatcher, *Edward Livingston: Jeffersonian Republican and Jacksonian Democrat* (University: Louisiana State University Press, 1940), 313–314.

8. Jackson party's superiority: Daniel Webster to Samuel Bell, 15 October 1827, in Charles M. Wiltse, ed., *The Papers of Daniel Webster, Correspondence*, vol. 2, *1825–1829* (Hanover, NH: University Press of New England, 1976), 244. Democratic Party press: Richard J. John, "Affairs of Office: The Executive Departments, the Election of 1828, and the Making of the Democratic Party," in *The Democratic Experiment: New Directions in American Political History*, ed. Meg Jacobs, William J. Novak, and Julian E. Zelizer (Princeton, NJ: Princeton University Press, 2003), 53. Clay supporters' lament: William L. Brent to Henry Clay, 5 December 1829, in Robert Seager II, ed., *The Papers of Henry Clay*, vol. 8 (Lexington: University of Kentucky Press, 1984), 8, 133.

9. Attack and defense: Henry Clay to Charles Hammond, 12 August 1829, in Seager, *The Papers of Henry Clay*, 8:87. Never give up: Henry Clay to Samuel L. Southard, 21 July 1832, in ibid., 8:555. Henry Clay to William Plumer Jr., 7 April 1828, in Robert Seager II, ed., *The Papers of Henry Clay*, vol. 7 (Lexington: University of Kentucky Press, 1982), 217.

10. Poisoned shirt: "Mr. Clay in Ohio," *United States' Telegraph*, 4 August 1830. Popular song: "The Glorious Victory in Maine," *Weekly Ohio Statesman*, 9 October 1844. Main reliance: Henry Clay to John Sloane, 21 May 1844, in *PHC*10, 62. Gravest error: Clay admitted it would have been "wiser and more politic" to refuse the secretaryship in Henry Clay, Speech in Lexington, 9 June 1842, in *PHC*9, 709. Clay on journey: Henry Clay to Charles Hammond, 23 May 1825, in *PHC*4, 387–388.

11. Invitations and toasts included in *PHC*4, 388–389, 398–399, 405, 406–407, 408–409, 412, 427, 436–437, 438–439,. Maysville residents: Maurice Langhorne and others to Henry Clay, 23 May 1825, in *PHC*4, 389.

12. "Mr. Clay," *United States' Telegraph*, 24 March 1829.

13. Be quite convenient: Henry Clay to Elisha Whittlesey, 24 March 1827, in *PHC*6, 349. Procured himself: "The Popularity Hunting," *Daily Louisville Public Advertiser*, 30 July 1830. "Would visit every State": Henry Clay, "Danger of the Military Spirit in a Republic," Baltimore, May 1828, in Calvin Colton, ed., *The Speeches of Henry Clay* (New York: Barnes, 1857), 1:358.

14. Henry Clay, "Fowler's Garden Speech," Lexington, 16 May 1829, in *PHC*8, 1984, 44.

15. *SE*, v–vi.

16. *An Account of Col. Crockett's Tour to the North and Down East, in the Year of Our Lord One Thousand Eight Hundred and Thirty-Four. His Object Being to Examine the Grand Manufacturing Establishments of the Country; and Also to Find Out the Conditions of Its Literature and Morals, The Extent of Its Commerce, and the Practical Operation of "The Experiment," Written by Himself* (Philadelphia: E. L. Carey and A. Hart, 1835). Surrounded: ibid., 40. Least idea: ibid., 78. Louisville: ibid., 159. Cincinnati: ibid., 150.

17. Richard Penn Smith, *Col. Crockett's Exploits and Adventures in Texas: Wherein Is Contained a Full Account of His Journey from Tennessee to the Red River and Natchitoches, and Thence across Texas to San Antonio, Written by Himself* (London: R. Kennett, 1837), 179.

18. Notoriety based on others: M. J. Heale, "The Role of the Frontier in Jacksonian Politics: David Crockett and the Myth of the Self-Made Man," *Western Historical Quarterly* 4 (1973): 407. Scholarly recognition of elusiveness: see, e.g., Walter Blair, "Six Davy Crocketts," *Southwest Review* 25, no. 4 (1940): 442–462; Howard Mumford Jones, "Foreword," in *Davy Crockett: American Comic Legend*, ed. Richard M. Dorson (New York: Rockland Editions, 1939), xiii.

19. Well born: "Davy Crockett's Early Days, Severe Courtships and Marriage," in Franklin J. Meine, *The Crockett Almanacks: Nashville Series, 1835–1838* (Chicago: Caxton Club, 1955), 4. Noble ancestry: *ANL*, 14. No chance: *ANL*, 16.

20. *ANL*, 137–138.

21. Ibid., 166–167.

22. Ibid., 168–170.

23. No superior claims: "Undated Letter to the *Jackson Gazette*, Published December 23 1826," in *DDC*, 204. Envy none: "Undated Letter Published in the *Jackson Gazette*, May 5, 1827," in *DCC*, 149.

24. Slaves: Clement Eaton, *Henry Clay and the Art of American Politics* (Boston: Little, Brown, 1957), 6. Connections: Carl Schurz, *Henry Clay*, vol. 1 (Boston: Houghton Mifflin, 1915), 8–9.

25. Move to Kentucky: Henry Clay, "Fowler's Garden Speech," in *PHC* 8, 54. Great Commoner: Prentice, *Biography of Henry Clay*, 23. Of the people: William Henry Milburn, *The Pioneers, Preachers and People of the Mississippi Valley* (New York: Derby and Jackson, 1860), 426. Backwoodsman: Sargent, *The Life and Public Services of Henry Clay*, 316. Oppressed: *Henry Clay Almanac, for the Year of Our Lord, 1843* (Philadelphia: T. K. and P. G. Collins, 1843), 18. Millboy: Colton, *The Life*, 19. Ashland: "Politics of the Day," *Daily National Intelligencer*, 24 May 1839. Banners: Nancy Rash, *The Painting and Politics of George Caleb Bingham* (New Haven, CT: Yale University Press, 1991), 26. Cincinnatus: *Henry Clay Almanac*, 32.

26. Obituary: "The Following Short Account," *St. Louis Commercial Bulletin*, 16 May 1836. *Ringtail Roarer* is the title of one *Crockett Almanack* identified in William R. Chemerka, *The Davy Crockett Almanac and Book of Lists* (Austin: Eakin Press, 2000), 159. Lungs: "Texas," *Times* (London), 12 June 1841. Melodrama: Frank Murdoch, "Davy Crockett; or, Be Sure You're Right, Then Go Ahead," in *Davy Crockett and Other Plays*, ed. Isaac Goldberg and Rubert Heffner (Princeton, NJ: Princeton University Press, 1940), 121. Travel: Franklin J. Meine, "Introduction," in *The Crockett Almanacks*, v. Chapman: John Gadsby Chapman, cited in Richard Boyd Hauck, *Crockett: A Bio-Bibliography* (Westport, CT: Greenport Press, 1982), 63.

27. Grammatical etc.: Ben Perley Poore, *Perley's Reminiscences of Sixty Years in the National Metropolis*, vol. 1 (Philadelphia: Hubbard Brothers Publishers, 1886), 152. Blunt: *SE*, 127. Rude: *SE*, 163. Unpolished: *SE*, 186. Simplest: *SE*, 176. Slang etc.: "The Following Short Account," *St. Louis Commercial Bulletin*, 16 May 1836. Phraseology: "Texas," *Times* (London), 12 June 1841. Dogs: "Speech Delivered in Boston, Early May, 1834 (as Part of Crockett's Tour to the North)," in *DCC*, 323. Fields: "Col. Crockett's Tour," *Daily National Intelligencer*, 1 April 1835. Swarm: "Col. Crockett's Last Speech," *New York Spectator*, 3 July 1834. Enemies: "Crockett Delivering His Celebrated War Speech," in *Davy Crockett: American Comic Legend*, ed. Richard M. Dorson (New York: Rockland Editions, 1939), 43–44. Warning: "Colonel Crockett Delivering His Celebrated Speech to Congress on the State of Finances, State Officers, and State Affairs in General," in ibid., 150–151. Fears and embrace:

ibid. Natural metaphors: "Crockett Delivering His Celebrated War Speech," in ibid., 43–44. Vulgar: *DCC*, 121. No pretensions: "Col Crockett," *Providence Patriot*, 10 May 1834. 28. Blunt: *SE*, 127. Language: *SE*, 186. Forcible: *DCC*, 51. Sensible: Blair, "Six Davy Crocketts," 449. Unpolished: *SE*, 186. Without trimmings: "Colonel Crockett Delivering His Celebrated Speech to Congress on the State of Finances, State Officers, and State Affairs in General," in Dorson, ed., *Davy Crockett*, 150. Straight: David Crockett, *The Life of Martin Van Buren, Heir-Apparent to the "Government" and the Appointed Successor of General Andrew Jackson* (Philadelphia: Robert Wright, 1836), 27. Oily words: "Speech Delivered in Boston, Early May, 1834 (as Part of Crockett's Tour to the North)," in *DCC*, 320. Plain etc.: "Letter Dated December 30, 1833, Published in the [Washington] *Daily National Intelligencer*, December 31, 1833," in *DDC*, 229. Homespun manner: "Political Circular, September 20, 1826, Published in the *Jackson Gazette*, October 7, 1826," in *DCC*, 295.

29. Plain and home style: *An Account*, 19, 25, 126. New York address: ibid., 43. Philadelphia address: ibid., 25. Boosters: Alex J. Dumas, "Preface," in Penn Smith, *Col. Crockett's Exploits*, iii. Press: *DCC*, 50. *Spectator*: "Col. Crockett's Last Speech," *New York Spectator*, 3 July 1834.

30. Henry Clay to Henry Clay Jr., 21 October 1828, in *PHC7*, 511.

31. Henry Clay, cited in Wrage, "Henry Clay," 607.

32. Extemporaneous: Wrage, "Henry Clay," 631. Battle: Edward G. Parker, *The Golden Age of American Oratory* (Boston: Whittmore, Niles and Hall, 1857), 29. Vocabulary: ibid., 28. Simple: Oliver Dyer, *Great Senators of the United States Forty Years Ago* (New York: Robert Bonner's Sons, 1889), 229. Plain: "Toasts and Speech at Public Dinner, Lewisburg, Virginia," 30 August 1826, in *PHC5*, 655. Child: Dyer, *Great Senators*, 229. Just enough: Colton, *The Life*, 68. Directness: Dyer, *Great Senators*, 244. Perspicuity etc.: Wrage, "Henry Clay," 631.

33. Cicero: "Barbecue and Speech of Mr. Clay," *Augusta Chronicle*, 22 July 1829. Lion: *New York Evening Post*, cited in "Look upon This Picture," *Pittsfield Sun*, 22 August 1839. Orator: "Reception of Mr. Clay," *Daily Herald and Gazette*, 19 July 1839. Jewel: "Extract from a Letter to the Editor," *Scioto Gazette*, 28 October 1829. Harry: "Fifteen Thousand Whigs at Madison, Geo," *Raleigh Register and North Carolina Gazette*, 20 August 1844. Consummate: Peterson, *The Great Triumvirate*, 17. Son: "Henry Clay and Liberty," in *Henry Clay Almanac, for the Year of Our Lord, 1844* (Philadelphia: T. K. and P. G. Collins, 1844), 4. Representative: Milburn, *The Pioneers*, 426. Josiah Quincy, cited in Remini, *Henry Clay*, 84. Stump orator: "The Democracy of Mr. Clay," *Extra Globe*, 21 August 1839. Pride: John Pemberton to Andrew Jackson, 15 February 1825, in Moser and Clifft, eds., *The Papers of Andrew Jackson*, 6:30. Cataline: "Henry Clay," *Richmond Enquirer*, 21 August 1832. Lord: "Webster in the West," *Globe*, 29 July 1837.

34. Formed: Poore, *Perley's Reminiscences*, 34; "Orators of Other Days," *Galveston Daily News*, 24 July 1886. Made: "Brooks Letters," *Connecticut Courant*, 1 February 1836. By nature: "Henry Clay: Personal Anecdotes, Incidents, Etc.," *Harper's New Monthly Magazine* 5 (1852): 393. Thunder: "Henry Clay," *Virginia Free Press*, 21 March 1839. Earthquake etc.: Prentice, *Biography of Henry Clay*, 193. Natural: Parker, *The Golden Age*, 40. Flame: "Henry Clay," *Virginia Free Press*, 21 March 1839. River: Prentice, *Biography of Henry Clay*, 273–274. Bayard's views: Margaret Bayard, *The First Forty Years of Washington Society* (New York: Charles Scribner's Sons, 1906), 285.

35. Physical descriptions: *Cincinnati Mirror and Western Gazette of Literature and Science*, 21 February 1835, cited in Chemerka, *The Davy Crockett Almanac*, 201; Poore, *Perley's Reminiscences*, 152. Clerk's description: *SE*, 115, 176.

36. Chapman portrait: Hauck, *Crockett*, 61–62. Crockett's weapons: *DCC*, 117. Reproduction of portrait available at http://en.wikipedia.org/wiki/File:Davy_Crockett_by_John_

Gadsby_Chapman.jpg. Colonel's clothing in portrait: Hauck, "The Man in the Buckskin Hunting Shirt," 5.

37. Brave soldier: "The Following Short Account," *St. Louis Commercial Bulletin*, 16 May 1836. Gun: *SE*, 67. Fighting British: *ANL*, 123. Native Americans: *ANL*, 77. Manly hunter: *SE*, 68. Hunting tally: *ANL*, 175, 179, 194. Heavy bear: *ANL*, 163–164. Stories devoted to hunting varied animals: Meine, *The Crockett Almanacks*. Jackson order: *SE*, 138. Vaulting etc.: *DCC*, 82.

38. "A Tongaferous Fight with an Alligator," in Meine, *The Crockett Almanacks*, 87–89. Vaulting etc.: *DCC*, 82.

39. Boasting: *SE*, 145. Jumping etc.: "'Go Ahead' Reader," in Meine, *The Crockett Almanacks*, 1955, 3. Whipping etc.: *SE*, 164. Eating etc.: "Stopping a Duel among His Brother Congressmen," in Dorson, ed., *Davy Crockett*, 84. Bear battle: "Col. Crockett Grinning a Grizzly out of Countenance," in ibid., 114. Sucking etc.: "Speech of Colonel Crockett in Congress," in Meine, *The Crockett Almanacks*, 106–107. Swallowing: "Speech of Colonel Crockett in Congress," in ibid., 106–107.

40. Outspeak etc.: "Speech of Colonel Crockett in Congress," in Meine, *The Crockett Almanacks*, 106–107. Voice etc.: "The Following Short Account," *St. Louis Commercial Bulletin*, 16 May 1836. Tennessee parliament: *SE*, 57–58.

41. Without gloves: Penn Smith, *Col. Crockett's Exploits*, 3. Let him have it: ibid., 55. Would suffer: "Undated Letter to the Southern Statesman, Published July 2, 1831," in *DCC*, 208.

42. Men fight: "Fight between an Alligator and a Bear," in Meine, *The Crockett Almanacks*, 34. Mighty droll: James N. Tidwell, ed., *The Lion of the West* (Stanford, CA: Stanford University Press, 1954), 55.

43. Kentucky boatman: *SE*, 143–145. Stage driver: "A Love Adventure and Uproarious Fight with a Stage Driver," in Meine, *The Crockett Almanacks*, 73–74. Yellow flower: "A Love Adventure and Uproarious Fight with a Stage Driver," in ibid., 74.

44. Never scared: "Col. Crockett's Adventure with a Grizzly Bear," *The Crockett Almanack* 2, no. 1 (1839): 3. Brier bushes story, included in *The Davy Crockett Almanack*, 1839, and cited in Carroll Smith-Rosenberg, "Davy Crockett as Trickster: Pornography, Liminality and Symbolic Inversion in Victorian America," *Journal of Contemporary History* 17, no. 2 (1982): 338. Riprorious females: Michael A. Lofaro, "Riproarious Shemales: Legendary Women in the Tall Tale World of the Davy Crockett Almanacs," in Michael A. Lofaro and Joe Cummings, eds., *Crockett at Two Hundred: New Perspectives on the Man and the Myth* (Knoxville: University of Tennessee Press, 1989), 114–152. Lampooning of family: Smith-Rosenberg, "Davy Crockett as Trickster," 342.

45. Taste etc.: Wrage, "Henry Clay," 620. Deep etc.: Sargent, *Life and Public Services*, 274. Great force: "Mr. Webster's Testimony in Favor of Mr. Clay," *Daily Atlas* (Boston), 28 November 1843. Assurance: John Botts, cited in "Celebration," *Cleveland Herald*, 17 April 1844. Manly: "Mr. Webster's Testimony in Favor of Mr. Clay," *Daily Atlas* (Boston), 28 November 1843. True man: Sargent, *Life and Public Services*, 316. Force: Wrage, "Henry Clay," 632. Energy: Dyer, *Great Senators*, 223. Action: "Great Orators," *Daily Evening Bulletin* (San Francisco), 9 March 1869; Bayard, *The First Forty Years*, 303. Forcible: William Plumer, Letter to Father, 12 February 1820, cited in Wrage, "Henry Clay," 633. Enchained: Poore, *Perley's Reminiscences*, 34. Resign themselves: Dyer, *Great Senators*, 229.

46. Fair ladies: Henry Clay, Speech in Charleston, SC, 6 April 1884, in *PHC*10, 17. Fair daughters: Henry Clay, Speech in Savannah, GA, 22 March 1844, in *PHC*10, 12. Flowers: Henry Clay, Speech at Yellow Springs, OH, 27 July 1830, in *PHC*8, 241–242. Kiss: The Honorable Waddy Thompson, cited in "Fifteen Thousand Whigs at Madison, Geo,"

Raleigh Register and North Carolina Gazette, 20 August 1844. Autographs and hair: Ramage and Watkins, *Kentucky Rising*, 20. Milburn: Milburn, *The Pioneers*, 426. Female participation in electioneering for Clay's Whigs: Elizabeth R. Varon, "Tippecanoe and the Ladies, Too: White Women and Party Politics in Antebellum Virginia," *Journal of American History* 82, no. 2 (1995): 494–521.

47. Veins and flesh: Sargent, *Life and Public Services*, 29. Gushing: Parker, *Golden Age*, 34. Drops: Prentice, *Biography of Henry Clay*, 98. Virile: Wrage, "Henry Clay," 609. Supernatural: Dyer, *Great Senators*, 223. Parker, *The Golden Age*, 1857, 34. Taller: Dyer, *Great Senators*, 223.

48. Every inch: Gansevoort Melville, cited in "A Rebuke to the Locofocos," *Daily National Intelligencer*, 12 July 1844. Assume responsibility: John C. Fitzpatrick, ed., "Autobiography of Martin Van Buren," in *Annual Report of the American Historical Association for the Year 1918*, vol. 2 (Washington, DC: Government Printing Office, 1920), 634. Strong will: Thomas Hart Benton, *Thirty Years' View; A History of the Working of the American Government for Thirty Years, from 1820 to 1850*, vol. 2 (New York: D. Appleton, 1856), 402. Sublime manhood: A nameless writer, cited in Sargent, *Life and Public Services*, 317. Manliness: J. O. Harrison, "Henry Clay: Reminiscences by His Executor," *Century Magazine* 33, no. 2 (1886): 179.

49. Open declaration: "Scaevola," "To Joseph Hamilton Daveiss," January 1803, in Hopkins, *The Papers of Henry Clay*, 1:93–94.

50. Frank, friendly, etc.: Henry Clay, Speech, Cincinnati, 30 August 1828, in *PHC*7, 452–453. Slave of the people: Henry Clay, cited in "Mr. Clay at Burlington," *Vermont Patriot* (Montpelier), 19 August 1839. I do not feel at liberty: Henry Clay, Speech in Raleigh, NC, 13 April 1844, in *PHC*10, 20. Seized by local committees: Henry Clay, cited in "Mr. Clay at Saratoga!" *Ohio Statesman*, 28 August 1839.

51. Henry Clay, Speech in Petersburg, VA, 19 April 1844, in *PHC*10, 47.

52. Right of speaking out: Henry Clay, Speech in New York City, 21 August 1839, in *PHC*9, 337. Brave risk for public good: Henry Clay, Speech in New York City, 21 August 1839, in *PHC*9, 337.

53. Table Orator: Peterson, *The Great Triumvirate*, 148. Selfish etc.: "Mr. Clay," *Louisville Public Advertiser*, 4 June 1828. Bad taste: *New York Courier and Enquirer*, cited in "War, Pestilence and Famine," *Louisville Public Advertiser*, 21 August 1830. Contemptible: "Mr. Bennett's Letters," *Morning Herald* (New York), 13 August 1839. Cunning: "The Last Dinner Speech of Mr. Clay," *Columbia Telescope* (Columbia, SC), 3 July 1829. Grossness: *New Orleans Courier*, cited in "A Travelling Speech Maker," *Mississippi Free Trader and Natchez Gazette*, 9 March 1844. Coarseness: ibid. Stoops to retail: *Richmond Enquirer*, cited in "The Table Orator," *Maryland Gazette*, 30 July 1829. Willing to descend: "A Friend from One," *United States' Telegraph*, 12 November 1829. To solicit a continuance: "We Copy To-day," *Louisville Public Advertiser*, 8 September 1827. Forget deference: "The Campaign Opened," *Vermont Patriot and State Gazette*, 30 March 1829.

54. *New York Enquirer*, cited in "Public Opinion on Clay's Speech," *United States' Telegraph*, 18 June 1828. "Mr. Clay's Doctors," *Delaware Patriot and American Watchman*, 8 July 1828. "Foreigners in This Country," *United States' Telegraph*, 5 July 1828. *Richmond Enquirer*, cited in "Not One of Our Presidents," *Louisville Public Advertiser*, 22 April 1829. Immediate public attack: *Richmond Enquirer*, cited in "The Table Orator," *Louisville Public Advertiser*, 1 April 1829.

55. A system: "The Last Dinner Speech of Mr. Clay," *Columbia Telescope*, 3 July 1829. Increasingly common: "Mr. Clay," *Louisville Public Advertiser*, 9 May 1829. An example: Specifically, the "Adams Party" rather than Clay is identified with this system in *Baltimore Republican*, cited in "Great Jackson Meeting in Baltimore," *Louisville Public Advertiser*, 4 June

1828. Comparator: see, e.g., Webster compared unfavorably with Clay: "Connecticut," *The Globe*, 10 April 1837. Patron saint (this is a position attributed to Stephen A. Douglas in later years): "'Henry Clay Is a Black-Hearted Villain,'" *New Hampshire Statesman*, 6 October 1860.

    56. Penn Smith, *Col. Crockett's Exploits*, 5–6, 8.

    57. Ibid., 6–7, 8, 34–36.

    58. "Letter to the Mississippi Congressional Delegation, February 24 1834, Published in the (Washington) *United States' Telegraph*, March 1, 1834," in *DCC*, 239.

    59. Angry disputes etc.: Crockett, *The Life of Martin Van Buren*, 178–179. Criticized political process: Hauck, *Crockett*, 33. Political weasels etc.: "Colonel Crockett Delivering His Celebrated Speech to Congress on the State of Finances, State Officers, and State Affairs in General," in Dorson, ed., *Davy Crockett*, 150–151. Sadly calculating etc.: "Col. Crockett's Tour," *Daily National Intelligencer*, 1 April 1835.

    60. Northern newspapers: see, e.g., "Life and Adventures of Colonel David Crocket[t] of West Tennessee," *Vermont Gazette*, 2 April 1833. Journal reproduction: see, e.g., "A Backwoodsman's Grin," *Bristol Mercury*, 28 December 1833; "Eloquence of the Stump," *New Hampshire Statesman and State Journal*, 22 August 1835; "Davy Crockett," *Vermont Watchman and State Gazette*, 29 September 1829. Unknown stump orator: "Stump Orator," *The Casket: Flowers of Literature Wit and Sentiment* (Philadelphia), no. 4 (1830): 186. Cicero's: see, e.g., "Stump Orators," *New England Farmer, and Horticultural Journal* 8 (1830): 288. *Almanack* editions: Michael Montgomery, "David Crockett and the Rhetoric of Tennessee Politics," in Lofaro and Cummings, *Crockett at Two Hundred*, 60. Popular songs: Charles K. Wolfe, "Davy Crockett Songs: Minstrels to Disney," in Michael Lofaro, ed., *Davy Crockett: The Man, the Legend, the Legacy 1786–1986* (Knoxville: University of Tennessee Press, 1985), 160–162. Melodrama: see, e.g., Murdoch, "Davy Crockett," 115–148.

    61. Downing was "patterned after" Crockett, according to Buddy Levy, *American Legend: The Real-Life Adventures of David Crockett* (New York: Putnam's Sons, 2005), 3. A play based on Downing was titled *The Lion of the East*—an obvious nod to Crockett. See Milton Rickels and Patricia Rickels, *Seba Smith* (Boston: Twayne Publishers, 1977), 139. Imaginary exchanges: *DCC*, 110. Elocution exercises: see, e.g., Robert Kidd, *Vocal Culture and Elocution: With Numerous Exercises in Reading and Speaking* (Cincinnati, OH: Wilson and Hinkle, 1857); Worthy Putnam, *The Science and Art of Elocution and Oratory* (New York: C. M. Saxton, 1858). On the place of the stump speech in minstrel shows, see Eric Lott, *Love and Theft: Blackface Minstrelsy and the American Working Class* (New York: Oxford University Press, 1993).

CHAPTER 2

    1. "The Stump," *Daily Herald and Gazette*, 5 September 1837. "Mr. N. P. Tallmadge," *North American*, 17 October 1839. *Boston Times*, cited in "The Following Remarks," *Dover Gazette and Strafford Advertiser*, 1 January 1839. Allen Nevins, ed., *The Diary of Philip Hone 1828–1851*, vol. 1 (New York: Dodd, Mead, 1927), 486. New England journals: see, e.g., "Wilson Preaching," *Dover Gazette and Strafford Advertiser*, 19 March 1839; "We Are Not Sorry," *New Bedford Mercury*, 28 August 1840.

    2. "Immense Assemblage of the Democracy of the City of New York," *New York Herald*, 17 September 1844. *New York Evening Mirror*, cited in Gil Troy, *See How They Ran: The Changing Role of the Presidential Candidate*, rev. ed. (Cambridge, MA: Harvard University Press, 1996), 40. "History of the Week," *Frank Leslie's Illustrated Newspaper*, 19 July 1856.

    3. Troy emphasizes often the political value of a presidential candidate embracing "tradition" and refusing to advocate his own election.

4. Northern contentious and less deferential: Robin L. Einhorn, *American Taxation, American Slavery* (Chicago: University of Chicago Press, 2006), 55; Amy Bridges, *A City in the Republic: Antebellum New York and the Origins of Machine Politics* (Cambridge, UK: Cambridge University Press, 1984), 22–23, 104; Gordon S. Wood, *Empire of Liberty: A History of the Early Republic, 1789–1815* (Oxford, UK: Oxford University Press, 2009), 27. Speeches: Jean H. Baker, *Affairs of Party: The Political Culture of Northern Democrats in the Mid-nineteenth Century* (Ithaca, NY: Cornell University Press, 1983), 49; "New York," *United States' Telegraph*, 9 August 1827; "Party Tactics and Intrigues," *New York Morning Herald*, 9 February 1838.

5. Literacy: Einhorn, *American Taxation*, 114–115. Organization, boss: Bridges, *A City in the Republic*, 61–62. Northern politics as organization rather than oratory, as compared with the South: Kenneth S. Greenberg, *Masters and Statesmen: The Political Culture of American Slavery* (Baltimore: John Hopkins University Press, 1985), 14.

6. William Alexander Caruthers, *The Kentuckian in New York, Or, the Adventures of Three Southerns*, vol. 1 (New York: Harper and Brothers, 1834), 19–20, 162–163.

7. Violence and fraud: "New York Elections," *National Advocate*, 26 May 1818; "Editorial," *Daily National Journal*, 16 November 1827; "New York Election," *New Hampshire Statesman and State Journal*, 19 April 1834. Organization: "New York Politics," *United States' Telegraph*, 4 November 1826; "New York Papers," *Carolina Observer*, 29 November 1826. Journalism: "New York Politics," *St. Louis Inquirer*, 9 October 1819; "The New York Election," *Daily National Intelligencer*, 9 November 1827.

8. On the convention, see Ronald P. Formisano, *The Birth of Mass Political Parties: Michigan, 1827–1861* (Princeton, NJ: Princeton University Press, 1971), 67. On the political camp meeting, see Richard J. Cawardine, *Evangelicals and Politics in Antebellum America* (New Haven, CT: Yale University Press, 1993), 52. For an example of a mass audience (an audience of one hundred thousand was claimed), see "The New York State Whig Convention," *Daily National Intelligencer*, 7 October 1844. For examples of urban gatherings that included these elements, see "Immense Assemblage of the Democracy of the City of New York Last Evening," *New York Herald*, 17 September 1844; "Mass Meeting of the Whigs of the Eight[h], Ninth and Fourteenth Wards, at the Corner of Grand Street and Broadway," *New York Herald*, 7 August 1844.

9. Partisan auditors: see, e.g., "Jackson's Birthday," *Weekly Ohio Statesman*, 27 March 1844. The custom was mocked in the political satire published in 1838: "Copy of Stump Speech," *National Gazette and Literary Register*, 31 May 1838. Reach undecided: See, e.g., Senator Stephen Douglas emphasized that he traveled the country "to enlighten the minds of these Republicans" during the famous Lincoln-Douglas debates, 17 July 1858, in *Political Debates between Abraham Lincoln and Stephen A. Douglas in the Celebrated Campaign of 1858 in Illinois, Including the Preceding Speeches of Each at Chicago, Springfield, Etc. Also, the Two Great Speeches of Abraham Lincoln in Ohio in 1859* (Cleveland, OH: Burrows Brothers, 1894), 56. Arouse existing supporters: see, e.g., Mr. M'Allister, cited in "Immense Assemblage of the Democracy of the City of New York Last Evening," *New York Herald*, 17 September 1844; Henry Clay, Speech at Lexington, 9 June 1842, in *PHC* 9, 715–716; S. S. Prentiss, Speech at Portland, Maine, 21 August 1840, in A. B. Norton, *The Great Revolution of 1840: Reminiscences of the Log Cabin and Hard Cider Campaign* (Mount Vernon, OH: A. B. Norton, 1888), 241–242.

10. On Jacksonian pioneers, see Kenneth Cmiel, *Democratic Eloquence: The Fight over Popular Speech in Nineteenth-Century America* (New York: William Morrow, 1990), 61; J. Jeffrey Auer, "Tom Corwin: 'King of the Stump,'" *Quarterly Journal of Speech* 30, no. 1 (1944): 48. For an attempt to link Federalists and stump oratory, see "Caucass Nominations," *National Advocate for the Country* (New York), 7 June 1822. For Whigs (emphasizing the novelty of

stump oratory in New Hampshire), see "Gen. Wilson's Caucus in Jefferson Hall," *New Hampshire Gazette*, 26 February 1839. For New York and anti-Jacksonians as leading mass oratory, see "New York," *Daily National Journal*, 5 November 1827; "Remarks of Colonel Rochester," *Daily National Intelligencer*, 11 July 1828; "Public Meeting at New York," *Boston Courier*, 13 February 1832; "The Whigs of New York," *Daily National Intelligencer*, 9 August 1834. On the Jacksonian machine (not oratory), see Walter A. McDougall, *Throes of Democracy: The American Civil War Era 1829–1877* (New York: Harper, 2008), 357. For the meticulous reconstruction of party mobilization in Oregon that emphasized organization, kinship, and the party ticket rather than speech, see Paul Bourke and Donald DeBats, *Washington County: Politics and Community in Antebellum America* (Baltimore: Johns Hopkins University Press, 1995), chap. 6 (esp. 166–167), chap. 7; Bourke and DeBats emphasized the importance of locality and neighborhood (chaps. 9–10).

11. On lifeless, small, managed meetings, see Glenn C. Altschuler and Stuart M. Blumin, "Limits of Political Engagement in Antebellum America: A New Look at the Golden Age of Participatory Democracy," *Journal of American History* 84, no. 3 (1997): 859–865. The unanimous adoption of resolutions was noted in "Jackson Meeting," *Berks and Schuykill Journal*, 18 September 1824. "Large and respectable" assemblage: "Jackson Meeting in Buckeys-Town," *Reservoir and Public Reflector*, 26 June 1827; "Jackson Meeting," *Richmond Enquirer*, 12 September 1826. False claims of "numerous and respectable" meetings: "From the National Journal," *Alexandria Gazette*, 25 June 1827. Adams's supporters dominate a Jackson meeting: "Jackson Meeting," *Alexandria Gazette*, 21 April 1827. Import of meetings in Jeffersonian period: David Hackett Fischer, *The Revolution of American Conservatism: The Federalist Party in the Era of Jeffersonian Democracy* (New York: Harper and Row, 1965), 97–98.

12. Contemporary observers: See, e.g., Ottilie Assing, Report, November 1860, in Christopher Lohmann, ed., *Radical Passion: Ottilie Assing's Reports from America and Letters to Frederick Douglass* (New York: Peter Lang, 1999), 200. Nasby: "Proposes to Celebrate the Fourth," June 1862, in *The Nasby Papers: Letters and Sermons Containing the Views on the Topics of the Day, of Petroleum V. Nasby, "Paster Uv the Church Uv the Noo Dispensashun"* (Indianapolis: C. O. Perrine, 1864), 47.

13. On violence at the polls, see Worden Pope to Andrew Jackson, 6 August 1831, in John Spencer Bassett, ed., *Correspondence of Andrew Jackson*, vol. 4, *1829–1832* (Washington, DC: Carnegie Institution of Washington, 1929), 326. On alcohol at Jacksonian events, see "Hickory Trees," *Spectator*, 18 October 1832. Confirmatory scholarship: Richard Franklin Bensel, *The American Ballot Box in the Mid-nineteenth Century* (Cambridge, UK: Cambridge University Press, 2004); Altschuler and Blumin, "Limits of Political Engagement in Antebellum America," 875–876. On "petty agents," etc., see "From Our Correspondent," *Spectator*, 15 October 1832. On local committees gathering names and votes, see Arthur Lee Campbell to Andrew Jackson, 4 September 1827, in Harold D. Moser and J. Clint Clifft, eds., *The Papers of Andrew Jackson*, vol. 6, *1825–1828* (Knoxville: University of Tennessee Press, 2002), 276. On tickets etc., see Bensel, *The American Ballot Box*, 2, 16, 296; Glenn C. Altschuler and Stuart M. Blumin, *Rude Republic: Americans and Their Politics in the Nineteenth Century* (Princeton, NJ: Princeton University Press, 2000), 71. Bone and tissue: Bensel, *The American Ballot Box*, 2. Thurlow Weed, cited in William E. Gienapp, "'Politics Seem to Enter into Everything': Political Culture in the North, 1840–1860," in *Essays on American Antebellum Politics, 1840–1860*, ed. Stephen E. Maizlish and John J. Kushma (Arlington: Texas A&M University Press, 1982), 52–53n.

14. Meetings resolved: see, e.g., "Jackson Meeting," *Baltimore Patriot*, 11 June 1824; "Fourth of March," *Richmond Enquirer*, 17 March 1829. Plan for address: "Jackson Meeting," *Southern Chronicle*, 17 December 1823; "Jackson Meeting," *Torch Light and Public Advertiser*,

22 March 1827; "Administration Meeting," *Augusta Chronicle and Georgia Advertiser*, 20 October 1827. Plan for written circular: "Jackson Meeting at Boston," *Baltimore Patriot*, 25 July 1826. Import of written tools of campaigning: Noble E. Cunningham Jr., *The Jeffersonian Republicans in Power: Party Operations, 1801–1809* (Chapel Hill: University of North Carolina Press, 1963), 101; Noble E. Cunningham Jr., *The Jeffersonian Republicans: The Formation of Party Organization, 1789–1801* (Chapel Hill: University of North Carolina Press, 1957), 157, 259. See also Andrew M. Robertson, *The Language of Democracy: Political Rhetoric in the United States and Britain, 1790–1900* (Ithaca, NY: Cornell University Press, 1995), which focuses on rhetoric in the press. Combustible materials etc.: John A. Dix to Azariah C. Flagg, 13 July 1832, *Azariah C. Flagg Papers*, New York Public Library, Box 1, 104 J-1.

15. Press central: Gienapp, "'Politics Seem to Enter into Everything,'" 41. Partisan press: Cunningham, *The Jeffersonian Republicans in Power*, 237. One of the new ventures was that the Whig Party established the *Log Cabin* for the 1840 campaign. The editor, Horace Greeley, claimed that sixty-two thousand copies were regularly printed. See Horace Greeley to Thurlow Weed, 27 July 1840, in Thurlow Weed Barnes, *Memoir of Thurlow Weed* (Boston: Houghton, Mifflin, 1884), 84–85. For complaints on allegedly unprincipled editors affiliated with Adams, see "Jackson Meeting at Lynchburg," *United States Telegraph*, 15 November 1827. Editor Amos Kendall became one of the symbols of the Jacksonian machine. See Donald B. Cole, *A Jackson Man: Amos Kendall and the Rise of American Democracy* (Baton Rouge: Louisiana State University Press, 2004). Editorial networks: Richard B. Kielbowicz, *News in the Mail: The Press, Post Office, and Public Information, 1700–1860s* (New York: Greenwood Press, 1989), 149. Newspapers and success: Martin Van Buren to Andrew Jackson, 14 September 1827, in Moser and Clifft, *The Papers of Andrew Jackson*, 6:392. Bulk copies: Elijah Hayard to Azariah C. Flagg, 21 February 1832, *Azariah C. Flagg Papers*, New York Public Library, Box 1, 104 J-1. Victory complete etc.: Robert P. Reynolds to James K. Polk, 18 February 1839, in Wayne Cutler, ed., *Correspondence of James K. Polk*, vol. 5, *1839–1841* (Nashville: Vanderbilt University Press, 1979), 74. On the overall import of the press to mass partisanship, see Andrew M. Robertson, "Voting Rites and Voting Acts: Electioneering Ritual, 1790–1820," in *Beyond the Founders: New Approaches to the Political History of the Early American Republic*, ed. Jeffrey L. Pasley, Andrew W. Robertson, and David Waldstreicher (Chapel Hill: University of North Carolina Press, 2004), 67.

16. Richard J. John, "Affairs of Office: The Executive Departments, the Election of 1828, and the Making of the Democratic Party," in *The Democratic Experiment: New Directions in American Political History*, ed. Meg Jacobs, William J. Novak, and Julian E. Zelizer (Princeton, NJ: Princeton University Press, 2003), 53.

17. Influence of patronage: Andrew Jackson to John Coffee, 12 May 1828, in Moser and Clifft, *The Papers of Andrew Jackson*, 6:458. For a satirical reference to Jackson's patronage, see Charles Augustus Davis, *Letters of J. Downing, Major, Downingville Militia, Second Brigade, to His Old Friend, Mr. Dwight, of the* New-York Daily Advertiser (New York: Harper and Brothers, 1834), 95–96. Permitted: Andrew Jackson to Martin Van Buren, 31 March 1829, in Bassett, ed., *Correspondence of Andrew Jackson*, 4:19. Stables: Andrew Jackson to Brigadier-General John Coffee, 30 May 1829, in ibid., 4:39. Rising offices: William R. Brock, *Parties and Political Conscience: American Dilemmas 1840–1850* (Millwood, NY: KTO Press, 1979), 76. Active agents: Michel Chevalier, *Society, Manners, and Politics in the United States: Letters on North America* (New York: Anchor Books, 1961), 193–194. See also "Fourth of July," *American Advocate*, 20 July 1832. Victor and spoils: Chevalier, *Society, Manners, and Politics in the United States*, 193. Jacksonians, patronage, and national party: John, "Affairs of Office," 60–63. Antebellum parties as patronage machines: Ronald P. Formisano, "The 'Party Period' Revisited," *Journal of American History* 86, no. 1 (1999): 94, 97.

18. Praise for caucus: "Caucass Nominations," *National Advocate for the Country*, 7 June 1822. On the origins of the caucus, see Frederick W. Whitridge, "Caucus System," in *Cyclopedia of Political Science, Political Economy, and the Political History of the United States*, ed. John J. Lalor (New York: Maynard, Merrill, 1899); Moisei Ostrogorski, *Democracy and the Organization of Political Parties* (New York: Macmillan, 1902). On the importance of Martin Van Buren in the consolidation of the modern party system, see Donald B. Cole, *Martin Van Buren and the American Political System* (Princeton, NJ: Princeton University Press, 1984). "First commandment" (Martin Van Buren's view, commonly shared): Michael E. McGerr, *The Decline of Popular Politics: The American North, 1865–1928* (New York: Oxford University Press, 1986), 13. Hone's lament: Nevins, *The Diary of Philip Hone 1828–1851*, 1:388. Press observation: "New York Election," *United States' Telegraph*, 16 April 1834; "New York Election," *New Hampshire Statesman and State Journal*, 19 April 1834; "Editorial," *Daily National Journal*, 16 November 1827.

19. Roughest man: Frances L. S. Dugan and Jacqueline P. Bull, eds., *Bluegrass Craftsman: Being the Reminiscences of Ebenezer Hiram Stedman, Papermaker 1808–1885* (Lexington: University of Kentucky Press, 1959), 71. Lost teeth: Andrew Jackson to Robert Paine et al., 30 September 1826, in Moser and Clifft, *The Papers of Andrew Jackson*, 6:220. Jackson's magnetism: Chevalier, *Society, Manners, and Politics in the United States*, 128; Nathan Sargent, *Public Men and Events in the United States: From the Commencement of Mr. Monroe's Administration in 1817 to the Close of Mr. Fillmore's Administration in 1853*, vol. 1 (1875; repr., New York: Da Capo Press, 1970), 246. Most popular man and idol: Nevins, *The Diary of Philip Hone 1828–1851*, 1:96, 1:452. Pressed forward: "The President in Lexington," *Richmond Enquirer*, 16 October 1832. Bayard's description related to the president's first inauguration: Margaret Bayard, *The First Forty Years of Washington Society* (New York: Charles Scribner's Sons, 1906), 295–296. Jackson's surprise: Andrew Jackson to Andrew Jackson Jr., 10 June 1833, in John Spencer Bassett, ed., *Correspondence of Andrew Jackson*, vol. 5, *1833–1838* (Washington, DC: Carnegie Institution of Washington, 1931), 109. Never before: Andrew Jackson to Andrew Jackson Jr., 14 June 1833, in ibid., 5:109.

20. Committee Letter, cited in Fletcher Melvin Green, "On Tour with President Andrew Jackson," in *Democracy in the Old South and Other Essays by Fletcher Melvin Green*, ed. Isaac Copeland (Kingsport, TN: Vanderbilt University Press, 1969), 160. Green suggested that only four of fifteen presidents between 1789 and 1861 undertook such tours (157–158). Party origin: *National Intelligencer*, cited in Green, "On Tour with President Andrew Jackson," 165. Subsequent confirmation, horse parade, dinner toasts, and gun salutes: Green, "On Tour with President Andrew Jackson," 160–161, 163, 166. Bows: Andrew Jackson to Andrew Jackson Jr., 14 June 1833, in Bassett, *Correspondence of Andrew Jackson*, 5:109. Wild beast: Duff Green, cited in Green, "On Tour with President Andrew Jackson," 164–165. Bamboozled: Letter 49, Boston, June 25, 1833, in Seba Smith (Major Jack Downing, pseud.), *My Thirty Years out of the Senate* (New York: Oaksmith, 1859), 212–213. Rheumatism: C. A. Davis, *Letters of J. Downing*, 15–16.

21. Fervor of people: See, e.g., the assessments of Chevalier, *Society, Manners, and Politics in the United States*, 128; Sargent, *Public Men and Events in the United States*, 246.

22. Jackson Dinners were celebrated on the anniversary of the Battle of New Orleans. See John William Ward, *Andrew Jackson: Symbol for an Age* (New York: Oxford University Press, 1955), 15. Their political uses are referenced in "Jackson Meeting in Windsor," *Farmers' Cabinet*, 29 December 1827. Anniversary celebrations: "Not a Drum Was Heard," *Portsmouth Journal and Rockingham Gazette*, 21 January 1832. Portraits etc.: "Great Democratic Meeting in Kennebec," *Age*, 11 July 1832.

23. These themes were developed in Ward, *Andrew Jackson*.

24. Old Hickory name: Ward, *Andrew Jackson*, 54. Versus oak: "The Hickory Tree," *Pittsfield Sun*, 1 November 1832. New World equality: Ward, *Andrew Jackson*. *Pittsfield Sun*: "The Hickory Tree," *Pittsfield Sun*, 1 November 1832.

25. Cut and trimmed: Sargent, *Public Men and Events in the United States*, 248. Resembled pole: Ben Perley Poore, *Perley's Reminiscences of Sixty Years in the National Metropolis*, vol. 1 (Philadelphia: Hubbard Brothers Publishers, 1886), 133. Earlier pole raisings: Baker, *Affairs of Party*, 297; Chevalier, *Society, Manners, and Politics in the United States*, 306–307. Party headquarters: Poore, *Perley's Reminiscences*, 133. Tammany Hall: "A Sign," *Philadelphia Inquirer*, 25 October 1832. *New York Evening Post*, cited in "The State of Pennsylvania," *Connecticut Herald*, 30 September 1828. Henry Clay, Speech in Raleigh, NC, 13 April 1844, in *PHC*10, 35–36. Labor: "Pole Worship—Pine Ward," *Philadelphia Inquirer*, 2 November 1832. Supporters: see, e.g., "Bucks County Meetings," *New Orleans Argus*, 8 October 1828. Children: Sargent, *Public Men and Events in the United States*, 248. Booze: "Hickory Trees," *Spectator*, 18 October 1832. Critics: "The Pennsylvanian," *Alexandria Gazette*, 30 October 1832. Coaches etc.: "Messrs. Gales and Seaton," *Daily National Intelligencer*, 18 October 1832. Jackson visits: *Washington Globe*, cited in "The President," *Vermont Gazette*, 16 October 1832; "The President in Lexington," *Richmond Enquirer*, 16 October 1832.

26. "The Hickory Tree," reproduced from *The Pennsylvanian* in "The Hickory Tree," *Pittsfield Sun*, 1 November 1832.

27. "The Hickory Tree," *Vermont Gazette*, 23 October 1832.

28. "Tammany Pledges," *Commercial Advertiser*, 31 October 1832.

29. No state without support: Brock, *Parties and Political Conscience*, 26. Metaphor of war: "The Noble Democracy of Ohio Pressing Forward in the Great Work of Free and Enlightened Principles," *Ohio Statesman*, 23 September 1840; Andrew Jackson to James K. Polk, 3 May 1828, in Herbert Weaver, ed., *Correspondence of James K. Polk*, vol. 1, *1817–1832* (Nashville: Vanderbilt University Press, 1969), 181. Arrayed: "Cincinnati," *Weekly Herald* (New York), 12 October 1844. Troops: "The Great Mass Meeting at the Capital," *Weekly Ohio Statesman*, 25 September 1844. General Jackson's success encouraged the recruitment of other military men, including Harrison, Scott, Pierce, and Taylor. Champions: "Old Virginia," *Boston Daily Atlas*, 5 September 1844. Keep armor: James K. Polk to Robert B. Reynolds, 19 August 1841, in Cutler, *Correspondence of James K. Polk*, 5:729. On martial language: Baker, *Affairs of Party*, 288.

30. Best indicators: see Daniel Webster's depressed assessment in Daniel Webster to Samuel Bell, 15 October 1827, in Charles M. Wiltse, ed., *The Papers of Daniel Webster, Correspondence*, vol. 2, *1825–1829* (Hanover, NH: University Press of New England, 1976), 244. Unexampled energy: "The Great Whig Meeting at Albany," *New York Herald*, 29 August 1844. Meeting resolutions: see "Kentucky: Jackson Meeting," *United States Telegraph*, 24 November 1827. Guiding principle: "Great Jackson Meeting in Baltimore," *Louisville Public Advertiser*, 4 June 1828.

31. Henry Clay to William Browne, 31 July 1840, in *PHC*9, 437. Henry Clay, Speech in Raleigh, NC, 13 April 1844, in *PHC*10, 35–36. James Kent, cited in McDougall, *Throes of Democracy*, 98.

32. The fullest discussion of the campaign was in Robert Gray Gunderson, *The Log-Cabin Campaign* (1957; repr., Westport, CT: Greenwood Press, 1977). Second Jackson: "Communications," *Ohio Statesman*, 24 June 1840. Mimicry: Marvin Meyers, *The Jacksonian Persuasion: Politics and Belief* (Stanford, CA: Stanford University Press, 1960), 8; McDougall, *Throes of Democracy*, 97.

33. Ronald P. Formisano, "The New Political History and the Election of 1840," *Journal of Interdisciplinary History* 23, no. 4 (1993): 661.

34. Democrats improve: Altschuler and Blumin, *Rude Republic*, 18. Revolution: William James Cooper, *The South and the Politics of Slavery 1828–1856* (Baton Rouge: Louisiana State University Press, 1978), 132. Newspaper dismissal: Harriet A. Weed, ed., *Autobiography of Thurlow Weed* (Boston: Houghton, Mifflin, 1883), 492–493.

35. Horace Greeley was the editor of the most famous *Log Cabin Herald* campaign newspaper. On the leading slogan, note the critical report of Clay's speech in "The Southwestern Whig Convention at Nashville," *Mississippian*, 11 September 1840. Hurrah: Nevins, *The Diary of Philip Hone 1828–1851*, 1:486. Thurlow Weed, cited in Barnes, *Memoir of Thurlow Weed*, 81.

36. Critics of repetition: see, e.g., "Mr. Medary," *Ohio Statesman*, 19 August 1840. Daniel Webster, Speech at the Great Mass Meeting at Saratoga, 19 August 1840, in Norton, *The Great Revolution of 1840*, 232. Song: "Gold Spoons vs. Hard Cider," in A. B. Norton, ed., *Tippecanoe Songs of the Log Cabin Boys and Girls of 1840* (Mount Vernon, OH: A. B. Norton., 1888), 73–74.

37. First mass deployment of songs: Poore, *Perley's Reminiscences*, 232. On song distribution, see the report from the *St. Louis New Era* on a Missouri procession in Norton, *The Great Revolution of 1840*, 144. Whig operatives: Weed, ed., *Autobiography of Thurlow Weed*, 467. Whigs ahead: Horace Greeley, *Recollections of a Busy Life* (New York: J. B. Ford, 1868), 134. Standard feature: Auer, "Tom Corwin," 50; Gienapp, "'Politics Seem to Enter into Everything,'" 33.

38. Upwards of ten thousand: see, e.g., "A Gathering of the People in Fayette," *Indiana Journal*, 18 April 1840. Missouri procession, as reported in *St. Louis New Era*, cited in Norton, *The Great Revolution of 1840*, 271. Long convoys: *New York Star* report of Utica Convention of 12 August 1840, cited in ibid., 261; "Medina Convention," *Cleveland Daily Herald*, 26 August 1840. Banners etc.: "A Gathering of the People in Fayette," *Indiana Journal*, 18 April 1840. Ballot boxes: "Zanesville Celebration," *Scioto Gazette*, 16 July 1840, citing a report from the *Log Cabin Herald*. Old Tip: *New York Star* report of Utica Convention of 12 August 1840, cited in Norton, *The Great Revolution of 1840*, 261. Raccoons: J. C. Guild, *Old Times in Tennessee, with Historical, Personal, and Political Scraps and Sketches* (Nashville: Tavel, Eastman, and Howell, 1878), 159–161. Other animals: "Mr. Medary," *Ohio Statesman*, 19 August 1840; "Communications," *Ohio Statesman*, 24 June 1840. The eagle: "The Presentation of the Fort Meigs Eagle," *North American and Daily Advertiser*, 30 March 1840.

39. On the convention, see Formisano, *The Birth of Mass Political Parties*, 67. At places of spiritual meeting: Cawardine, *Evangelicals and Politics in Antebellum America*, 52. The role of party champions is discussed in depth later in this chapter. One notable example is Tom Corwin of Ohio, who allegedly delivered six major speeches in the final week of August 1840 to an estimated fifty-three thousand persons. See Auer, "Tom Corwin," 50. Press promotion: Brock, *Parties and Political Conscience*, 3–4. Delegate elections: Reuben Davis, *Recollections of Mississippi and Mississippians*, rev. ed. (n.p.: University and College Press of Mississippi, 1972), 113. Long journeys and alcohol: Poore, *Perley's Reminiscences*, 233–234. Arriving processions: Formisano, *The Birth of Mass Political Parties*, 133. Speaker rotation: Cawardine, *Evangelicals and Politics in Antebellum America*, 52. Without parallel: "The Corwin Meeting," *Cleveland Daily Herald*, 2 September 1840. Splendid affair: "Democratic Mass Meeting!" *Weekly Ohio Statesman*, 25 September 1844. Thronging Whigs: "A Whig Jubilee in Georgia," *Daily National Intelligencer*, 6 August 1844. Inflated estimates (one report listed "acre meetings" across the country from Tennessee to New York, some allegedly drawing as many as fifteen thousand): "Acre Meetings," *Cleveland Daily Herald*, 15 June 1840. American women: Elizabeth R. Varon, "Tippecanoe and the Ladies, Too: White Women and Party Politics in Antebellum Virginia," *Journal of American History* 82 (1995): 494–521.

40. Urban meetings: Joel H. Silbey, *The Partisan Imperative: The Dynamics of American Politics before the Civil War* (New York: Oxford University Press, 1985), 65. Earlier meetings:

see, e.g., "Great Jackson Meeting in New York," *New Hampshire Patriot and State Gazette*, 12 November 1827. Log cabins (the estimate was for the New York Log Cabin): Nevins, *The Diary of Philip Hone 1828–1851*, 1:486. For references to cabins elsewhere, see, e.g., "Harrison, Tyler and Corwin," *Cleveland Daily Herald*, 12 May 1840; "Saturday Evening," *Cleveland Daily Herald*, 16 June 1840. Later Whig campaigns: John W. Bear, *The Life and Travels of John W. Bear, "The Buckeye Blacksmith"* (Baltimore: Binswanger, 1879), 110, 118; Benjamin French to James K. Polk, 1 July 1844, in Wayne Culter, ed., *Correspondence of James K. Polk*, vol. 7, *January–August 1844* (Nashville: Vanderbilt University Press, 1989), 304–305; "Hon. Joshua R. Giddings on the Stump," *Cleveland Herald*, 5 August 1844; William Henry Russell to Henry Clay, 7 May 1844, in *PHC*10, 55–56. Party headquarters: McGerr, *The Decline of Popular Politics*, 24.

41. Tammany Hall: "Great Jackson Meeting in New York," *New Hampshire Patriot and State Gazette*, 12 November 1827. Silk banner: "Mass Meeting of the Whigs of the Eight[h], Ninth and Fourteenth Wards, at the Corner of Grand Street and Broadway," *New York Herald*, 7 August 1844.

42. See the reports earlier cited: "The Stump," *Daily Herald and Gazette*, 5 September 1837; "Mr. N. P. Tallmadge," *North American*, 17 October 1839; *Boston Times*, cited in "The Following Remarks," *Dover Gazette and Strafford Advertiser*, 1 January 1839; "Wilson Preaching," *Dover Gazette and Strafford Advertiser*, 19 March 1839; "We Are Not Sorry," *New Bedford Mercury*, 28 August 1840.

43. Henry Clay to John Sloane, 27 July 1840, in *PHC*9, 435. Daniel Webster, cited in Irving H. Bartlett, *Daniel Webster* (New York: Norton, 1978), 163–164.

44. Biography: "A Brief Sketch of Thomas Corwin," *Cleveland Daily Herald*, 22 April 1840. Sarcastic reply: *Boston Herald*, cited in "Thomas Corwin," *Cleveland Daily Herald*, 12 March 1840. Campaign document: Poore, *Perley's Reminiscences*, 234–235. Stump talent: "A Looker On," Letter to the Editor, *Ohio Statesman*, 21 February 1840.

45. Acre meetings: "Acre Meetings," *Cleveland Daily Herald*, 15 June 1840. Speaking engagements: "Thomas Corwin," *Scioto Gazette*, 30 July 1840. Corwin's claims: Thomas Corwin, cited in Auer, "Tom Corwin," 49. Ludicrous: "Thomas Corwin," *Cleveland Daily Herald*, 12 March 1840. Exuberant etc.: "Tom Corwin of Ohio," *Harper's New Monthly Magazine* 35 (June–November 1867): 80. Prince of wags: "General Grant as an Orator," *Daily Evening Bulletin*, 8 October 1874.

46. Natural eloquence: "Harrison and Corwin," *Scioto Gazette*, 5 March 1840. Influences: Auer, "Tom Corwin," 54. Playful etc.: "Reception and Visit of Thomas Corwin," *Scioto Gazette*, 13 August 1840. Exhibit sunshine etc.: "Mr. Corwin, of Ohio," *New Hampshire Statesman*, 13 August 1847.

47. Dumbstruck etc.: See, e.g., "Tom Corwin," *Ohio Statesman*, 8 July 1840; "Messrs. Hamer and Corwin," *Ohio Statesman*, 15 July 1840. Disgusting: *Cleveland Advertiser*, cited in "Federal Decency," *Ohio Statesman*, 2 September 1840. Power of eloquence etc.: "Medina Convention," *Cleveland Daily Herald*, 26 August 1840; "Thomas Corwin," *Cleveland Daily Herald*, 27 August 1840. Breathless silence: "Thomas Corwin," *Cleveland Daily Herald*, 27 August 1840.

48. On the capacity of press and orator to work in harness in other contexts, such as the later Lincoln-Douglas debates, see, e.g., Robertson, *The Language of Democracy*, 88–90.

49. Warren: "The Corwin Meeting," *Cleveland Daily Herald*, 2 September 1840. Zanesville: "Zanesville Celebration," *Scioto Gazette*, 16 July 1840. Democratic prey: "Old Pickaway," "Last Lay of the Minstrel," *Scioto Gazette*, 29 October 1840.

50. "Thomas Corwin," in *Bench and Bar of Ohio*, vol. 1, ed. George Irving Reed (Chicago: Century Publishing and Engraving, 1897), 247.

51. Auer, "Tom Corwin," 47–55.

52. Parents and service: *Bear*, 7. Clay: ibid., 9. Pugilistic victory: ibid., 10–11. African Americans: ibid., 12. Slavery: ibid., 24.

53. Tone and principle (e.g., Bear claimed never to have voted for the Democrats, owing to their support for slavery): *Bear*, 24. Best posted: ibid., 40. Small meetings: ibid., 35. Friendly talks: ibid., 37. Ratification meeting: ibid., 42.

54. Called to stage: *Bear*, 42. Congratulated: ibid., 43–44. Main stand: ibid., 45. Ohio: ibid., 46–47. Kentucky, Virginia: ibid., 49. Pennsylvania: ibid., 60. New York: ibid., 68–69.

55. *Bear*, 62.

56. Blacksmith stumper: "Log Cabin Meeting," *Cleveland Daily Herald*, 15 May 1840. Appointment: "John W. Bear, Sub Indian Agent," *Ohio Statesman*, 2 June 1841. Party committees: *Bear*, 52. Local gossip: ibid., 48.

57. Props: *Bear*, 46. Horseshoe: ibid., 59. Greatest shout: ibid., 69–70.

58. Kellogg: "Log Cabin Meeting," *Cleveland Daily Herald*, 15 May 1840. Full of inspiration: Mr. Bradford, cited in "Meeting in Monument Square," 5 May 1840, in Norton, *The Great Revolution of 1840*, 132–133. Itinerant preachers: "Wilson Preaching," *Dover Gazette and Strafford Advertiser*, 19 March 1839. Whig roster: Robert G. Gunderson, "The Southern Whigs," in *Oratory of the Old South: 1828–1860*, ed. Waldo W. Braden (Baton Rouge: Louisiana State University Press, 1970), 137. Sargent: ibid., 118.

59. Merrill D. Peterson, *The Great Triumvirate: Webster, Clay, and Calhoun* (New York: Oxford University Press, 1987), 293.

60. Liberty: Daniel Webster, "Bunker Hill Monument," in *Daniel Webster Reader*, ed. Bertha M. Rothe (New York: Oceana Publications, 1956), 89. Guarded etc.: ibid., 92. A model (included, for example, in the literature curriculum of the University of Chicago in the late nineteenth century): Cmiel, *Democratic Eloquence*, 190. Webster's closing words: Daniel Webster, "Webster-Hayne—2nd Speech," in Rothe, ed., *Daniel Webster Reader*, 230.

61. Forehead: William Henry Milburn, *The Pioneers, Preachers and People of the Mississippi Valley* (New York: Derby and Jackson, 1860), 426. National ideal: Edward G. Parker, *The Golden Age of American Oratory* (Boston: Whittmore, Niles and Hall, 1857), 51. Dark etc.: Cyril Thornton, in Rothe, ed., *Daniel Webster Reader*, 51. Piercing etc.: "'Take the Ruffian Bellows by the Top,'" *Herald* (New York), 17 March 1837. Clear etc.: Cyril Thornton, in Rothe, ed., *Daniel Webster Reader*, 51. Deep etc.: Oliver Dyer, *Great Senators of the United States Forty Years Ago* (New York: Robert Banner's Sons, 1889), 253. Very English: Parker, *The Golden Age of American Oratory*, 117. Formal dress: Henry Hilliard, in Rothe, ed., *Daniel Webster Reader*, 56. Leonine: ibid., 56. Godlike: Dyer, *Great Senators of the United States*, 251. Majestic: Parker, *The Golden Age of American Oratory*, 64. Cold etc.: William M. Morrison, in Rothe, ed., *Daniel Webster Reader*, 57. Stern: sterner than Clay, according to Greeley, *Recollections of a Busy Life*, 250. Speeches: Cyril Thornton, in Rothe, ed., *Daniel Webster Reader*, 51. Language: Cmiel, *Democratic Eloquence*, 57. Exactness: Parker, *The Golden Age of American Oratory*, 108. No gaudiness: Cyril Thornton, in Rothe, ed., *Daniel Webster Reader*, 52.

62. Want of passion: William M. Morrison, in Rothe, ed., *Daniel Webster Reader*, 57. Uphill effort: "Connecticut," *The Globe*, 10 April 1837. Clay comparison: ibid.

63. At barbecues: Bartlett, *Daniel Webster*, 163. *Missouri Democrat*, cited in "Daniel Webster," *The Globe*, 31 July 1837.

64. Frontier barbecue: Bartlett, *Daniel Webster*, 163. Inflammatory harangues: *Missouri Democrat*, cited in "Daniel Webster," *The Globe*, 31 July 1837. Talked a good deal: *New Orleans Bee*, cited in "Webster in the West," *The Globe*, 29 July 1837. Cannot take: "Communications," *The Globe*, 24 July 1837.

65. Advice: Cmiel, *Democratic Eloquence*, 61. Changing style: Bartlett, *Daniel Webster*, 163. New light: Peterson, *The Great Triumvirate*, 294. Lightening of manner: ibid., 295.

Spectacle: Daniel Webster, Address to Young Men's Whig National Convention at Baltimore May 4 1840, in Norton, *The Great Revolution of 1840*, 123. Great movement: Daniel Webster, Speech at the Great Mass Meeting at Saratoga, 19 August 1840, in ibid., 225. New revolution: Daniel Webster, Address to Young Men's Whig National Convention at Baltimore May 4 1840, in ibid., 123.

66. Hard cider: Daniel Webster, Address to Young Men's Whig National Convention at Baltimore May 4 1840, in Norton, *The Great Revolution of 1840*, 123. Saratoga: Daniel Webster, Speech at the Great Mass Meeting at Saratoga, 19 August 1840, in ibid., 226. Log cabin: Daniel Webster, Speech at the Great Mass Meeting at Saratoga, 19 August 1840, in ibid., 233.

67. Richmond promise: Daniel Webster, Address to Virginia Convention at Richmond, October 1840, in Norton, *The Great Revolution of 1840*, 334. Syracuse: Bartlett, *Daniel Webster*, 163. A liar: Daniel Webster, Address to New York Merchants Meeting, in Norton, *The Great Revolution of 1840*, 323. Challenge: Daniel Webster, Address to New York Merchants Meeting, in ibid., 323.

68. Webster's rank as stump speaker: Gil Troy, *See How They Ran: The Changing Role of the Presidential Candidate*, rev. ed. (Cambridge, MA: Harvard University Press, 1996), 53. Tactic vindicated: John Sloane to Henry Clay, 24 November 1840, in *PHC9*, 454. Refined orator: "Stump Speaking," *New-Orleans Commercial Bulletin*, 17 August 1844. Whigs descend: "Eastman's Wakefield Speechification," *Dover Gazette and Strafford Advertiser*, 5 March 1839.

69. Adam Huntsman to James K. Polk, 26 January 1840, in Cutler, *Correspondence of James K. Polk*, 5:374.

70. Thrilling eloquence: "The Noble Democracy of Ohio Pressing Forward in the Great Work of Free and Enlightened Principles," *Ohio Statesman*, 23 September 1840. Democratic leaders promise: Sam Medary, paraphrased in "National Convention," *Ohio Statesman*, 27 May 1840. Claim to have taken the stump: "Specie Clause," *Ohio Statesman*, 8 April 1840. Greater prominence of public speaking: Harry L. Watson, *Jacksonian Politics and Community Conflict: The Emergence of the Second American Party System in Cumberland County, North Carolina* (Baton Rouge: Louisiana State University Press, 1981), 270.

71. Early and active part: David Burford to James K. Polk, 14 November 1840, in Cutler, *Correspondence of James K. Polk*, 5:584. Course of our opponents: Lucien B. Chase to James K. Polk, 28 November 1843, in ibid., 5:363. Into Africa: Gainsevoort Melville, cited in "Jackson's Birthday," *Weekly Ohio Statesman*, 27 March 1844.

72. Superior organization: James K. Polk to David Burford, 7 November 1840, in Cutler, *Correspondence of James K. Polk*, 5:576–577. Polk's suggestion: James K. Polk to Cave Johnson, 24 June 1844, in Wayne Cutler, ed., *Correspondence of James K. Polk*, vol. 7, *January–August 1844* (Nashville: Vanderbilt University Press, 1989), 275–276.

73. Attendance: "The Great National Democratic Mass Convention at Nashville," *New York Herald*, 27 August 1844. Battalions: ibid. Fifty acres: *Nashville Union*, cited in "Camp Hickory," *Weekly Ohio Statesman*, 4 September 1844. Dinner table: "The Great National Democratic Mass Convention at Nashville," *New York Herald*, 27 August 1844. Largest assemblage: "Camp Hickory," *Weekly Ohio Statesman*, 4 September 1844. Most brilliant: "The Great Democratic Mass Convention at Nashville," *New York Herald*, 27 August 1844. Great encampment: ibid.

74. Mass meetings: Allen Nevins, ed., *The Diary of Philip Hone 1828–1851*, vol. 2 (New York: Arno Press, 1970), 714. Outpouring: "Immense Assemblage of the Democracy of the City of New York Last Evening," *New York Herald*, 17 September 1844.

75. Cheap edition: "Democratic Celebration," *New York Herald*, 18 March 1844. Circulation: "Two Spirits from the Vast Deep," *New York Herald*, 22 March 1844. One of the

ablest: William E. Cramer to James K. Polk, 21 July 1844, in Cutler, *Correspondence of James K. Polk*, 7:376. For Melville in Nashville: "The Great Democratic Mass Convention at Nashville," *New York Herald*, 27 August 1844. In Ohio: "Zanesville Whiggery," *Weekly Ohio Statesman*, 2 October 1844. In New Jersey: "Great Meeting of the Democracy at Newark," *New York Herald*, 5 November 1844. For the description as "Tammany Hall Orator": "'A Nut for the New York Anti-Texas Democrats to Crack,'" *Cleveland Herald*, 7 October 1844. Jackson's presence: "Great Meeting of the Democracy at Newark," *New York Herald*, 5 November 1844.

76. Into southern fashion: Amasa J. Parker (of Albany, New York) to James K. Polk, 17 August 1844, in Cutler, *Correspondence of James K. Polk*, 5:455. Stolen music, cited in Troy, 30.

77. Troy, 6. The difference with Troy's impressive interpretation may be a product of his specific concern with the stumping of presidential candidates rather than its overall use within the polity.

78. On Crockett: See, e.g., "Stump Speech," *American Advocate*, 23 September 1831 (reproduced from the *Illinois Gazette*). Wolf's Creek: See, e.g., "Stump Speaking in Arkansas," *New York Herald*, 29 April 1844. San Francisco: "A Stump Speech," *Fayetteville Observer*, 5 August 1851. Promising genius: "Racy Stump Speech," *Fayetteville Observer*, 15 June 1854. Downing's travels: Jack Downing, Letter 61, Telegraph Wires, 31 October 1848, in Smith, *My Thirty Years Out of the Senate*, 309–310.

79. Downing as model for Ward: Melville D. Landon, "A Biographical Sketch by Melville D. Landon," in Charles Farrar Browne, *The Complete Works of Artemus Ward* (Project Gutenberg, 2004), available at www.gutenberg.org/files/6946/6946-h/6946-h.htm. Indiana: "Fourth of July Oration," in ibid., 60. Show business: "Among the Spirits," in ibid., 23. July Fourth: "Fourth of July Oration," in ibid., 60.

80. Minstrel show form: Eric Lott, *Love and Theft: Blackface Minstrelsy and the American Working Class* (New York: Oxford University Press, 1993), 5–6. Popularity: Paul Gilmore, *The Genuine Article: Race, Mass Culture, and American Literary Manhood* (Durham, NC: Duke University Press, 2001), 38. First mass culture: Catherine M. Cole and Tracy Davis, "Routes of Blackface," *TDR: The Drama Review* 57, no. 2 (2013): 8.

81. Not in earliest performances: Note that published reviews of leading troupes in the 1850s do not reference the performance of stump speeches. See "Peel's Minstrels," *New Orleans Daily Creole*, 15 November 1856; "Christy's Minstrels," *New Orleans Daily Creole*, 2 October 1856. First act: Hans Nathan, "The Performance of the Virginia Minstrels," in *Inside the Minstrel Mask: Readings in Nineteenth-Century Blackface Minstrelsy*, ed. Annemarie Bean, James V. Hatch, and Brooks McNamara (Hanover, NH: Wesleyan University Press/University Press of New England, 1996), 37. Second act: Lott, *Love and Theft*, 5–6. Contemporary program: Charles Townsend, "Negro Minstrels," in Bean, Hatch, and McNamara, eds., *Inside the Minstrel Mask*, 122–123.

82. Variety of subjects and Lyceum as model: Jules Zanger, "The Minstrel Show as Theater of Misrule," *Quarterly Journal of Speech* 60, no. 1 (1974): 35–36, 37. Subjects: Nathan, "The Performance of the Virginia Minstrels," 40. Slavery etc., canvased: Lott, *Love and Theft*, 87. Citation: Byron Christy, "Burlesque Political Stump Speech," in *Christy's New Songster and Black Joker*, ed. E. Byron Christy and William E. Christy (New York: Dick and Fitzgerald Publishers, 1863), 9. A "celebrity": "Byron Christy's Burlesque Stump Speech," in *Beadle's Dime Patriotic Speaker* (New York: Beadle, 1863), 27.

83. Filthy scum etc.: "The Hutchison Family—Hunkerism," *Frederick Douglass' Paper*, 27 October 1848. Inverse relationship: *Pacific Appeal*, cited in Tavia Nyong'o, *Amalgamation Waltz: Race, Performance, and the Ruses of Memory* (Minneapolis: University of Minnesota Press, 2009), 119. Minstrelsy's rise and black mobilization: Constance Rourke, *American Hu-*

mor: A Study of the National Character (Tallahassee: Florida State University Press, 1959), 98. Antislavery as minstrelsy: *New York Sunday Era*, reprinted in "Garrison's Nigger Minstrels," *The Liberator*, 31 May 1850. White assertion and bulwark: Douglas A. Jones Jr., "Black Politics but Not Black People," *TDR: The Drama Review* 57, no. 2 (2013): 28.

84. Sensitivity and richness of African American culture: Carl Bryan Holmbert and Gilbert D. Schneider, "Daniel Decatur Emmett's Stump Sermons: Genuine Afro-American Culture, Language and Rhetoric in the Negro Minstrel Show," *Journal of Popular Culture* 19, no. 4 (1986): 28; Martha S. Jones, *All Bound Up Together: The Woman Question in African American Public Culture, 1830–1900* (Chapel Hill: University of North Carolina Press, 2007), 101. Transgressive glee: Lott, *Love and Theft*, 77. Radical etc.: W. T. Lhamon Jr., "Turning Around Jim Crow," in *Burnt Cork: Traditions and Legacies of Blackface Minstrelsy*, ed. Stephen Johnson (Amherst: University of Massachusetts Press, 2012), 27. Targets: Thomas L. Riis, "Minstrelsy and Theatrical Miscegnation," in *The Oxford Companion to the American Musical*, ed. Raymond Knapp, Mitchell Morris, and Stacy Wolf (Oxford, UK: Oxford University Press, 2011), 72; William John Mahar, *Behind the Burnt Cork Mask: Early Blackface Minstrelsy and Antebellum American Popular Culture* (Urbana: University of Illinois Press, 1999), 89.

85. American Eagle: Byron Christy, "Ain't I Right, Eh?" in Christy and Christy, *Christy's New Songster*, 33. Logically: J. B. Murphy, "Burlesque Stump Oration," in ibid., 56–57. Rats: Christy, "Burlesque Political Stump Speech," 10. Representatives: "The Olio—a Stump Speech," in Dailey Paskman, *"Gentlemen, Be Seated!" A Parade of the American Minstrels* (New York: Clarkson N. Potter, 1976), 129. Stump speakers: "Speech on Women's Rights," in Bean, Hatch and McNamara, eds., *Inside the Minstrel Mask*, 136. Song: "Money a Hard Thing to Borrow," in Christy and Christy, *Christy's New Songster*, 66.

86. Most popular entertainment: Alexander Saxton, "Blackface Minstrelsy and Jacksonian Ideology," *American Quarterly* 27, no. 1 (1975): 3–4. Minstrel fever: Riis, "Minstrelsy and Theatrical Miscegnation," 66. Popularity of stump speeches: See Charles Townsend, "Negro Minstrels," in Bean, Hatch, and McNamara, eds., *Inside the Minstrel Mask*, 122; Nathan, "The Performance of the Virginia Minstrels," 40. Elocution guides: See Robert Kidd, *Vocal Culture and Elocution: With Numerous Exercises in Reading and Speaking* (Cincinnati, OH: Wilson and Hinkle, 1857); Worthy Putnam, *The Science and Art of Elocution and Oratory* (New York: C. M. Saxton, 1858); Albert J. Spencer, ed., *Spencer's Book of Comic Speeches and Humorous Recitations* (New York: Dick and Fitzgerald, 1867); Nathaniel K. Richardson, *One Hundred Choice Selections in Poetry and Prose* (Philadelphia: P. Garrett, 1868); Oliver Optic, ed., *Our Boys and Girls* (Boston: Lee and Shepard, 1868).

87. A new power: *Charleston Patriot*, reproduced in "Stump Speaking," *New-Orleans Commercial Bulletin*, 17 August 1844. Essential American: "'The Stump' as an Educator," *Frank Leslie's Illustrated Newspaper*, 19 July 1856. General John L. Swift, paraphrased in "City and Vicinity," *Lowell Daily Citizen and News*, 30 January 1868.

CHAPTER 3

1. Suffrage: Dorothy Thompson, *The Chartists* (Hounslow, UK: Temple Smith, 1984), 11. On boisterous British elections: Charles Tilly, *Popular Contention in Great Britain, 1758–1834* (Cambridge, MA: Harvard University Press, 1995); Jon Lawrence, *Electing Our Masters: The Hustings in British Politics from Hogarth to Blair* (Oxford, UK: Oxford University Press, 2009); Frank Gorman, *Voters, Patrons and Parties: The Unreformed Electorate of Hanoverian England, 1734–1832* (Oxford, UK: Clarendon Press, 1989).

2. Hustings definition: *The Oxford English Dictionary* (online) definition of "husting" (noun). Popular expectation of address: Lawrence, *Electing Our Masters*, 24. "The Election,

a Poem," cited in Joseph Grego, *A History of Parliamentary Elections and Electioneering in the Old Days* (London: Chatto and Windus, 1886), 11.

3. Lawrence, *Electing Our Masters*, 29. David Moore, *The Politics of Deference: A Study of the Mid-nineteenth Century English Politics System* (Hassocks, UK: Harvester Press, 1976); H. J. Hanham, *Elections and Party Management: Politics in the Time of Disraeli and Gladstone* (London: Longmans, 1959). Andrew W. Robertson notes that British electioneering in the early nineteenth century, unlike American electioneering, remained focused on the character and conduct of candidates for Parliament. See Andrew W. Robertson, *The Language of Democracy: Political Rhetoric in the United States and Britain, 1790–1900* (Ithaca, NY: Cornell University Press, 1995), 66.

4. Mr. Newdegate, MP, cited in "The Policy of Non-intervention," *Times* (London), 25 December 1866; "Mr. Sala's Diary in America," *Pall Mall Gazette*, 16 March 1865.

5. *Times* assessment: "It Would Be Affectation," *Times* (London), 6 May 1857. Radicals: Emma Macleod, *British Visions of America, 1775–1820: Republican Realities* (London: Pickering and Chatto, 2013), 132.

6. On the dominance of economic rather than political motives for most Americans and Britons in this period, see P. J. Marshall, *Remaking the British Atlantic: The United States and the British Empire after American Independence* (Oxford, UK: Oxford University Press, 2012), 320. Frank Thistlethwaite calls radical migrants from Britain arriving in the United States only a "significant few": Frank Thistlethwaite, *The Anglo-American Connection in the Early Nineteenth Century* (Philadelphia: University of Pennsylvania Press, 1959), 45. On the importance of utilitarian and political concerns, note the organization of Nevins's discussion into three periods: Allan Nevins, ed., *America through British Eyes* (New York: Oxford University Press, 1948), esp. 8–9. Steam travel: ibid., 9. Steam travel and the wealthy: ibid., 79. Increasing travel: R. J. M. Blackett, *Divided Hearts: Britain and the American Civil War* (Baton Rouge: Louisiana State University Press, 2001), 178. Publications: John S. Whitley and Arnold Goldman, "Introduction," in Charles Dickens, *American Notes for General Circulation* (Harmondsworth, UK: Penguin, 1972), 11.

7. Initial radical acclaim: Gregory Claeys, "The Example of America a Warning to England? The Transformation of America in British Radicalism and Socialism, 1790–1850," in *Living and Learning: Essays in Honour of J. F. C. Harrison*, ed. Malcolm Chase and Ian Dyck (Aldershot, UK: Scolar Press, 1995), 66–80; Claeys noted a growing radical criticism of economic inequality in the United States. British conservatives: Macleod, *British Visions of America*, 79. England's aristocracy: Alexander MacKay, cited in Benjamin P. Thomas, *"Lincoln's Humor" and Other Essays*, ed. Michael Burlingame (Urbana: University of Illinois Press, 2002), 52. Middle- and upper-class Britons: Kathleen Burk, *Old World, New World: Great Britain and America from the Beginning* (New York: Atlantic Monthly Press, 2007), 278. Increasing criticism (note that Nevins dated the Age of Tory Condescension from 1825): Nevins, *America through British Eyes*. Characterization of America: Paul Langford, "Manners and Character in Anglo-American Perceptions, 1750–1850," in *Anglo-American Attitudes: From Revolution to Partnership*, ed. Fred M. Leventhal and Roland Quinault (Aldershot, UK: Ashgate, 2000), 76.

8. American government as weaker: Henry Pelling, *America and the British Left: From Bright to Bevan* (London: Adam and Charles Black, 1956), 13–14. Election fever: Frances Trollope, *Domestic Manners of the Americans* (1832; repr., London: Penguin Books, 1997), 197. Rise of the politician: "All Americans Agree," *Times* (London), 23 October 1866. Dwindling statesmen and wide echo: "Mr. Spence on American Union and Secession," *Times* (London), 6 January 1862. Vulgarity and coarseness: "Mr. Sala's Diary in America," *Pall Mall Gazette*, 16 March 1865. Shallow and rambling: Basil Hall, *Travels in North America in the*

Years 1827 and 1828, vol. 1 (Philadelphia: Carey, Lea and Carey, 1829), 236. Abusive: "Modern Speakers," *Saturday Review* 2, no. 20 (9 June 1866): 1. Manichean: Trollope, *Domestic Manners of the Americans*, 197. Truth etc. and aggression: "The United States and Slavery," *Sheffield and Rotherham Independent*, 5 October 1850. Word "Republican," etc.: Lieutenant Francis Hall, *Travels in Canada and the United States*, 2nd ed. (London: Longman, Hurst, Rees, Orme and Brown, 1819), n.p. Demagogues: Michel Chevalier, *Society, Manners, and Politics in the United States: Letters on North America* (New York: Anchor Books, 1961), 62. American elections: John Gifford (1800), cited in Macleod, *British Visions of America*, 81.

9. Macleod noted an overwhelming admiration of Americans among British radicals up to 1820: Macleod, *British Visions of America*, 150. On continuing radical enthusiasm, see James Epstein, "'America' in the Victorian Cultural Imagination," in *Anglo-American Attitudes*, 107–123. On Paine and Cobbett's praise for republican principles, see Claeys, "The Example of America," 66–72. Cobbett was initially critical of the United States but began to praise American institutions from about 1812; ibid., 71.

10. On electioneering, see Frances Wright D'Arusmont, *Life, Letters and Lectures 1834/1844* (New York: Arno Press, 1972), 133–134. Rejects party politics: ibid., 152.

11. Greatest good: Alexis de Tocqueville, *Democracy in America*, ed. J. P. Mayer (New York: Harper and Row, 1966), 232. Restless activity: ibid., 244. Shortage of guarantees: ibid., 252. Disappearing statesmen: ibid., 197. "Hasty judgements," etc.: ibid., 198. Superior men: ibid., 198–199. Darker view dominates: Pelling, *America and the British Left*, 3; e.g., "Mr. Spence on American Union and Secession," *Times* (London), 6 January 1862.

12. *Sketches*: "Davy Crocket[t]," *Belfast News-Letter*, 13 February 1829. Colonies (Australian): Richard Waterhouse, "The Minstrel Show and Australian Culture," *Journal of Popular Culture* 24, no. 3 (1990): 159. Reviews: see, e.g., "Hurrah for Old Kentuck!" *Derby Mercury*, 18 December 1833. Hackett: "Mr. Hackett," *Morning Post*, 25 January 1833; "Theatre Royal," *Manchester Times and Gazette*, 22 June 1833; "Adelphi," *Bell's Life in London and Sporting Chronicle*, 6 October 1839.

13. "Celebrated": "Letters from New York," *Bristol Mercury*, 3 October 1835; "The Bowie Knife," *Glasgow Herald*, 18 May 1846. Death: "The Texas," *Belfast News-Letter*, 17 May 1836. Schooner: "Ship News," *Morning Post*, 23 February 1841. Racehorses: "Hampton Races," *Daily News*, 11 June 1860; "Huntingdon Summer Meeting," *Sheffield and Rotherham Independent*, 18 July 1871. "The Literary Examiner," *Examiner*, 7 August 1841. "Traits of American Humour," *Morning Post*, 5 January 1852. Stock principles: "London Correspondence," *Leeds Mercury*, 21 April 1857. Principles: "Amity," Letter to the Editor, "Tories and Reform," *Dundee Courier and Argus*, 1 August 1867.

14. Presidential dinner: "Davy Crocket[t]," *Belfast News-Letter*, 13 February 1829. Grin: "A Backwoodsman's Grin," *Bristol Mercury*, 28 December 1833. Treats: "Electioneering Tactics in the United States," *Bradford Observer*, 11 May 1837; "An American Election," *Derby Mercury*, 24 May 1837. Texas Memoir: "How to Secure an Election," *Blackburn Standard*, 24 May 1837; "Electioneering in America," *Figaro in London*, 4 August 1838; "How to Secure an Election," *Belfast News-Letter*, 30 September 1853.

15. Downing in Britain: see, e.g., "General Jackson," *Morning Post*, 27 October 1836; "The New American President," *Glasgow Herald*, 26 January 1861; "The Question," *Daily News*, 18 December 1868. Australia: "American Squib," *Sydney Gazette and New South Wales Advertiser*, 4 August 1835; "The New Council," *South Australian Gazette and Colonial Register*, 8 December 1838. India: "The Colloquial Language of America," *Oriental Observer and Literary Chronicle*, 2 November 1839. Commentator on Australian events: "Jack Downing in Australia to His Cousin in New York," *Brisbane Courier*, 8 December 1854. Nasby in Britain: "Mr. Nasby Shows That a War Platform Won't Do for the Democracy," *Dundee Courier*

and Argus, 18 August 1864; "The Nasby Papers," *Daily News*, 10 October 1865. Nasby's stump oratory advice: "Occasional Notes," *Pall Mall Gazette*, 30 September 1871; "Petroleum Nasby's Advice to Stump Orators," *Birmingham Daily Post*, 2 October 1871.

16. Haliburton's background: Richard A. Davies, *Inventing Sam Slick: A Biography of Thomas Chandler Haliburton* (Toronto: University of Toronto Press, 2005), 8, 11. Judge: ibid., 3. Legislator, ibid., 28. Downing inspiration: ibid., 54. London successes, printings, and Dickens: ibid., 56, 62. *Blackwood's Magazine*, reprinted in "Yankeeism," *Penny Satirist*, 11 November 1837. "Slicings from Slick," *Blackburn Standard*, 16 October 1839. "Literature," *Daily News*, 9 February 1849. "The Literary Examiner," *Examiner*, 8 July 1843. English Earls: Earl of Dartmouth, cited in "South Staffordshire Election," *Daily News*, 20 February 1849.

17. Boastful nationalist: Thomas Chandler Haliburton, "Conversations at River Philip," in *The Clockmaker, or, the Sayings and Doings of Samuel Slick, of Slickville*, Project Gutenberg e-book (1836) 2002, 9, available at www.gutenberg.org/cache/epub/5817.html; and "A Body without a Head," 70. Go ahead: Haliburton, "Go Ahead," in ibid., 13. American customs: Haliburton, "Conversations at River Philip," in ibid., 10. Learning: Thomas Chandler Haliburton, "Dining Out," in *The Attaché, or, Sam Slick in England* (Project Gutenberg [1843–1844] 2009), 70, available at www.gutenberg.org/files/7823/7823-h/7823-h.htm. Teaching grownups: Haliburton, "The American Eagle," in *The Clockmaker*, 26. Jumping cats: Haliburton, "Cumberland Oysters Produce Melancholy Forebodings," in ibid., 24. Talking big: Haliburton, "The Blowin Time," in ibid., 111.

18. African Americans: Haliburton, "The White Nigger," in *The Clockmaker*, 65. Violent doggerel: Haliburton, "Taming a Shrew," in ibid., 62. Politics corrupting and electioneering a poor business: Haliburton, "The Dancing Master Abroad," in ibid., 33. Teaches to stoop: Haliburton, "Sayings and Doings in Cumberland," in ibid., 30. Politicians lay it on: A Sam Slick story, cited in "Mr. Williams and His Moral Difficulty," *Huddersfield Chronicle and West Yorkshire Advertiser*, 11 June 1853. Nature ordained: Haliburton, "A Body without a Head," in *The Clockmaker*, 71.

19. Mixture of republican and monarchical: Haliburton, "A Body without a Head," in *The Clockmaker*, 71. Haliburton versus liberal-democratic reforms: This was argued in Haliburton's book, *The English in America*, as discussed in "Literature," *Morning Post*, 6 August 1851. On the English constitution: Haliburton, cited in "Launceston Election," *Royal Cornwall Gazette, Falmouth Packet*, and *General Advertiser*, 22 April 1859. Slick versus American freedoms: Haliburton, "A Body without a Head," in *The Clockmaker*, 70. Less political talk: Haliburton, "Setting Up for Governor," in ibid., 48–49. Leveling down: Haliburton, "The Grahamite and the Irish Plot," in ibid., 41. True patriot: Sam Slick story, cited in "Patriots," *Hull Packet*, 31 December 1841.

20. Sackville House: Sam Slick story, cited in "Sam Slick," *Hampshire Telegraph and Sussex Chronicle*, 16 November 1840. Squashed to death etc.: Sam Slick story, cited in "Slicings from Slick," *Blackburn Standard*, 25 November 1840. Illusory bubble etc.: Thomas Chandler Haliburton, cited in Davies, *Inventing Sam Slick*, 32. Clock making better: Sam Slick story, cited in "Slicings from Slick," *Blackburn Standard*, 25 November 1840.

21. See the discussion of the etymology of "buncombe," in *The Oxford English Dictionary* (online).

22. Thomas Chandler Haliburton, "Bunkum," in *The Attaché*, 108–109.

23. See, e.g., "Thoughts on Municipal Matters," *Sheffield and Rotherham Independent*, 23 December 1854; "English Extracts. Bunkum," *Sydney Morning Herald*, 28 May 1844.

24. On etymology and Slick's use, see www.worldwidewords.org/qa/qa.sof1.htm. Politician's soft sawder: Sam Slick story, cited in "Mr. Williams and His Moral Difficulty," *Huddersfield Chronicle and West Yorkshire Advertiser*, 11 June 1853.

25. For examples of linking or comparison, see "Major Crockett Best," *Morning Post*, 25 March 1837; "National and Historical Novels," *Court Magazine and La Bella Assemblée* (London), 1 June 1837; "Yankee Humour," *Cleave's Gazette of Variety* (London), 15 December 1838. For examples of confusion between the characters, see "Mr. Disraeli's Task," *Liverpool Mercury*, 24 September 1852; "Major Jack Downing on Secession," *Glasgow Herald*, 26 January 1861.

26. On Clay and half-horse etc., see Haliburton, "The Clockmaker Quilts a Blue Nose," in *The Clockmaker*, 44–45. Hard cider: Haliburton, "The Blowin Time," in ibid., 55. Clay's policies as applied: Davies, *Inventing Sam Slick*, 58–59. Crockett speeches: "Sam Slick in England," reproduced in "Crocket[t]'s Last Speech," *Morning Post*, 11 August 1843. Attaché: Haliburton, "Uncorking a Bottle," in *The Attaché*, 6.

27. Reality enough: "Yankee Humour," *Cleave's Gazette of Variety* (London), 15 December 1838. "The Literary Examiner," *Examiner* (London), 13 January 1839. "The Old Judge; or, Life in a Colony," *Morning Chronicle*, 31 January 1849. "Literature," *Daily News*, 23 March 1855. "Editorial," *Sydney Morning Herald*, 24 June 1859. For a rare argument that Haliburton was "by no means a reliable authority," see Dr. J. A. Lang, cited in "Legislative Assembly," *Empire*, 16 September 1859.

28. Crossing the Atlantic: George F. Rehin, "Harlequin Jim Crow: Continuity and Convergence in Blackface Clowning," *Journal of Popular Culture* 9, no. 3 (1975): 687. Immediate acclaim: ibid., 685; Alexander Saxton, "Blackface Minstrelsy and Jacksonian Ideology," *American Quarterly* 27, no. 1 (1975): 5. In Australia: Waterhouse, "The Minstrel Show and Australian Culture," 147. Success of local troupes: Melissa Bellanta, "Leary Kin: Australian Larrikins and the Blackface Minstrel Dandy," *Journal of Social History* 42, no. 3 (2009): 682. Global circuit: Waterhouse, "The Minstrel Show and Australian Culture," 158. Australian allusions: ibid., 152. Local books: ibid., 148.

29. Music halls etc.: see, e.g., "London Music Halls," *Era* (London), 21 June 1863; "The Christy Minstrels," *Liverpool Mercury*, 4 January 1865; Nathalie Rosset, "The Birth of the 'African Glen': Blackface Minstrelsy between Presentation and Representation," *Rethinking History* 9, no. 4 (2005): 416–417. Working-class haunts: Bellanta, "Leary Kin," 681; Rehin, "Harlequin Jim Crow," 687–688. But on an audience also beyond the male working class, see Michael Pickering, *Blackface Minstrelsy in Britain* (Aldershot, UK: Ashgate, 2009), 4. Enjoyment of mockery of elites: Waterhouse, "The Minstrel Show and Australian Culture," 151. Frederick Douglass, cited in Blackett, *Divided Hearts*, 37. Stereotypes: R. J. M. Blackett, *Building an Antislavery Wall: Black Americans in the Atlantic Abolitionist Movement, 1830–1860* (Baton Rouge: Louisiana State University Press, 1983), 160. Epithets: Waterhouse, "The Minstrel Show," 148–149. Mocking electioneering: Richard Waterhouse noted the reworking of a minstrel stump speech in an exchange between candidates in Albury, New South Wales, in 1859. See ibid., 148–149. Melissa Bellanta noted the appearance of the character of "an electioneer" in a local farce and suggested the influence of the minstrel show: Bellanta, "Leary Kin," 679. On minstrels, abolitionist literature, and sentiment, see Pickering, *Blackface Minstrelsy in Britain*, 22–23.

30. This is an account indebted to some excellent work on Carlyle's life and scholarship, including Michael Levin, *The Spectre of Democracy: The Rise of Modern Democracy as Seen by Its Critics* (Houndmills, UK: Macmillan, 1992); Michael Levin, *The Condition of England Question: Carlyle, Mill, Engels* (Houndmills, UK: Macmillan, 1998); Chris R. Vanden Bossche, *Carlyle and the Search for Authority* (Columbus: Ohio State University Press, 1991); John Morrow, *Thomas Carlyle* (London: Hambledon Continuum, 2006); Fred Kaplan, *Thomas Carlyle: A Biography* (Berkeley: University of California Press, 1983); Simon Heffer, *Moral Desperado: A Life of Thomas Carlyle* (London: Weidenfeld and Nicolson, 1995).

31. Thomas Carlyle, ed., "The Present Time," in *Latter-Day Pamphlets* (1850; repr., London: Chapman Hall, 1887), 5.

32. "Tremulous affection": Thomas Carlyle, cited in Morrow, *Thomas Carlyle*, 137. "Sick": Thomas Carlyle, *Reminiscences of My Irish Journey in 1849* (London: Sampson, Low, Marston, Searle, and Rivington, 1882), 4. "Savagery": ibid., 159. "Brawling," etc.: ibid., 34.

33. Sick and dispirited: Thomas Carlyle, cited in Kaplan, *Thomas Carlyle*, 332; Carlyle's tour was motivated by the view that Ireland "really is my problem" and a topic for his future work: Carlyle, *Reminiscences of My Irish Journey*, v.

34. Thomas Carlyle, ed., "Stump-Orator," in *Latter-Day Pamphlets* (Boston: Phillips, Sampson, 1855), 238.

35. Public haranguer: Thomas Carlyle, ed., "The Present Time," 6. Platform: Thomas Carlyle, ed., "Model Prisons," in ibid., 60. Stumps and taverns: Carlyle, "Stump-Orator," 223. Universal suffrage: Thomas Carlyle, ed., "The New Downing Street," in *Latter-Day Pamphlets* (1850; repr., London: Chapman and Hall, 1887), 113. Highest stump: Carlyle, "The Present Time," 6.

36. Convocation not seen: Thomas Carlyle, ed., "Parliaments," in *Latter-Day Pamphlets* (1850; repr., London: Chapman and Hall, 1887), 187. Sham-excellent: Carlyle, "Stump-Orator," 222. Education: ibid., 228. Premiership etc.: ibid., 238.

37. Pseudo-virtues: Carlyle, "Model Prisons," 60. Mouthpiece: Carlyle, "Stump-Orator," 224. Envious etc.: Carlyle, "Model Prisons," 60.

38. Noxious habit: Carlyle, "Stump-Orator," 246. Grand Doer: ibid., 250. Incendiary madness: ibid., 229. Moral life: ibid., 254. Destruction and annihilation: ibid., 265. Tongues: ibid., 267. Not an orator: ibid., 270–271.

39. Father's words: Thomas Carlyle, cited in Vanden Bossche, *Carlyle and the Search for Authority*, 37. Coleridge: Thomas Carlyle, cited in ibid., 84. *Past and Present*: Thomas Carlyle, cited in ibid., 113. *On Heroes*: ibid., 100–101. Cromwell: Morrow, *Thomas Carlyle*, 177.

40. Beggars: Carlyle, *Reminiscences of My Irish Journey*, 71. Independence from reformers: Morrow, *Thomas Carlyle*, 139. Peel: John Morrow, "The Paradox of Peel as Carlylean Hero," *Historical Journal* 40, no. 1 (1997): 97–110; Kaplan, *Thomas Carlyle*, 361. Regretting literature: Vanden Bossche, *Carlyle and the Search for Authority*, 140.

41. On dislike of pamphlets: Kaplan, *Thomas Carlyle*, 355–356. Wrong side: John Greenleaf Whittier, "Thomas Carlyle on the Slave Question," *Literary Recreations and Miscellanies* (Boston: n.p., 1854), collected in Jules Paul Seigel, ed., *Thomas Carlyle: The Critical Heritage* (London: Routledge and Kegan Paul, 1971), 317. Brain: "Thomas Carlyle," *Plain Dealer*, 14 March 1850. Raven: "Latter Day Pamphlets," *New Hampshire Patriot and State Gazette*, 24 October 1850. Sublime grumbler: "The Present Time," *Gloucester Telegraph*, 27 March 1850. Practical ability: "Literature," *Trewman's Exeter Flying Post or Plymouth and Cornish Advertiser*, 6 June 1850. Humbug: "The Ideas Seems," *Gloucester Telegraph*, 24 August 1850.

42. Intellectual production: David Mason, an unsigned review, *North British Review*, November 1850, collected in Seigel, *Thomas Carlyle*, 364. Wise and pleasant: *Eclectic Review*, 1450, new series, 28 (1850): 401. Hard-worker: *Eclectic Review*, 402. Deterioration of government: Elizur Wright, *Perforations in the "Latter-Day Pamphlets," by One of the "Eighteen Millions of Bores"* (Boston: Phillips, Sampson, 1850), 7. Universal suffrage: ibid., 13.

43. Turning point: Jules Paul Seigel, "Introduction," in Seigel, *Thomas Carlyle*, 2. Punch: "Two Parodies of Carlyle," *Punch* (January–June 1850), collected in ibid., 318. Truthlessly eccentric: "Carlyle on American Democracy," *Daily Ohio Statesman*, 22 April 1850. Incoherent: "Thomas Carlyle," *Vermont Journal*, 27 June 1851. Unfortunate turn: "Thomas Carlyle," *Liberator*, 26 April 1850. Never recover: Kaplan, *Thomas Carlyle*, 355–356.

44. Notoriety: "Literature," *Trewman's Exeter Flying Post or Plymouth and Cornish Advertiser*, 6 June 1850. Extensively read: Thomas Carlyle, cited in Kaplan, *Thomas Carlyle*, 355.

Howl of astonishment: Thomas Carlyle, cited in Charles Gavan Duffy, *Conversations with Carlyle* (London: Sampson, Low, Marston, 1892), 154. Defenders: see, e.g., "A Carlylian," *Blackwood v. Carlyle: A Vindication* (London: Effingham Wilson, 1850). Evidence that some leading newspapers supported Carlyle is registered in Siegel, "Introduction," 18. Later vogue: Morrow, *Thomas Carlyle*, 221. Journalistic attribution: see, e.g., "Mr. Gavan Duffy in Belfast," *Argus*, 29 May 1856. See also "Sentimental Politics," *Mercury* (Hobart), 15 March 1865. Quoting Carlyle: see, e.g., *Mount Alexander Mail*, cited in "Political Adventurers," *Argus*, 25 July 1856. Historical influence: note, for example, the sudden appearance of the character of the "Stump-Orator" (with the spelling resembling Carlyle's) in the satirical London weekly *Punch* only after the publication of the *Latter-Day Pamphlets*. For the first uses of the term, see "A Stump-Orator with His Bone from the French," *Punch*, 27 November 1852; "Sir John Key for Stump-Orator!" *Punch*, 4 June 1853. Coining term: Morrow, *Thomas Carlyle*, 140.

45. Fields and parks (as James Epstein notes, this was part of a broader claiming of a right to move in public space): James Epstein, *Radical Expression: Political Language, Ritual and Symbol in England, 1790–1850* (New York: Oxford University Press, 1994), 151. Mass platform: see, e.g., J. C. Belchem, "Henry Hunt and the Evolution of the Mass Platform," *English Historical Review* 93, no. 369 (1978): 773. Agitators in election campaigns: Henry Hunt's electioneering speeches were noted in "Mr. Hunt's Canvassing," *Morning Post*, 17 June 1818; "Somerset," *Morning Chronicle*, 2 June 1826; "County of Somerset," *Morning Chronicle*, 22 June 1826. Celebratory dinners: see, e.g., "Crown and Anchor Dinner to Henry Hunt," *Morning Post*, 14 September 1819. The centrality of the "mass platform" to "extra-parliamentary 'constitutional' agitation" is noted in John Belchem, "1848: Feargus O'Connor and the Collapse of the Mass Platform," in *The Chartist Experience: Studies in Working-Class Radicalism and Culture, 1830–60*, ed. James Epstein and Dorothy Thompson (London: Macmillan, 1982), 270. Hunt as pioneer: see, e.g., Belchem, "Henry Hunt and the Evolution of the Mass Platform," 740. O'Connor as successor: Boyd Hilton, *A Mad, Bad, Dangerous People? England 1783–1846* (Oxford, UK: Clarendon Press, 2006), 614. James Epstein, O'Connor's biographer, emphasized O'Connor's debt to Hunt and Chartism's status as a platform movement: James Epstein, *The Lion of Freedom: Feargus O'Connor and the Chartist Movement, 1832–1842* (London: Croom Helm, 1982), 90–93. John Bright and dynasty: a designation from Eugenio F. Biagini, *Liberty, Retrenchment and Reform: Popular Liberalism in the Age of Gladstone 1860–1880* (Cambridge, UK: Cambridge University Press, 1992), 379.

46. Charisma (note Dorothy Thompson's account of Feargus O'Connor's speaking tours): Thompson, *The Chartists*, 33. Public gatherings increase: Charles Tilly, "The Rise of the Public Meeting in Great Britain, 1758–1834," *Social Science History* 34, no. 3 (2010): 292, 295. Open air meetings: See reports and commentary in "Chartism and Its Results at Sheffield," *Sheffield and Rotherham Independent*, 17 August 1839; "The Chartist and Other Meetings," *Age* (London), 7 August 1842. Itinerant orators: Miles Taylor, "Rethinking the Chartists: Searching for Synthesis in the Historiography of Chartism," *Historical Journal* 39, no. 2 (1996): 492, 495; David Jones, *Chartism and the Chartists* (New York: St. Martin's Press, 1975), 102–103. Camp meetings: Jones, *Chartism and the Chartists*, 53–54. A privilege: Henry Hunt, cited in Belchem, "Henry Hunt and the Evolution of the Mass Platform," 747–748. Own park: a claim expressed by a speaker in "Meeting in Hyde Park," *Glasgow Herald*, 24 October 1855.

47. Challenge to earlier customs: George Rudé claimed that "mass oratory" was the "exception" up until the Chartist agitation of the late 1830s onward in Britain and until 1848 in France: George Rudé, *The Crowd in History: A Study of Popular Disturbances in France and England 1730–1848* (New York: John Wiley and Sons, 1964), 249. Elite alarm (see responses to Hunt's oratory): Stephen H. Browne, "Contesting Political Oratory in Nineteenth Century

England," *Communication Studies* 43, no. 3 (1992): 201. New legislation: Belchem, "Henry Hunt and the Evolution of the Mass Platform," 771. Cavalry massacre (note the report of the conservative press): "Manchester Meeting," *Morning Chronicle*, 20 August 1819. Later studies of the event, dubbed "Peterloo," include Donald Read, *Peterloo: The "Massacre" and Its Background* (Manchester, UK: Manchester University Press, 1973); Robert Poole, "The March to Peterloo: Politics and Festivity in Late Georgian England," *Past and Present* 192, no. 1 (2006): 109–153. Police restrictions: see, e.g., "The Chartists," *Morning Post*, 12 June 1848; "The Hyde-Park Meeting of Yesterday," *Morning Post*, 12 November 1855. *Times* (London), cited in "The Building Trades' Hyde Park Meeting," *Glasgow Herald*, 6 August 1859.

48. Demagogue: see, e.g., "Orator Hunt," *Morning Post*, 24 December 1816; "The Manchester Meeting," *Royal Cornwall Gazette, Falmouth Packet and Plymouth Journal*, 21 August 1819; "Chartist Baptisms," *Essex Standard*, 5 February 1841; "A Demagogue," *Bradford Observer*, 23 June 1841; "The Popular Excitement," *Age* (Melbourne), 29 August 1860. Mob orator: "Anti Corn Law Meeting," *Leicester Chronicle*, 19 January 1839; "Defence of the Press," *Standard* (London), 22 April 1848; "The McCulloch Government," *Argus* (Melbourne), 26 September 1865. Waggon orator: "Spirit of the Press," *Leicester Chronicle*, 24 August 1839; "Public Entry of Mr. Pakington into Stourbridge," *Berrow's Worcester Journal*, 25 October 1832; "From the Standard," *Lancaster Gazette*, 17 November 1832; "Aspect of Chartism," *Leicester Chronicle*, 24 August 1839; "North Wales Circuit," *Morning Chronicle*, 12 August 1852. Traveling orator: "'Orator Hunt,'" *Morning Post*, 3 December 1816; "Manchester Meeting," *Morning Chronicle*, 19 August 1819. A near synonym was "itinerant orator": "The Chartist and Other Meetings," *Age* (London), 7 August 1842. Agitators: "On the Proceedings at Manchester," *Morning Post*, 20 August 1819; "Deliverance Promises," *Argus* (Melbourne), 15 May 1860. Hyde Park: "The Building Trades' Hyde Park Meeting," *Glasgow Herald*, 6 August 1859; "The Right Hon. Mr. Cowper and Hyde Park Orators," *Essex Standard*, 17 August 1860. Eastern Market: "The Popular Excitement," *Age*, 29 August 1860; "The Discreditable Disturbances," *Age*, 30 August 1860. Tap-room: "Melbourne Punch to Charles Jardine Don, MLA," *Melbourne Punch*, 9 February 1860.

49. Aristocratic pleasure ground: "Sunday Afternoon in Hyde-Park," *Morning Chronicle*, 13 August 1860. Horse racing: "Facts about Epsom," *Freeman's Journal and Daily Commercial Advertiser*, 3 June 1870. Primary arena for discussion: "The Government and the Hyde Park Meeting," *Essex Standard and General Advertiser for the Eastern Counties*, 10 May 1867. Stump orator in 1850s: see, e.g., "Meeting in Hyde Park," *Glasgow Herald*, 24 October 1855. Stump of tree: "The Hyde-Park Riots," *Morning Posts*, 26 July 1855. Slick: Haliburton, "Dining Out," 70. Dozen or so orators and crowd: "Hyde Park Oratory," *Examiner*, 8 September 1860.

50. Successful defiance: "The Hyde Park Meeting," *Newcastle Courant*, 10 May 1867. Commendations of gatherings: "Another Great Reform Meeting in Hyde Park," *Hampshire Telegraph and Sussex Chronicle*, 7 August 1867; "The Reform Meeting in Hyde Park," *Leeds Mercury*, 6 August 1867; "Reform Meeting in Hyde Park," *Leicester Chronicle and the Leicestershire Mercury*, 27 April 1867. Firmness etc.: "Another Hyde Park Meeting," *Penny Illustrated Paper*, 19 August 1871. Brave future controls: Note the resolutions carried in a meeting described in "Demonstration in Hyde-Park," *Daily News*, March 1872.

51. J. Brinsley-Richards, "Hyde Park Corner," *Graphic* (London), 31 March 1883. Reformers' Tree: "The Irish Church Meeting in Hyde-Park," *Cheshire Observer and Chester, Birkinhead, Crewe and North Wales Times*, 25 July 1868. Tree cut: "The Fenian Amnesty Meeting in Hyde Park," *Penny Illustrated Paper*, 30 October 1869. Sacred spot: "Meeting in Hyde Park," *Daily News*, 14 August 1871. Fallen relic: "The Fenian Amnesty Meeting in Hyde Park," *Penny Illustrated Paper*, 30 October 1869. Customary site: "Anti-coercion Meeting in Hyde Park," *North Wales Chronicle*, 19 February 1881. Relative freedom: Lisa Keller contrasted Lon-

don's freedom as compared with New York's in Lisa Keller, *Triumph of Order: Democracy and Public Space in New York and London* (New York: Columbia University Press, 2009).

52. Chartist: "Differences among Those Who Labour," *Sheffield and Rotherham Independent*, 26 August 1854. Working men: "Demonstration in Hyde-Park," *Daily News*, 4 March 1872. Inequality theme: see, e.g., H. F. T., "Stump Oratory," Letter to the Editor, *Standard*, 6 April 1863.

53. Samuel Owen: "Hyde Park Oratory," *Examiner*, 8 September 1860. Professional speaker: "Extraordinary Scene in Hyde Park," *Jackson's Oxford Journal*, 8 September 1860. Note that he was charged with begging when attempting to collect money. See "Domestic and General News," *Lancaster Gazette and General Advertiser*, 29 September 1860. Owen's attack on Cowper: "Mr. Cowper," *Lloyd's Weekly Newspaper*, 19 August 1860; "The Right Hon. Mr. Cowper and Hyde Park Orators," *Essex Standard and General Advertiser for the Eastern Counties*, 17 August 1860; "Mr. Cowper," *Lloyd's Weekly Newspaper*, 19 August 1860; "The Right Hon. Mr. Cowper," *Reynolds's Newspaper*, 20 August 1860. William Cowper, cited in "House of Commons," *Reynolds's Newspaper*, 19 August 1860.

54. Vindicating equity: "Sunday Afternoon in Hyde-Park," *Morning Chronicle*, 13 August 1860. Socialism etc.: "House of Commons," *Reynolds's Newspaper*, 19 August 1860. Astonished crowd etc.: "Sunday Afternoon in Hyde-Park," *Morning Chronicle*, 13 August 1860. Proper and manly: William Cowper, cited in "House of Commons," *Reynolds's Newspaper*, 19 August 1860. Manliness: "Peeps into Parliament, and Elsewhere," *Reynolds's Newspaper*, 19 August 1860. Pluck: "The Kensington Gardens Question," *Examiner*, 18 August 1860. Commons: "House of Commons," *Reynolds's Newspaper*, 19 August 1860. "A Minister on the Stump," *Reynolds's Newspaper*, 19 August 1860. Red mark in calendar: "The Right Hon. Mr. Cowper," *Reynolds's Newspaper*, 20 August 1860.

55. "From Our London Correspondence," *Daily National Intelligencer*, 3 September 1860. Cowper's apology: "Mr. Cowper and the Working Classes," *Bradford Observer*, 16 August 1860.

56. On electoral reform in period: For a discussion of electoral reform in this period and its ties to contention, see Sean Scalmer, "Containing Contention: A Reinterpretation of Democratic Change and Electoral Reform in the Australian Colonies," *Australian Historical Studies* 42 (2011): 337–356. On the frontier of Great Britain, see James Bellich, *Replenishing the Earth: The Settler Revolution and the Rise of the Anglo-World, 1783–1939* (Oxford, UK: Oxford University Press, 2009).

57. Not English: "Literature," *Daily News*, 9 February 1849. Effervescent: "Some Three or Four Years," *Argus*, 25 August 1859. Take the lead: Duffy describes the colony in these terms in Sir Charles Gavan Duffy, *My Life in Two Hemispheres*, vol. 2 (Shannon: Irish University Press, 1969), 141. Sir Charles Dilke, cited in John Tregenza, *Professor of Democracy: The Life of Charles Henry Pearson, 1830–1894* (Carlton: Melbourne University Press, 1968), 2. "Australia," *Times* (London), 18 May 1863.

58. Bunkum: "Bunkum," *Sydney Morning Herald*, 28 May 1844. Soft sawder: see, e.g., "The Yatala Election—the Nominees," *South Australian*, 12 August 1851; "The Portland Election," *Melbourne Punch*, 6 August 1857. Quoting Slick: see, e.g., "Legislative Council," *Maitland Mercury and Hunter River General Advertiser*, 7 September 1853; "The Victorian Parliament," *Argus*, 27 July 1860. Radicals from stump: Peter Lalor, "To the Colonists of Victoria," Statement in *Argus*, 10 April 1855, reproduced in *Historical Studies: Eureka Centenary Supplement*, December 1954, 9. Governor: "Despatch of Lieutenant-Governor, Sir Charles Hotham to the Right Honourable Sir George Grey," 20 December 1854, in ibid., 3, 7.

59. Suffrage: see, e.g., "Universal Suffrage (or Suffering). By a repentant Stump Orator," *Launceston Examiner*, 26 February 1861. Diggings: "When the Imperial Government," *Argus*, 29 February 1860.

60. On the Market: "A Visit to Paddy's Market," *Melbourne Punch*, 25 January 1866; "The Lions of Melbourne; or, The New Chum's Handbook," *Melbourne Punch*, 27 December 1866. Unemployed: "The Unemployed," *Argus*, 25 September 1857.

61. Almost nightly meetings: "The Late C. J. Don," *Argus*, 29 September 1866. The very name: J. Harris, Letter to the Editor, *Argus*, 6 December 1860. Useful claptrap etc.: "General Speech, Address, and Letter Composing Company," *Melbourne Punch*, 1 November 1860. Don's blustering: "'Vox, et praeterea nihil,'" *Melbourne Punch*, 4 October 1860. Burn stump: "Serenade," *Melbourne Punch*, 10 November 1859.

62. Prophets of stump: "Deliverance Promises," *Argus*, 15 May 1860. Widespread epithet: Mr. Scotchmere, cited in "The Political Crisis," *Age*, 7 June 1860. R. D. Balfour, Letter to Editor, *Courier*, 22 September 1862. "Melbourne," *Sydney Morning Herald*, 14 September 1857.

63. Don's size and lung power: Des Shiel, *The People's Man: Charles Jardine Don, Australian Labour's First Parliamentarian* (North Melbourne: Garravembi Press, 1996), 37. Description: *Argus*, cited in ibid., 35. Dark visage: "Punch's Parliamentary Biographies: No. XI. Mr. Don," *Melbourne Punch*, 8 March 1860. Egotistical manner: "Under the Patronage of Don," *Melbourne Punch*, 16 February 1860. "'Won't that Young Critter . . . ,'" *Argus*, 10 March 1858. "Don on the English Aristocracy," *Melbourne Punch*, 19 February 1863. "The Victorian Parliament," *South Australian Register*, 3 November 1859.

64. Election: Sam Merrifield, "Don, Charles Jardine (1820–1866)," in *Australian Dictionary of Biography*, available at http://adb.anu.edu.au/biography/don-charles-jardine-3423. Address to House: Charles Jardine Don, cited in "The Death of Charles Jardine Don," *Age*, 29 September 1866. Hostile scribes: E. J. Whitby, cited in "The Late C. J. Don," *Argus*, 29 September 1866.

65. Class prejudices etc.: "Melbourne Punch to Charles Jardine Don, MLA," *Melbourne Punch*, 9 February 1860. Baron etc.: "On Dits," *Melbourne Punch*, 17 May 1860. Mob's cheer: "Valentines for Legislators," *Melbourne Punch*, 13 February 1862.

66. Legislative opponents use "stump orator" label: see, e.g., Mr. Stephen, cited in "The Victorian Parliament," *Argus*, 27 July 1860; Thomas Embling claimed to look forward to the decline of stump oratory in a way that drew a retort from Don. See "The Victorian Parliament—Mr. Don," *Argus*, 28 April 1860. Don on Slick: Charles Jardine Don, cited in "The Victorian Parliament," *Argus*, 27 July 1860. No stump orator: ibid.

67. Star of stump: Charles Jardine Don, cited in "Nicholson Land Bill—Monster Meeting at the Eastern Market," *Age*, 5 June 1860. In the Eastern Market: Charles Jardine Don, cited in "The Ministerial Crisis," *Age*, 28 August 1860. To unionists: Charles Jardine Don, cited in Shiel, *The People's Man*, 95. Advanced portion of working class: Charles Jardine Don, cited in "The Victorian Parliament: Legislative Assembly," *Argus*, 28 April 1860.

68. "Laid foundation," "strong foundation" "as far as people," etc.: Charles Jardine Don, cited in "The Victorian Parliament: Legislative Assembly," *Argus*, 28 April 1860.

69. "Punch's Essence of Parliament," *Melbourne Punch*, 3 May 1860. "The Oracle of the Stump," *Argus*, 30 April 1860.

70. "The Oracle of the Stump," *Argus*, 30 April 1860.

71. Not ashamed: Mr. Scotchmere, cited in "The Political Crisis," *Age*, 7 June 1860. "No professed": Mr. Hunter, cited in "Victorian Convention," *Argus*, 28 April 1858.

CHAPTER 4

1. Frontier, settlement, and growth: James Bellich, *Replenishing the Earth: The Settler Revolution and the Rise of the Anglo-World, 1783–1939* (Oxford, UK: Oxford University Press, 2009), 79, 85–86. Social equality: Sir Charles Gavan Duffy, *My Life in Two Hemispheres*, vol.

2 (Shannon: Irish University Press, 1969), 203. Democratic feeling: Governor Sir George Bowen to Sir Michael Hicks-Beach, 25 January 1879, cited in J. E. Parnaby, "The Economic and Political Development of Victoria, 1877–1881" (PhD diss., University of Melbourne, 1951), 407.

2. On colonial democratization and its limits, see Ann Curthoys and Jessie Mitchell, "The Advent of Self-Government, 1840s–90," in *The Cambridge History of Australia*, vol. 1, *Indigenous and Colonial Australia*, ed. Alison Bashford and Stuart Macintyre (Cambridge, UK: Cambridge University Press, 2013), 149–169; Sean Scalmer, "Containing Contention: A Reinterpretation of Democratic Change and Electoral Reform in the Australian Colonies," *Australian Historical Studies* 42 (2011): 337–356.

3. Neo-Britains and greater democracy: Carl Bridge and Kent Fedorowich, eds., "Mapping the British World," in *The British World: Diaspora, Culture and Identity* (London: Frank Cass, 2003), 5. New parliamentarians: "Mr. Graham Berry," *Argus*, 18 October 1865. Catastrophic collapse: John Hirst, *Australia's Democracy: A Short History* (Crows Nest, Australia: Allen and Unwin, 2002), 258.

4. Committee in Hotel: Hirst, *Australia's Democracy*, 66; Parnaby, "Economic and Political Development," 284. Requisition: Geoffrey Bartlett, "Political Organisation and Society in Victoria 1864–1883" (PhD diss., Australian National University, 1964), 150. Canvas most effective: John Hirst, *The Sentimental Nation: The Making of the Australian Commonwealth* (Melbourne: Oxford University Press, 2000), 260. Radicals and wealthy in canvasing: Bartlett, "Political Organisation and Society," 141.

5. Placards: Walter A. Cooper to Henry Parkes, 7 March 1872, PC, 50:180–186; John Wearne to Henry Parkes, 19 December 1874, PC, 43:140–143. Rumors: Editorial, *Brisbane Courier*, 13 January 1882. Letters: Walter A. Cooper to Henry Parkes, 26 November 1873, PC, 8:7–8. Governmental patronage: Henry Parkes, "The First Years of Responsible Government," in *Speeches on Various Occasions Connected with the Public Affairs of New South Wales 1848–1874* (Melbourne: George Robertson, 1876), 175. Treating: James Rodd to Henry Parkes, 4 February 1864, PC, 33:329–343; Parnaby, "Economic and Political Development," 284–285. Newspapers: Alfred Deakin, 19 February 1901, in Alfred Deakin, *Federated Australia: Selections from Letters to the Morning Post 1900–1910* (Carlton: Melbourne University Press, 1968), 40. The two leading statesmen of nineteenth-century Victoria and New South Wales (Graham Berry and Henry Parkes) both owned newspapers.

6. Meeting most effective: Henry Parkes, *The Electoral Act and How to Work It* (Sydney: G. T. Thornton, 1859), 16. Duty: Henry Parkes, "State of Politics in 1860," in *Speeches on Various Occasions*, 114. Reporting election speeches: Carol Fort, *Electing Responsible Government, South Australia 1857* (Rose Park, Australia: State Electoral Office, 2001), 27. Ready pen: "Election Meetings: City of Adelaide District," *South Australian Register*, 2 February 1857.

7. Talent for speaking: Parkes, *Electoral Act*, 12. Manner: Alfred Deakin in *"And Be One People": Alfred Deakin's Federal Story*, ed. Stuart Macintyre (Carlton: Melbourne University Press, 1995), 52. Daniel Deniehy, *The Attorney-General of New Barataria* (1860; repr., Sydney: Sunnybrook Press, 1932), 41.

8. No stumping: D. Cassin to Henry Parkes, 16 December 1871, PC, 9:295–297. Cassin calls himself an "old stager" in D. Cassin to Henry Parkes, 20 December 1871, PC, 9:319–322.

9. Candidate's qualities: Parkes, *Electoral Act*, 12. Bombastic: "Election Notice," *South Australian Register*, 27 February 1857. Plain spoken: see, e.g., "Mr. Francis at Richmond," *Age*, 19 August 1859. Practical: "Election Notices," *South Australian Register*, 14 February 1857. Common sense: "Election Meetings," *South Australian Register*, 26 January 1857. NSW candidate: "Representation of the Glebe Electorate," *Sydney Morning Herald*, 12 May 1859.

10. On Duffy's biography: Joy E. Parnaby, "Duffy, Sir Charles Gavan," *Australian Dictionary of Biography*, 1972, available at http://adb.anu.edu.au/biography/duffy-sir-charles-gavan-3450. Examples of name dropping: Duffy, *My Life*, 2:317–318. Serene etc.: Charles Gavan Duffy, *Conversations with Carlyle* (London: Sampson, Low, Martson, 1892), 6.

11. Principles: Charles Gavan Duffy, *Four Years of Irish History, 1845–1849* (Melbourne: George Robertson, 1883), 22. Education: ibid., 25. "Wanted, a Few Workmen!": reproduced in Duffy, *Conversations with Carlyle*, 136–145. Statesman and demagogue: Charles Gavan Duffy, *My Life in Two Hemispheres*, vol. 1 (Shannon: Irish University Press, 1969), 245. Popular oratory and platform: Duffy, *Four Years of Irish History*, 536. Recognized leader: Leon Ó Broin, *Charles Gavan Duffy: Patriot and Statesman* (Dublin: James Duffy, 1967), 28.

12. Horse face: Jane Carlyle, cited in Ó Broin, *Charles Gavan Duffy*, 12. Brow: D'Arcy McGee, cited in ibid., 65–66. Vein: Cyril Pearl, *The Three Lives of Gavan Duffy* (Kensington: University of New South Wales Press, 1979), 111. Sphinx: D'Arcy McGee, cited in Ó Broin, *Charles Gavan Duffy*, 65–66. Fragile ascetic: Pearl, *The Three Lives*, 180. Cold eyes and voice: Deakin in Macintyre, ed., *"And Be One People,"* 4. Unfitness and voice: Pearl, *The Three Lives*, 195.

13. Integrity and character: Pearl, *The Three Lives*, 118. Contribution to Empire: *Spectator*, cited in Duffy, *My Life*, 2:324.

14. O'Connell's novel combination of these three methods is identified in Garry Owens, "Nationalism without Words: Symbolism and Ritual Behaviour in the Repeal 'Monster Meetings' of 1843–5," in *Irish Popular Culture 1650–1850*, ed. James S. Donnelly Jr. and Kirby A. Miller (Dublin: Irish Academic Press, 1998), 248.

15. Fergus O'Ferrall, *Catholic Emancipation: Daniel O'Connell and the Birth of Irish Democracy, 1820–30* (Dublin: Gil and Macmillan, 1985), 271.

16. O'Connell's energy: Duffy, *My Life*, 1:80. O'Connell's intensity: ibid., 1:85. League banquets and meetings: Duffy, *My Life*, 2:92, 2:97. Australian convention: ibid., 2:193. Melbourne rights: Duffy, *Victorian Hansard Session 1859–60*, 1746, available at www.parliament.vic.gov.au/hansard.

17. Advertising: Henry Gyles Turner, *A History of the Colony of Victoria*, vol. 2 (London: Longmans Green, 1904), 66. Hotels and Omnibus: Duffy, *My Life*, 2:143. Melbourne as capital: Duffy, cited in Parnaby, "Duffy, Sir Charles Gavan." Funds: Turner, *A History*, 2:68.

18. Property qualification: Turner, *A History*, 2:74. Land: Duffy, *My Life*, 2:228. Defense of Australia: C. G. Duffy, *Popular Errors Concerning Australia at Home and Abroad* (Melbourne: W. B. Stephens, 1866), 5.

19. Unscrupulous: "How Are the Mighty Fallen!" *Hobart Mercury*, 29 May 1872. Mole: Jerry Braham, "A Soliloquy," *Melbourne Punch*, 18 January 1877. Duffy's obstacles and achievement: Parnaby, "Duffy, Sir Charles Gavan."

20. Stop-gap: "Talk on 'Change,'" *Australasian*, 24 June 1871. Ministerial makeup etc.: Parnaby, "Duffy, Sir Charles Gavan." Graham Berry, cited in "The Ministerial Elections: The Treasurer at Geelong," *Argus*, 29 June 1871.

21. Duffy's past and attacks: Pearl, *The Three Lives*, 203. Hostile parliament: John Waugh, "'The Inevitable McCulloch' and His Rivals, 1863–1877," in *The Victorian Premiers, 1856–2006*, ed. Paul Strangio and Brian Costar (Annandale, NSW: Federation Press, 2006), 41. Fierce etc.: Duffy, *My Life*, 2:332. Virulent: *Kyneton Guardian*, cited in "The Victorian Press and the Duffy Ministry," *Freeman's Journal*, 1 July 1871. Parliamentary majorities: *Age*, reproduced in "The Ministry and Their Critics," *Geelong Advertiser*, 20 April 1872.

22. Tramp of people: "The Ministerial Banquet at Sandhurst," *Australasian*, 22 July 1877. Great towns etc.: Duffy, *My Life*, 2:332.

23. Even hostile outlets admitted that invitations had been extended: see, e.g., "Summary for Europe—Introduction," *Argus Supplement*, 23 April 1872. For a fuller sketch of the

patrician as an ideal type of politician and its survival into the twentieth century, see Sean Scalmer and Nathan Hollier, "'I Diarist': Examining Australian Politics from the 'Inside,'" *Australian Journal of Politics and History* 55, no. 2 (2009): 170–189. Popular sympathy: *My Life*, 2:332.

24. Ballarat: "Banquet to the Ministry at Ballarat," *Daily Telegraph*, 22 December 1871. Complimentary: "Ministerial Banquet at Clunes," *Argus*, 31 January 1872. Friends: "Summary for Europe—Introduction," *Argus*, 1 February 1872. Banquet committees: see, e.g., "In regard to the Ministerial Banquets," *Argus*, 17 January 1872; "The Ministry," *Mount Alexander Mail*, reprinted in *Geelong Advertiser*, 27 February 1872; "Ministerial Banquet at Creswick," *Australasian*, 3 February 1872; "Ministerial Banquet at Kilmore," *Age*, 17 April 1872. Demonstration committees: "The Ministerial Banquet at Maryborough," *Australasian*, 17 April 1872. *Argus*: "Yet More Ministerial Banquets," *Argus*, 18 January 1872.

25. Chairs and major speakers: see, e.g., "Banquet to the Ministry at Ballarat," *Daily Telegraph*, 22 December 1871; "The Ministerial Visit to Ballarat," *Argus*, 23 December 1871; "The Ministerial Banquet at Castlemaine," *Daily Telegraph*, 21 March 1872; "Ministerial Banquet at Creswick," *Australasian*, 3 February 1872; "The Banquet," *Australasian*, 24 February 1872; "The Ministers in the Country," *Australasian*, 2 March 1872; and "The Ministry at Clunes," *Australasian*, 13 April 1872. MPs accompany: "Banquet to the Ministry at Ballarat," *Daily Telegraph*, 22 December 1871; "The Ministry at Castlemaine," *Melbourne Age*, 21 March 1872; "The Ministry at Clunes," *Daily Telegraph*, 5 April 1872; "Ministerial Banquet at Creswick," *Australasian*, 3 February 1872. On MPs as welcoming, see "The Ministerial Banquet at Maryborough," *Australasian*, 17 April 1872.

26. Noted in "The News of the Day—the Dejeuner," *Age*, 5 April 1872.

27. Special train: "Mr. Duffy," *Daily Telegraph*, 22 December 1871; "Ministers Are to Start for This Evening's Castlemaine Banquet," *Argus*, 20 March 1872. Upon arrival: "The Ministerial Banquet at Ballarat," *Argus*, 22 December 1871; "Ministerial Banquet at Clunes," *Argus*, 31 January 1872. Maryborough: "To-day the Maryborough Ministerial Banquet," *Argus*, 18 April 1872; "The Ministry at Maryborough," *Ballarat Courier*, 19 April 1872; "The Ministerial Banquet at Maryborough," *Geelong Advertiser*, 19 April 1872. Stawell: "The Ministry at Stawell," *Argus*, 21 February 1872; "The Stawell Banquet," *Age*, 20 February 1872. Similar elsewhere: "The News of the Day—the Dejeuner," *Age*, 5 April 1872. Clunes: "The Ministry at Clunes," *Australasian*, 13 April 1872. Castlemaine: "The Ministerial Banquet at Castlemaine," *Daily Telegraph*, 21 March 1872; "The Ministry at Castlemaine," *Age*, 21 March 1872. Flags and evergreens: "The Ministry at Ararat," *Age*, 23 February 1872; "The Ministry at Carisbrook," *Age*, 20 April 1872.

28. Kilmore and Maryborough: "Summary for Europe—Introduction," *Argus Supplement*, 23 April 1872. Ballarat: "Mr. Duffy," *Daily Telegraph*, 22 December 1871. Ararat: "The Ministry at Ararat," *Argus*, 23 February 1872. Sale: "A Merry Life," *Daily Telegraph*, 23 February 1872. Stawell: "Topics of the Week—We Can but Think," *Australasian*, 24 February 1872.

29. Maryborough: "The Ministry at Maryborough," *Ballarat Courier*, 19 April 1872. Ballarat: "The Ministerial Banquet at Ballarat," *Argus*, 22 December 1871. Clunes: "The News of the Day—the Dejeuner," *Age*, 5 April 1872. Ticket prices and women: "Mr. Duffy," *Daily Telegraph*, 22 December 1871; "On the Tramp," *Daily Telegraph*, 15 April 1872; "The Ministry at Carisbrook," *Age*, 20 April 1872; "The Banquet to the Ministry at Castlemaine," *Geelong Advertiser*, 21 March 1872.

30. Ballarat: "There Were Great Complaints," *Ballarat Courier*, 23 December 1871. Maryborough: "Sad News," *Argus*, 9 April 1872. Creswick: "In Point of Numbers," *Ballarat Courier*, 30 January 1872. Beaufort: "Beaufort," *Australasian*, 13 April 1872.

31. Duffy's speeches were sometimes very long. The Castlemaine oration was timed at ninety minutes: "The News of the Day—Whatever Opinions May Have Been Entertained," *Age*, 21 March 1872. In a few cases, Duffy was unable to attend, and his speeches and ceremonial duties were performed by his senior ministers.

32. Preparation: "Topics of the Week—Mr. Duffy Is Always Excellent," *Australasian*, 30 December 1871. Closet: "Mr. Duffy's Castlemaine Speech," an article reproduced from the *Ballarat Post*, *Geelong Advertiser*, 25 March 1872. Solitude: excerpt from the *Bendigo Advertiser* in "The Country Press on Mr. Duffy," *Argus*, 5 February 1872. Weak voice: "The Ministry and Its Critics," *Geelong Advertiser*, 22 April 1872. Very pleasant: "Oh, You Gods," *Daily Telegraph*, 31 January 1872. Different order: "Australian Notes for English Circulation," *Age*, 28 March 1872. Graceful: "Australia," *London Times*, 18 June 1872. Able: "Charles Gavan Duffy," *Freeman's Journal and Daily Commercial Advertiser* (Dublin), 23 March 1872. Lucid: "Ballarat Courier— with the Revival," *Ballarat Courier*, 22 March 1872. Luminous: "This Month's Gossip," *Geelong Advertiser*, 28 March 1872. Admirable: "Australian Notes for English Circulation—Political," *Age*, 1 January 1872. Elegant: "Mr. Duffy's Castlemaine Speech," an article reproduced from the *Ballarat Post*, *Geelong Advertiser*, 25 March 1872. Magnificent: "Mr. Duffy's Castlemaine Speech" (an excerpt from the *Ballarat Mail*), *Geelong Advertiser*, 25 March 1872. Charming: "The Australasian—the Castlemaine Manifesto," *Australasian*, 30 March 1872.

33. 1871 letter and 1872 letter: Duffy, *Conversations with Carlyle*, 243, 247. Best self: Duffy, *My Life*, 2:336–337.

34. Class legislation etc.: "When Greek Meets Greek," *Hamilton Spectator*, 15 November 1871. Stump etc.: "A Victorian Ministerial Banquet," *Wagga Wagga Advertiser and Riverine Reporter*, 9 March 1872. Selected beef eaters: "Portland," *Border Watch* (Mount Gambier, Australia), 15 May 1872. *Telegraph*: "On the Tramp," *Daily Telegraph*, 15 April 1872; "The People at Stawell," *Daily Telegraph*, 21 February 1872. Average newspaper writer: *Mount Alexander Mail*, cited in "Impartial Criticism and Unprincipled Hostility," *Advocate* (Melbourne), 20 January 1872.

35. *Telegraph*: "On the Tramp," *Daily Telegraph*, 15 April 1872. *Argus*: "The Argus— Intelligent Observers," *Argus*, 29 February 1872. Unfavorable criticism: "Summary for Europe—the Ministry Have Been Feted," *Argus Supplement*, 28 March 1872.

36. "The People at Stawell," *Daily Telegraph*, 21 February 1872.

37. Ibid.

38. English constitution: "The Argus—Intelligent Observers," *Argus*, 29 February 1872. House as people's committee: "The Chief Secretary," *Daily Telegraph*, 19 April 1872. *Australian*: "Topics of the Week—Mr. Duffy Is Always Excellent," *Australasian*, 30 December 1871. *Argus*: "The Approaching Session," *Argus*, 27 April 1872.

39. Mere convention: "The Chief Secretary," *Daily Telegraph*, 19 April 1872. Overawe Parliament: "On the Tramp," *Daily Telegraph*, 15 April 1872. Outside and above plus constitutional government ending: "Are We to Have a Dictator?" *Riverine Herald*, 15 May 1872. *Daily Telegraph*: "The Bendigo Advertiser," *Daily Telegraph*, 23 March 1872. Experiment: "But for People Being Occupied," *Daily Telegraph*, 28 December 1871.

40. Ballarat: "The Ministerial Banquet at Ballarat," *Australasian*, 30 December 1871. Castlemaine: "The Ministerial Banquet at Castlemaine," *Daily Telegraph*, 21 March 1872.

41. Creswick: "Ministerial Banquet at Creswick," *Australasian*, 3 February 1872. Maryborough: "The Ministerial Banquet at Maryborough," *Australasian*, 27 April 1872.

42. These were advanced as criteria indicating the "great success" of the banquet at Maryborough in "Geelong Advertiser—the Banquet," *Geelong Advertiser*, 19 April 1872.

43. "The Ministry at Maryborough," *Ballarat Courier*, 19 April 1872; "The Banquets to the Ministry" (an excerpt from the *Bendigo Independent*), *Geelong Advertiser*, 28 February

1872 (it refers to "demonstrations"); "Ministerial Banquet at Kilmore," *Age*, 17 April 1872; "The Ministry" (an excerpt from the *Mount Alexander Mail*), *Geelong Advertiser*, 27 February 1872 (it refers to "demonstrations").

44. *Ballarat Post*: "The Ministry and Their Critics" (an excerpt from the *Ballarat Post*), *Geelong Advertiser*, 20 April 1872. *Bendigo Advertiser* and *Kyneton Guardian*: "The Ministry and Its Critics," *Geelong Advertiser*, 22 April 1872. Gratifying: "The Age—the Speech," *Age*, 23 December 1871. *Advertiser*: "The Month's Gossip—Parliament Will Not Meet," *Geelong Advertiser*, 1 February 1872; "Geelong Advertiser—the Banquet," *Geelong Advertiser*, 19 April 1872.

45. Democratic practice (toast offered by Mr. R. Richardson, JP): see "Ministerial Banquet at Creswick," *Australasian*, 3 February 1872. Fountainhead: "Geelong Advertiser—the Ministerial Banquet," *Geelong Advertiser*, 2 February 1872. Own eyes etc.: "Geelong Advertiser—the Series of Ministerial Banquets," *Geelong Advertiser*, 26 February 1872. Mutual recognition: "Shoddy," *Geelong Advertiser*, 27 February 1872.

46. "Geelong Advertiser—the Banquet," *Geelong Advertiser*, 19 April 1872.

47. Education policy: "How Are the Mighty Fallen!" *Hobart Mercury*, 29 May 1872. Appointments and scandals: Turner, *A History*, 2:160–161; Duffy, *My Life*, 2:337.

48. Duffy, *My Life*, 2:342.

49. Leading studies of Duffy's life largely ignore these events. See J. E. Parnaby, "Sir Charles Gavan Duffy in Victoria 1856–1880" (master's thesis, University of Melbourne, 1943); Pearl, *The Three Lives*; Ó Broin, *Charles Gavan Duffy*.

50. Berry's biography: "The Hon. Graham Berry," *Australasian Sketcher with Pen and Pencil*, 7 July 1877. Reading: Alfred Deakin, *The Crisis in Victorian Politics, 1879–1881: A Personal Retrospect* (Carlton: Melbourne University Press, 1957), 13–14. Chess: "The Game," *Argus*, 21 December 1874. Aspirates and grammar: "Topics of the Week," *Australasian*, 20 May 1871. Persevering grocer: "Town Twaddle," *Melbourne Punch*, 29 November 1860.

51. Career beginnings: Bartlett, "Political Organisation and Society," 116. Garibaldi: "The Story of the Political Riots," *Hobart Mercury*, 1 September 1860. Press: "The Ministerial Crisis," *Age*, 28 August 1860. *Argus*: "Geelong," *Argus*, 5 October 1860. Defense of stump: "East Geelong Election," *Argus*, 4 October 1860.

52. Sequentially: "The Meeting To-Night," *Ballarat Star*, 4 August 1865; "Summary for Europe: Political," *Ballarat Star*, 22 May 1868; "We Have Not Been Able," *Argus*, 13 November 1865; "It Is Encouraging," *Argus*, 31 August 1867; "The New Treasurer," *Telegraph*, *St. Kilda, Prahran and South Yarra Guardian*, 29 January 1870; "The Geelong Advertiser," *Melbourne Punch*, 11 May 1876.

53. Early public meetings on protection included Berry alongside fellow speakers Charles Jardine Don and Wilson Gray at the Eastern Market. See "Great Public Meeting: Revision of the Tariff," *Ballarat Star*, 20 July 1861. *Punch*: "Pritchard Disowns His 'Friends,'" *Melbourne Punch*, 31 January 1878. Exhausted: "Protection to Native Industry," *Argus*, 5 July 1861. Berry as "father of protection": "Our Melbourne Letter," *Brisbane Courier*, 3 March 1877. On Syme, see Stuart Macintyre, *A Colonial Liberalism: The Lost World of Three Victorian Visionaries* (South Melbourne: Oxford University Press, 1991); Elizabeth Morrison, *David Syme: Man of the Age* (Clayton, Australia: Monash University Publishing, 2014).

54. The lectures were reputedly at his own cost: "We Have Been Curious," *Argus*, 5 September 1867. For examples of the term "lecture," see "At Castlemaine," *Ballarat Star*, 1 June 1865; "A Lecture," *Bendigo Advertiser*, 29 May 1865. Not a lecture: "Graham Berry on Protection," *Bendigo Advertiser*, 2 June 1865. Great gun: "The Pro-tariff Meeting," *Ballarat Star*, 8 March 1865.

55. Technically, the Kerferd government's policies still had a majority of one on the floor of the assembly, although this was registered by James Service as a loss of confidence in the

government's future. See Geoffrey Bartlett, "Berry, Sir Graham," *Australian Dictionary of Biography*, 1969, available at http://adb.anu.edu.au/biography/berry-sir-graham-2984. *Age*: "Mr. Berry," *Age*, 6 August 1875. Promises etc.: "The Chief Secretary at Geelong," *Argus*, 17 August 1875. Threat to speak: "The Ministerial Elections," *Argus*, 19 August 1875. Crude etc.: "Intercolonial News," *West Australian Times*, 21 September 1875. A Victorian crisis: see, e.g., "The Colony of Victoria," *Brisbane Courier*, 30 August 1875.

56. "An Old Liberal," *Bendigo Advertiser*, 27 January 1877.

57. Get up an agitation: "The 'Right Hand,'" *Argus*, 21 September 1875. Out-of-door: *Ararat Advertiser*, cited in "The Ministerial Crisis: Opinions of the Country Press," *Argus*, 24 September 1875. Jerry Braham, "Worthy of Ken," *Melbourne Punch*, 2 December 1875.

58. Meetings estimate: "Mr. Berry at Warrnambool," *Argus*, 5 November 1875. *Argus*: "The Elections. The Hon. Graham Berry at Geelong," *Argus*, 13 February 1877. Delegation: "Mr. Berry at Warrnambool," *Argus*, 5 November 1875. Fiercest: Alfred Deakin, cited in John Tregenza, *Professor of Democracy: The Life of Charles Henry Pearson* (Carlton: Melbourne University Press, 1968), 97.

59. "Mr. Berry at Warrnambool," *Argus*, 5 November 1875.

60. George Higinbotham was unable to support Berry's course, although he equally opposed the new Government; he resigned.

61. No sleep: "Protectionist Meeting," *Riverine Herald*, 8 March 1877. To Geelong auditors: "The Elections. The Hon. Graham Berry at Geelong," *Argus*, 13 February 1877.

62. Amalgamation: Bartlett, "Political Organisation," 268. Importance of organization: "The National Reform League," *Argus*, 2 June 1876. Uses of organization: Tregenza, *Professor of Democracy*, 105; Bartlett, "Political Organisation," 270–271. Opinion focused: "The Elections: Mr. Berry at Echuca," *Argus*, 8 March 1877.

63. Berry visits: "The Honourable Sir Graham Berry," in *Jubilee History of Victoria and Melbourne*, vol. 1 (Melbourne: Leavitt and Lilbum, 1888), n.p. Never refused: "Protectionist Meeting," *Riverine Herald*, 8 March 1877. Parnaby, "Economic and Political Development," 281.

64. McCulloch: "The Ministerial Elections," *Argus*, 4 November 1875. *Argus* correspondent: "Berry, Dow, Pearson, and Co," *Argus*, 29 December 1876. G. P. Smith, cited in Bartlett, "Political Organisation and Society," 113; "Mr. G. P. Smith at Hawthorn," *Argus*, 24 February 1877.

65. Stumping country: "Legislative Assembly," *Argus*, 18 November 1875; "Bendigo Summary for Europe," *Bendigo Advertiser*, 23 February 1876. Stump to stump: "Prunes and Prisms," *Bendigo Advertiser*, citing *Daily Telegraph*, 28 August 1877. Expedition: "Melbourne," *Kapunda Herald and Northern Intelligencer*, 13 March 1877. Done duty: "A Vagabond," "A Reform Tea-Fight," *Argus*, 24 October 1876. Chief stump orator etc.: "Mr. Francis on a Windbag," *Melbourne Punch*, 27 March 1879. *Punch* satire: "Cabinet Council," *Melbourne Punch*, 27 December 1877.

66. "Song of Graham Berry," *Freeman's Journal*, cited in "An Outside Opinion of a Demagogue," *Melbourne Punch*, 12 June 1879.

67. Tammany: "Vagabond," "Notes on Current Events," *Melbourne Punch*, 18 October 1877. Bug: "The Berrylalor Vastator; or, Mammoth Bug," *Melbourne Punch*, 3 January 1878. Traveling company: "A Yankee Notion," *Melbourne Punch*, 18 December 1879.

68. Results: Tregenza, *Professor of Democracy*, 115. Rout: "Our Melbourne Letter," *Queenslander*, 2 June 1877. Calamity: "Victoria," *Freeman's Journal*, 26 May 1877. People in power: "The Ministerial Policy: The Chief Secretary at Geelong," *Argus*, 31 May 1877.

69. Berry and mass party: see, e.g., P. Loveday and A. W. Martin, "Colonial Politics," in *The Emergence of the Australian Party System*, by P. Loveday, A. W. Martin, and R. S. Parker

(Sydney: Hale and Iremonger, 1977), 14. Admitted bungling: "The Results of the Various Elections," *Argus*, 12 May 1877. Conservative versions of stump tour: Bartlett, "Political Organisation and Society," 560.

70. Parkes in Cudal: "The Banquet," *Sydney Morning Herald*, 7 October 1880. Orange: "The Premier at Orange," *Evening News*, 30 October 1880. A manifesto: "Editorial," *Sydney Morning Herald*, 2 November 1880. Parkes like Berry: "Intercolonial News," *Queenslander*, 30 October 1880. Parkes as stumping: see, e.g., "Sir Henry Parkes," *Wagga Wagga Advertiser*, 2 November 1880. For a later speech-making visit, see "John Trying It Again," *Australian Town and Country Journal*, 9 December 1882. Stumping in other colonies (e.g., Ebenezer Ward in South Australia): see "Rural Notes and Comments," *Adelaide Observer*, 17 January 1880. Samuel Walker Griffith in Queensland: see "Messrs. Griffith and Dickson," *Queenslander*, 13 January 1883.

CHAPTER 5

1. H. C. G. Matthew, ed., *The Gladstone Diaries, with Cabinet Minutes and Prime-Ministerial Correspondence*, vol. 9, *January 1875–December 1880* (Oxford, UK: Clarendon Press, 1986), 466.

2. Like to write: W. E. Gladstone to Lord Rosebery, 10 April 1880, LRB. Stunned: Matthew, *The Gladstone Diaries*, 471. Will of God: W. E. Gladstone, cited in Richard Shannon, *Gladstone: Heroic Minister 1865–1898* (London: Allen Lane, 1999), 229.

3. Historic: "Mr. Gladstone and the Nation," *British Quarterly Review* 71 (January 1880): 171. Great event: "Mr. Gladstone's Visit to Mid-Lothian," *Scotsman*, 1 December 1879. Foremost: Edward A. Freeman, "The Election and the Eastern Question," *Contemporary Review* 37 (June 1880): 957. Extraordinary: "Mr. Gladstone's Pilgrimage," *Blackwood's Edinburgh Magazine* 127, no. 800 (1880): 124. Magnitude: "Conservative Demonstration in Leeds," *Scotsman*, 22 December 1879.

4. First major statesman: H. J. Hanham, *Elections and Party Management: Politics in The Time of Disraeli and Gladstone*, 2nd ed. (Sussex, UK: Harvester Books, 1978), 202. Initiator of new method: Maurice Bailey, "The Heyday of Elections and Electioneering," *Transactions of the Leicester Literary and Philosophical Society* 87 (1993): 3. Eastern shores: Eugenio F. Biagini, *Liberty, Retrenchment and Reform: Popular Liberalism in the Age of Gladstone 1860–1880* (Cambridge, UK: Cambridge University Press, 1992), 405. Unprecedented: John M. Morley, *The Life of William Ewart Gladstone*, vol. 2 (New York: Macmillan, 1903), 613. First modern: Humphrey Southall, "Agitate! Agitate! Organize! Political Travellers and the Construction of National Politics, 1839–1880," *Transactions of the Institute of British Geographers* 21, no. 1 (1996): 187; see also Douglas Hurd, "In the Battle Royal," *New Statesman*, 8 January 2007, 52. New age: Leo McKinstry, *Rosebery: Statesman in Turmoil* (London: John Murray, 2005), 87. New departure: Ronald Butt, *The Power of Parliament* (London: Constable, 1967), 90. New era: Niall Ferguson, "What America Needs Now Is a Mighty Blast of Fire and Gladstone," *Daily Telegraph*, 5 March 2006. *Oxford History*: R. C. K. Ensor, *England, 1870–1914*, cited in Newell D. Boyd, "Gladstone, Midlothian, and Stump Oratory," *Central States Speech Journal* 30, no. 2 (1979): 154. Matter of course: "Current Topics," *Ipswich Journal*, 17 October 1882.

5. Stump tour: "Though We Might Be Prematurely Congratulating Ourselves," *Edinburgh Courant*, 8 December 1879. Electioneering raid: "Is Mr Gladstone," *Edinburgh Courant*, 28 November 1879. Gladstone on stump: "Lord George Hamilton, M.P., in Edinburgh," *Scotsman*, 15 January 1880. Queen Victoria, cited in Newell D. Boyd, "Gladstone, Midlothian, and Stump Oratory," *Central States Speech Journal* 30, no. 2 (1979): 154. "Wan-

dering Willie," *Edinburgh Courant*, 21 November 1879. Roving statesman: "The Colossus of Words," *Punch*, 13 December 1879, 270.

6. "Election Squibs and Cartoons," *Pall Mall Gazette*, 22 October 1885. Reference to Byron Christy: Byron Christy, "Burlesque Political. Stump Speech; or, 'Any Other Man,'" in E. Byron Christy and William E. Christy, *Christy's New Songster and Black Joker* (New York: Dick and Fitzgerald Publishers, 1863), 9–11.

7. Joseph S. Meisel, *Public Speech and the Culture of Public Life in the Age of Gladstone* (New York: Columbia University Press, 2001), 248–249; Sydney C. Buxton, "Can the Cost of Elections Be Reduced?" *Fortnightly Review*, no. 158, new series, 1 February 1880, 261.

8. M. R. D. Foot, "Introduction," in W. E. Gladstone, *Midlothian Speeches 1879* (New York: Humanities Press, 1971), 15.

9. This was the case especially with regard to attempts by large landowners to manipulate their property holdings to allow tenants to qualify for the franchise. This practice was called the manufacture of "faggot" votes.

10. R. H. Hutton, "The Political Character of the Working Class," in *Essays on Reform* (London: Macmillan, 1867), 43.

11. Newspapers and interest in oratory: Meisel, *Public Speech and the Culture of Public Life*, 78. Provincial press: H. C. G. Matthew, "Rhetoric and Politics in Britain, 1860–1950," in *Politics and Social Change in Modern Britain: Essays Presented to A. F. Thompson*, ed. P. J. Waller (Sussex UK: Harvester Press, 1987), 46–47; J. R. Vincent, *The Formation of the British Liberal Party 1857–1868*, 2nd ed. (Sussex, UK: Harvester Press, 1976), 64. Central news agencies: Matthew, "Rhetoric and Politics in Britain," 43–44. Telegraph: Meisel, *Public Speech and the Culture of Public Life*, 277–278. For thoughtful commentary on the connections between changes in the franchise and an expanding press, see Andrew W. Robertson, *The Language of Democracy: Political Rhetoric in the United States and Britain, 1790–1900* (Ithaca, NY: Cornell University Press, 1995), 129–131.

12. Pullman carriage: Ian Bradley, "How Gladstone's 'Whistle-Stop' Campaign Rocked the Tories," *Times*, 24 November 1979. "Electioneering á la Mode," *Punch*, 27 March 1880, 133. Whistle stop: Christopher Harvie, "Gladstonianism, the Provinces, and Popular Political Culture, 1860–1906," in *Victorian Liberalism: Nineteenth-Century Political Thought and Practice*, ed. Richard Bellamy (London: Routledge, 1990), 160.

13. Manhattan Club: A. R. C. Grant, ed., *Lord Rosebery's North American Journal—1873* (Hamden, CT: Archon Books, 1967), 86–87. Convention: Lord Rosebery, cited in McKinstry, *Rosebery*, 82.

14. Convince Gladstone: W. P. Adam to J. J. Reid, 28 May 1878, JJR. Organize banquet: Lord Rosebery to J. J. Reid, 27 December 1878, JJR. Regular contact: Lord Rosebery to J. J. Reid, 5 September 1879, JJR. Six engagements: W. E. Gladstone to Lord Rosebery, 4 November 1879, LRB. Funding: J. J. Reid to Lord Rosebery, 18 April 1880, LRB. Great care: W. E. Gladstone to Lord Rosebery, 30 October 1879, LRB. Midlothian meetings description partly drawn from E. F. Biagini, *Gladstone* (Basingstoke, UK: Macmillan, 1999), 70.

15. W. E. Gladstone to Lord Rosebery, 10 April 1880, LRB.

16. Duffy on commentary: Sir Charles Gavan Duffy, *My Life in Two Hemispheres*, vol. 2 (Shannon: Irish University Press, 1969), 333. Berry's victory: see, e.g., *Pall Mal Gazette*, cited in "The Prospect in Victory," *Sydney Morning Herald*, 22 September 1877.

17. "News by the Mail: The Victorian Embassy," *South Australian Register*, 13 June 1879.

18. C. H. Pearson, "On the Working of Australian Institutions," in *Essays on Reform*, 191–216. Charles H. Pearson, "The Functions of Modern Parliaments," *Fortnightly Review*, new series, no. 151, 1 July 1879, 70, 71, 79, 81.

19. John Tregenza, *Professor of Democracy: The Life of Charles Henry Pearson* (Carlton: Melbourne University Press, 1968), 148.

20. Ibid., 149.

21. Politics subordinate: Morley, *The Life of William Ewart Gladstone*, 2:200. Sermons and training: ibid., 2:100. Impressed with Americans: Meisel, *Public Speech and the Culture of Public Life*, 160. Historians on influence: Harvie, "Gladstonianism, the Provinces, and Popular Political Culture," 158; H. C. G. Matthew, *Gladstone: 1875–1898* (Oxford, UK: Clarendon Press, 1995), 58.

22. Duty: W. E. Gladstone, "Address to Electors of Midlothian," 11 March 1880, in Gladstone, *Midlothian Speeches 1879*, 258. Inner call: Matthew, *Gladstone*, 33. Moral demonstration: W. E. Gladstone, "Perth," in Gladstone, *Midlothian Speeches 1879*, 168. "Pilgrimage" (this was in planning the tour): W. E. Gladstone to W. Adams, 11 January 1879, GP, Add. 56444, 128–129ff. Inner conscience: W. E. Gladstone, "First Midlothian Speech," 25 November 1879, in Gladstone, *Midlothian Speeches 1879*, 57. Conscience of community: W. E. Gladstone, "St. Andrew's Hall, Glasgow," 5 December 1879, in ibid., 210. Duty: W. E. Gladstone, "Taymouth Speech," 2 December 1879, in ibid., 182. Shame: W. E. Gladstone, "Perth," in ibid., 174. Honor: W. E. Gladstone, "St. Andrew's Hall, Glasgow," 5 December 1879, in ibid., 209. See also Gladstone's written reply to the invitation to stand as a candidate: W. E. Gladstone to John Cowan Esq., 30 January 1879, GP, Add. 56444, 130–131ff. Revivalist preachers: Biagini, *Liberty, Retrenchment and Reform*, 391. Old Testament prophet: Ruth Clayton Windscheffel, *Reading Gladstone* (Houndmills, UK: Palgrave Macmillan, 2008), 213.

23. Hustings speeches: Jon Lawrence, *Electing Our Masters: The Hustings in British Politics from Hogarth to Blair* (Oxford, UK: Oxford University Press, 2009); Meisel, *Public Speech and the Culture of Public Life*, 226–227; Ellen Reid Gold, "Gladstone's Role in the Development of Stump Oratory," *Central States Speech Journal* 33, no. 2 (1982): 382. Banquets: Marc Baer, "Political Dinners in Whig, Radical and Tory Westminster, 1780–1880," *Parliamentary History* 24 (2005): 186. Radical mass platform: John Belchem, *Popular Radicalism in Nineteenth-Century Britain* (Houndmills, UK: Palgrave Macmillan, 1996), 38. On Hunt and O'Connor as exemplars of this platform, see Meisel, *Public Speech and the Culture of Public Life*, 235–236. See, more generally, John Belchem, *"Orator" Hunt: Henry Hunt and English Working-Class Radicalism* (Oxford, UK: Oxford University Press, 1985); James Epstein, *The Lion of Freedom: Feargus O'Connor and the Chartist Movement, 1832–1842* (London: Croom Helm, 1982).

24. John Bright: Meisel, *Public Speech and the Culture of Public Life*, 237–238. Biagini, *Liberty, Retrenchment and Reform*, 259. On the broader Anti-Corn Law campaign: Paul A. Pickering and Alex Tyrell, *The People's Bread: A History of the Anti-Corn Law League* (London: Leicester University Press, 2000). Radical oratory's impact: Meisel, *Public Speech and the Culture of Public Life*, 8. Radicals and precedents: Gold, "Gladstone's Role in the Development of Stump Oratory," 382.

25. Tamworth Manifesto: Robert Peel, cited in David Thomson, "The United Kingdom and Its World-Wide Interests," 333–356, in *The New Cambridge Modern History*, ed. J. P. T. Bury, vol. 10, *The Zenith of European Power, 1830–1870* (Cambridge, UK: Cambridge University Press, 1960), 339. Mansion house: Gold, "Gladstone's Role in the Development of Stump Oratory," 385. Later addresses: Meisel, *Public Speech and the Culture of Public Life*, 231. On the broader import of Tamworth, see Robertson, *Language of Democracy*, 98–99. Russell: Meisel, *Public Speech and the Culture of Public Life*, 232–233. Palmerston: Matthew, "Rhetoric and Politics in Britain," 40–41.

26. Disraeli's speaking: Lionel A. Tollemache, *Gladstone's Boswell: Late Victorian Conversations* (Sussex, UK: Harvester Press, 1984), 62. Address at Free Trade Hall: Roy Jenkins,

Gladstone (London: Macmillan, 1995), 353. Lord Rosebery suggested a "Liberal banquet" for Gladstone, "on the model of that given to Ld Beaconsfield in 1868." See Lord Rosebery to J. J. Reid, 27 December 1878, GP, Add. 56444, 52–53ff. Gladstone on opponents: W. E. Gladstone, "Aberfeldy Speech," in Gladstone, *Midlothian Speeches 1879*, 178.

27. Change from 1860s: Matthew, "Rhetoric and Politics in Britain," 40–41, 45. Terms used: see, e.g., "The Usual Autumnal Session," *Morning Chronicle*, 22 August 1860; "Extra Parliamentary Utterances," *Glasgow Herald*, 9 December 1863 (reproducing a piece from the *Saturday Review*). Grouse: "Parliament in the Provinces," *Aberdeen Journal*, 13 January 1864. Deer: "The Season of Extra Parliamentary Utterances," *Huddersfield Chronicle*, 9 September 1871. Leaves: "Notes of the Week," *Essex Standard*, 17 October 1866.

28. Vent: "Extra Parliamentary Utterances," *Glasgow Herald*, 9 December 1863 (reproducing a piece from the *Saturday Review*). Rechauffe: "The 'Morning Post' on Extra Parliamentary Utterances," *Dundee Courier and Argus*, 24 August 1864. Identified as stump speeches: see, e.g., "Mr. Bright in His Element," *Cheshire Observer*, 15 January 1870; "Radical Members," *North Wales Chronicle*, 2 September 1871; "M," Letter to the Editor, "Poetical Politics," *Pall Mall Gazette*, 5 February 1873. Electioneering purpose: "Speeches out of Parliament," *Dundee Courier and Argus*, 11 December 1873. Extra-parliamentary utterances (e.g., including attribution to the *Times*): "News of the Day," *Birmingham Daily Post*, 3 December 1863; "Extra Parliamentary Utterances," *Glasgow Herald*, 9 December 1863 (reproducing piece from *Saturday Review*). Defense of speech: "Sir John Trelawny," *Bradford Observer*, 25 August 1864; "Newcastle," *Newcastle Courant*, 15 September 1865. The rule: "The Recess," *Western Mail* (Cardiff), 28 August 1871. No peace: "The Extra Parliamentary Campaign," *Huddersfield Chronicle*, 15 August 1874.

29. Great assemblage: Meisel, *Public Speech and the Culture of Public Life*, 223–224. Later addresses: Jenkins, *Gladstone*, 175. Early 1860s: ibid., 237–239. Diary, cited in Philip Magnus, *Gladstone: A Biography* (London: John Murray, 1954), 165.

30. Unmuzzled: Magnus, *Gladstone*, 172. 1868 and over-stumped: Meisel, *Public Speech and the Culture of Public Life*, 242.

31. R. T. Shannon, *Gladstone and the Bulgarian Agitation 1876*, 2nd ed. (Sussex, UK: Harvester Press, 1975).

32. W. E. Gladstone, "Introductory—Carlisle Speech," 24 November 1879, in Gladstone, *Midlothian Speeches 1879*, 18.

33. Shannon, *Gladstone*, 116–117n.

34. Morley, *The Life of William Ewart Gladstone*, 2:587.

35. Not written in advance: Matthew, *Gladstone*, 48–49. Main heads: D. W. Bebbington, *The Mind of Gladstone: Religion, Homer, and Politics* (Oxford, UK: Oxford University Press, 2004), 258. Studies as resource: Windscheffel, *Reading Gladstone*, 147. Watch audience: Morley, *The Life of William Ewart Gladstone*, 2:192. Spontaneity: George Jacob Holyoake, *Public Speaking and Debate: A Manual for Advocates and Agitators* (London: T. Fisher Unwin, n.d.), 251. Gladstone, cited in Magnus, *Gladstone*, 165–166.

36. R. H. Hutton, cited in D. A. Hamer, "Gladstone: The Making of a Political Myth," *Victorian Studies* 22, no. 1 (1978): 45.

37. Body and tree felling: W. T. Stead, *1809–1898. Gladstone. A Character Sketch* (1898; repr., London: Review of Reviews Office, n.d.), 10, 13. Gestures: Morley, *The Life of William Ewart Gladstone*, 2:191–192; Sir Henry Lucy, *Sixty Years in the Wilderness: More Passages by the Way* (London: Smith, Elder, 1912), 42; Earl Curzon of Kedleston (Chancellor of the University of Oxford), *Modern Parliamentary Eloquence: The Rede Lecture, Delivered before the University of Cambridge November 6, 1913* (London: Macmillan, 1913), 27. Fingers: Matthew, *Gladstone*, 2–3.

38. Voice: Matthew, *Gladstone*, 2–3. Northern burr: a thinly veiled version of Gladstone is described this way in H. D. Traill, *The New Lucian. Being a Series of Dialogues of the Dead*

(London: Chapman and Hall, 1884), 199. Clearness etc.: Holyoake, *Public Speaking and Debate*, 251. Silver: Lord Rosebery, cited in "Mr. Gladstone's Visit to Mid-Lothian," *Scotsman*, 1 December 1879. Bell-like: Boyd, "Gladstone, Midlothian, and Stump Oratory," 146. Emphasis: Stead, *1809–1898. Gladstone*, 14. Pausing: Boyd, "Gladstone, Midlothian, and Stump Oratory," 146. Rolling: Curzon, *Modern Parliamentary Eloquence*, 24.

39. Perpetual motion: Stead, *1809–1898. Gladstone*, 13. Forehead and eyebrows: Morley, *The Life of William Ewart Gladstone*, 2:194. Hair: Matthew, *Gladstone*, 2–3. Bright eyes: Goldwin Smith, *My Memory of Gladstone* (London: T. Fisher Unwin, 1904), 2. Imperious flash: Morley, *The Life of William Ewart Gladstone*, 2:191–192. Magnetic quality and gaze: Jenkins, *Gladstone*, 13. W. E. H. Lecky, cited in Hamer, "Gladstone," 35–36.

40. Earnestness: "Mr. Gladstone's Visit to Mid-Lothian," *Scotsman*, 27 November 1879. Belief and impress upon: Morley, *The Life of William Ewart Gladstone*, 2:193. Soul: Stead, *1809–1898. Gladstone*, 14. Exaltation: Tollemache, *Gladstone's Boswell*, 187. T. P. O'Connor, "The Candour of Mr. Gladstone," *Contemporary Review* 56 (September 1889): 362. Transmuted: Patrick Joyce, *Visions of the People: Industrial England and the Question of Class, 1848–1914* (Cambridge, UK: Cambridge University Press, 1991), 43. Moral force: Curzon, *Modern Parliamentary Eloquence*, 206.

41. Cult: Joyce, *Visions of the People*, 49–50. Name reconfigured: Biagini, *Liberty, Retrenchment and Reform*, 396; Letter: "Agricola," "The Gladstone Bonfires," *Edinburgh Courant*, 27 November 1879. Champion of finance: "Mr. Gladstone at West Calder," *Edinburgh Courant*, 28 November 1879. Honest man: "Mr. Gladstone in Edinburgh," *Edinburgh Courant*, 1 December 1879. Portraits etc.: Michael Winstanley, *Gladstone and the Liberal Party* (Florence, KY: Routledge, 1990), 65. Hawarden and woodchips: Hamer, "Gladstone," 37. Biographies appear annually: ibid., 31. Pamphlet: Ralph Richardson to Lord Rosebery, LRBB, 24 December 1878.

42. Grace and queen: David Brooks, "Gladstone and Midlothian: The Background to the First Campaign," *Scottish Historical Review* 64, no. 177 (1985): 57. Never national cult: Harvie, "Gladstonianism, the Provinces, and Popular Political Culture," 153. Based on misunderstanding: Vincent, *The Formation of the British Liberal Party*, 224. Galahad etc.: as noted in "Mr. Gladstone's Indictment of the Ministry," *Edinburgh Courant*, 3 December 1879.

43. Robert Kelley, "Midlothian: A Study in Politics and Ideas," *Victorian Studies* 4, no. 2 (1960): 122.

44. Operation as a whole: W. E. Gladstone to Lord Rosebery, 4 November 1879, LRB. Anvil hot: W. E. Gladstone to Lord Rosebery, 21 August 1879, LRB. More telling plan: W. E. Gladstone to Lord Rosebery, 30 October 1879, LRB. On arrangement of tour, compare Hanham, *Elections and Party Management*, 205. Wonderful: Stead, *1809–1898. Gladstone*, 16. Astounding: Henry, "Mr. Gladstone," *Fortnightly Review*, no. 157, new series, 1 January 1880: 51. Toil: O'Connor, "The Candour of Mr. Gladstone," 369. "The Colossus of Words," *Punch*, 13 December 1879, 270.

45. Rail route: J. J. Reid to Lord Rosebery, 5 October 1879, LRBC. Matching speeches and venues: Lord Rosebery to W. E. Gladstone, 17 November 1879, GP, Add. 56444, 194ff. Addressing multitude: Lord Rosebery to W. E. Gladstone, 29 October 1879, GP, Add. 56444, 181–184ff. Enable crowds: Lord Rosebery to W. E. Gladstone, 29 October 1879, GP, Add. 56444, 181–184.

46. For examples, see "Mr. Gladstone at West Calder," *Edinburgh Courant*, 28 November 1879; "Mr. Gladstone in Edinburgh," *Edinburgh Courant*, 1 December 1879; and "Mr. Gladstone in the North," *Scotsman*, 2 December 1879.

47. Gladstone mania: see Letter, "A Trades' Union Official," "The Trades' Council and the Gladstone Mania," *Edinburgh Courant*, 3 November 1879. Platform: Lucy, *Sixty Years in the Wilderness*, 191–192. Bonfires: see Letter, "Agricola," "The Gladstone Bonfires," *Edinburgh*

Courant, 27 November 1879. Candles: Lord Rosebery, cited in "Mr. Gladstone's Visit to Mid-Lothian," *Scotsman,* 1 December 1879. One-tenth of applicants: "Mr. Gladstone's Visit to Mid-Lothian: Departure from Hawarden," *Scotsman,* 24 November 1879. Crowds: "Mr. Gladstone in Edinburgh," *Edinburgh Courant,* 1 December 1879. Coachmen trampled: "Mr. Gladstone at West Calder," *Edinburgh Courant,* 28 November 1879. Hats and handkerchiefs: "Mr. Gladstone's Visit to Mid-Lothian," *Scotsman,* 27 November 1879. Mary Gladstone, cited in Shannon, *Gladstone,* 236–237. Gifts: "Over the Border," *Punch,* 6 December 1879, 263.

48. Grave errand: W. E. Gladstone, "Perth," in Gladstone, *Midlothian Speeches 1879,* 167. Far from ordinary: W. E. Gladstone to John Cowan, 30 January 1879, GP, Add. 56444, 130–131ff. Note that this letter was a reply to the invitation to stand for Midlothian, and it was widely circulated. System of government: W. E. Gladstone, "First Midlothian Speech," 25 November 1879, in Gladstone, *Midlothian Speeches 1879,* 50. Most important crisis: W. E. Gladstone, "Introductory—Carlisle Speech," 24 November 1879, in ibid., 18–19. Detailed exposition: W. E. Gladstone, "Motherwell Station," 6 December 1879, in ibid., 211. Grounds of principle: W. E. Gladstone, "First Midlothian Speech," 25 November 1879, in ibid., 48. Foreign policy: W. E. Gladstone, "Third Midlothian Speech," 27 November 1879, in ibid., 115–117. Look to proofs: W. E. Gladstone, "Second Midlothian Speech," 26 November 1879, in ibid., 61. Endeavor to be intelligible: W. E. Gladstone, "Speeches in the Corn Exchange and Waverley Market, Edinburgh," 29 November 1879, in ibid., 145.

49. High seriousness: Foot, "Introduction," 13. Never playing down: G. T. Garratt, *The Two Mr. Gladstones* (London: Macmillan, 1936), 162. Stillness and interest: W. E. Gladstone, "Introductory—Carlisle Speech," 24 November 1879, in Gladstone, *Midlothian Speeches 1879,* 21. Uninformed cheers: W. E. Gladstone, "First Midlothian Speech," 25 November 1879, in ibid., 39. Rational freedom: W. E. Gladstone, "Speeches in the Corn Exchange and Waverley Market, Edinburgh," 29 November 1879, in ibid., 133.

50. Failed in steam: "Our London Letter," *Edinburgh Courant,* 2 December 1879. London journals skeptical: As noted in "Though We Might Be Prematurely Congratulating Ourselves," *Edinburgh Courant,* 8 December 1879. Discharge of musketry: "Conservative Demonstration in Leeds," *Scotsman,* 22 December 1879. Lord Dalkeith: "Editorial," *Scotsman,* 5 December 1879. Harangues: Boyd, "Gladstone, Midlothian, and Stump Oratory," 153. Wildness etc.: "Editorial," *Scotsman,* 1 December 1879, citing other (unnamed) outlets. *Times,* cited in Kelley, "Midlothian," 126.

51. Newspaper coverage: Biagini, *Liberty, Retrenchment and Reform,* 411. *Times* reportage: Bradley, "How Gladstone's 'Whistle-Stop' Campaign Rocked the Tories." Pictorials: Boyd, "Gladstone, Midlothian, and Stump Oratory," 151. Speeches: "Mr. Gladstone's Speeches," *Scotsman,* 17 December 1879.

52. Astounding: Henry Dunckley, "Mr. Gladstone," *Fortnightly Review* 157 (1880): 51. Extraordinary: "The Recess," *Blackwood's Edinburgh Magazine* 126 (1879): 629. Most wonderful: "Mr. Gladstone and the Nation," *British Quarterly Review* 71 (January 1880): 173. "The Recess," 629. Surpassed hopes: W. E. Gladstone to Lord Rosebery, 10 April 1880, LRB. Admirably effective: Ralph Richardson to W. E. Gladstone, 14 February 1880, GP, Add. 44462, 89–90. Conquest: Bright, cited in Morley, *The Life of William Ewart Gladstone,* 2:601. Triumphs: Lord Rosebery in "Mr. Gladstone's Visit to Mid-Lothian," *Scotsman,* 1 December 1879.

53. Lord Salisbury to Arthur Balfour, 10 April 1880, in Robert Rhodes James, *Lord Randolph Churchill* (London: Phoenix, 1994), 71–72.

54. James R. Thursfield, "The Liberal Majority," *Macmillan's Magazine,* May 1880, 77. *Manchester Guardian,* cited in "The Press on the Mid-Lothian Election," *Scotsman,* 7 April 1880. *Daily News,* cited in "The Press on the Mid-Lothian Election."

55. Personal majority admitted: Morley, *The Life of William Ewart Gladstone*, 2:618. *Times*, cited in Robertson, *Language of Democracy*, 144, and embedded in his careful analysis of the campaign. "The Bagpiper of Midlothian," *Punch*, 1 May 1880, 204.

56. Economic downturn: Ralph Richardson to Lord Rosebery, 24 December 1878, LRBB. National Liberal Federation: Hanham, *Elections and Party Management*, 133; Jenkins, *Gladstone*, 441. Election costs: Ralph Richardson to Lord Rosebery, 7 May 1880, LRBD. Electioneering agents: John J. Reid to Lord Rosebery, 26 February 1880, LRBC. Handbills: John J. Reid to Lord Rosebery, 13 March 1880, LRBC. Pamphlets etc.: "Mr. Gladstone," *Edinburgh Courant*, 3 November 1879. Rosebery's power as landowner: Foot, "Introduction," 15; Ralph Richardson to Lord Rosebery, 10 December 1879, LRBC. Commentary on narrowness: *Standard*, cited in "The Press on the Mid-Lothian Election," *Scotsman*, 7 April 1880. Estimates and poll: Ralph Richardson to Lord Rosebery, 6 April 1880, LRBC.

57. Model: Meisel, *Public Speech and the Culture of Public Life*, 245.

58. Ibid., 250.

59. Lord Salisbury, cited in Bailey, "The Heyday of Elections and Electioneering," 3. Gladstone's secretary: Dudley W. R. Bahlman, ed., *The Diary of Sir Edward Walter Hamilton 1880–1885*, vol. 2 (Oxford, UK: Clarendon Press, 1972), 697. "'Staffy' on the Stump!" *Fun* (London), 17 October 1883.

60. "The Man about Town," *County Gentleman*, 26 January 1895. Voice: Curzon, *Modern Parliamentary Eloquence*, 37–38. Gestures: T. H. Escott, *Randolph Spencer-Churchill, as a Product of His Age. Being a Personal and Political Monograph* (London: Hutchinson, 1895), 302; "The Man about Town," *County Gentleman*, 26 January 1895. Churchill cited: James, *Lord Randolph Churchill*, 115. Criticisms: Curzon, *Modern Parliamentary Eloquence*, 37–38. Pluck: "The Game of Toryism," *Reynold's Newspaper*, 20 April 1884.

61. Continuous attack: Escott, *Randolph Spencer-Churchill*, 301. *The Wondrous Adventures of St. William the Woodcutter. The Genuine Grand Old Man* (London: John Heywood, 1884), 7. Match for Gladstone: Escott, *Randolph Spencer-Churchill*, 195–196. Publication of speeches: "Plain Politics for the Working Classes," *Morning Post*, 6 November 1885.

62. First conservative hustings orator: Hanham, *Elections and Party Management*, 206. An end to false modesty: Robert Blake, *Disraeli* (London: Eyre and Spottiswoode, 1966), 701.

63. "The Monster Meeting," *Morning Post*, 2 October 1883; "Perhaps One of the Most Marked of the Many Changes," *Morning Post*, 8 October 1887. "Topics of the Week," *Graphic* (London), 27 April 1889. "Occasional Notes," *Pall Mall Gazette*, 27 August 1883. Order of day: "Extra Parliamentary Utterances," *Essex Standard*, 8 October 1881. Less exception: "No More Interesting Unofficial Manifesto," *County Gentleman*, 29 November 1884. "Current Topics," *Ipswich Journal*, 17 October 1882.

64. Inciter of Irish disturbances: "The Political Status Quo," *Cambridge Independent Press*, 7 January 1882. Foreign wars: "Parliament out of Session," *Times*, 9 September 1882. Poisoner of German relations: "Lord G. Hamilton, M.P., at Kilburn," *Times*, 8 November 1883. Rabid orations: "Extra Parliamentary Utterances," *Essex Standard*, 8 October 1881. Floated into power: "Lord Cranbrook at Huddersfield," *Times*, 30 January 1884. Traill, *The New Lucian*, 188–189.

65. Gladstone as solely responsible as party myth: Ian St. John, *Gladstone and the Logic of Victorian Politics* (London: Anthem Press, 2010), 250; M. A. Fitzsimons, "Midlothian: The Triumph and Frustration of the British Liberal Party," *Review of Politics* 22, no. 2 (1960): 198. Table donated: "News in Brief," *Times*, 19 January 1952. Party publications: Duncan Brack, "Report: Speeches and Speech-makers," *Journal of Liberal Democrat History*, nos. 34/35 (Spring/Summer 2002): 35. Websites: see the website of the Liberal Democrat His-

tory Group at www.liberalhistory.org.uk/. Later Liberal leaders: "Ashdown Starts Whirlwind Tour," *Times*, 25 April 1997.

66. On Gladstone biographies, see Hamer, "Gladstone," 31–32. Response to Morley's publication: M. R. D. Foot, "A Revealing New Light on Gladstone," *Times*, 6 November 1970. Morley, *The Life of William Ewart Gladstone*, 2:594. Morley as classic account: Brooks, "Gladstone and Midlothian," 42.

67. On Jephson: Meisel, *Public Speech and the Culture of Public Life*, 224. Henry Jephson, *The Platform: Its Rise and Progress*, vol. 2 (London: Macmillan, 1892), 512–513.

68. Memoir echoes: see, e.g., Lucy, *Sixty Years in the Wilderness*, 191–192; Curzon, *Modern Parliamentary Eloquence*, 26. Plays: "Gladstone as the Author Intended," *Times*, 19 October 1960. Radio and TV: "Radio 1," *Times*, 4 April 1992; Andrew Billen, "TV and Radio," *Times*, 4 March 2009. Hardy perennial and textbooks specified: Simon Lemieux (Head of History, Portsmouth Grammar School), "Survival Skills: Gladstone and Disraeli," *History Review*, September 2001, 9. School curriculum: see, e.g., Curriculum Document: "Focus: Britain 1865–1915, Unit 13. Title: Gladstone's Midlothian Campaign." Part of "Teacher Resource Bank/GCE History/A2 Scheme of Work HIS3G/Version 1.0."

69. Time of Midlothian etc.: see, e.g., Lord Chorley, "Sir John Hope Simpson," *Times*, 22 April 1961; David Wood, "MPs Tense on Eve of Final EEC Debates," *Times*, 7 June 1971. Invoking Midlothian (Michael Foot on a campaign to oust Thatcher): "Nationwide Campaign to Oust Government," *Times*, 30 October 1980. Michael Gove on education: Michael Gove, Speech to Cambridge University, 24 November 2011, available at https://www.gov .uk/government/speeches/michael-gove-to-cambridge-university. Political commentators: see, e.g., Ferguson, "What America Needs Now Is a Mighty Blast of Fire and Gladstone"; John Russell, "A Dream of Orators Past," *New York Times*, 22 August 1984; Jason Cowley: "Once We Had Gladstone and Disraeli. Now We Have Clegg and Cameron," *New Statesman*, 14 February 2011.

70. Campaign in American sense: "Midlothian Notes," *Boston Daily Advertiser*, 7 October 1884. Democratic triumph etc.: "Mr. Gladstone's Triumph," *New York Daily Tribune*, 7 April 1880. Long stride: "Editorial Suggestions," *Boston Daily Advertiser*, 30 May 1898. Comparison with American presidential candidates: see, e.g., "Current Political Notes," *Milwaukee Sentinel*, 9 October 1884.

71. "Few Developments Are More Striking," *Argus* (Melbourne), 29 March 1890.

72. "Going on the Stump," *Wanganui Herald*, 12 March 1883.

73. As noted in "Mr. Gladstone's Visit to Midlothian," *Scotsman*, 1 December 1879.

74. Max Weber, "Politics as a Vocation," in *From Max Weber: Essays in Sociology*, ed. H. H. Gerth and C. Wright Mills (London: Routledge and Kegan Paul, 1948), 106.

CONCLUSION

1. Oratory mattered: Conor Cruise O'Brien, "Putting New Bounce into Labour," *Times*, 10 June 1987. Speakers demand: "No Thanks," *Times*, 2 October 2008. Moral case possible: "The Art of Persuasion," *Times*, 7 March 2003. Alternative to soundbite: Alice Thomson, "Major Calls for End to Soundbite Politics," *Times*, 14 September 1996. Roy Jenkins, cited in Duncan Brack, "Report: Speeches and Speech-makers," *Journal of Liberal Democrat History*, nos. 34/35 (2002): 37.

2. Deterioration of stump speaking: "A Recent Article," *St. Louis Globe-Democrat*, 20 September 1885; "A Lost Art," *Atchison Daily Champion*, 22 November 1891. Pioneer condition: "The Revolution of Platform Oratory," *Daily Evening Bulletin* (San Francisco), 30 June 1888. Never to return: "Political Orators," *Los Angeles Times*, 11 October 1887.

3. Lincoln as youthful auditor: A. H. Chapman (written statement), 8 September 1865, in Douglas L. Wilson and Rodney O. Davis, ed., *Herndon's Informants: Letters, Interviews, and Statements about Abraham Lincoln* (Urbana: University of Illinois Press, 1998), 102. Quite good stump speeches: John Hanks to William H. Herndon, 13 June 1865, in ibid., 43. Against visiting electioneers: Lincoln biographers John G. Nicolay and John Hay reference two cases in Lincoln's boyhood, cited in Paul M. Angle, ed., *The Lincoln Reader* (New Brunswick: Rutgers University Press, 1947), 47.

4. Turned Whig: Dennis Hanks (William H. Herndon interview), 8 September 1865, in *Herndon's Informants*, 105. Enduring admiration for Clay: Usher F. Linder (part of statement for J. G. Holland), enclosed in letter, Josiah G. Holland to William H. Herndon, 19 August 1867, in ibid., 569; Abraham Lincoln, "Eulogy on Henry Clay Delivered in the State House at Springfield, Illinois," 6 July 1852, in Joseph R. Fornieri, ed., *The Language of Liberty: The Political Speeches and Writings of Abraham Lincoln* (Washington, DC: Regnery Publishing, 2003), 128–140.

5. Sophistry and vituperation: *Cincinnati Commercial*, cited in Saul Sigelschiffer, *The American Conscience: The Drama of the Lincoln-Douglas Debates* (New York: Horizon Press, 1973), 182. Protagonist interruptions etc.: events recorded in Roy Morris Jr., *The Long Pursuit: Abraham Lincoln's Thirty-Year Struggle with Stephen Douglas for the Heart and Soul of America* (New York: Harper Collins, 2008), 107–113. Deep and profound etc.: "A Lost Art," *Atchison Champion*, 22 November 1891. Glorious: "Some Noted Speeches," *Atchison Daily Globe*, 8 June 1892. Sacred events: "Lincoln and Douglas," *Milwaukee Sentinel*, 8 October 1899. Affirmed their greatness: "Lincoln-Douglas Memorial," *New York Times*, 22 March 1903. William McKinley, cited in *Milwaukee Sentinel*, 8 October 1899. Theodore Roosevelt, cited in "President's Tribute to Lincoln's Character," *New York Times*, 4 June 1903.

6. Bronze tablet: "In Abe Lincoln's Pulpit," *New York Times*, 8 October 1896. Boulders: "Odd Freeport Monument," *Washington Post*, 5 June 1903; "Where Lincoln Met Douglas," *New York Times*, 22 August 1908. Cottage: "Lincoln Shrine Arranged," *New York Times*, 29 July 1947. Pageants: "Lincoln-Douglas Pageant," *New York Times*, 27 August 1922; "Knox Again Hears Lincoln Debate," *New York Times*, 7 October 1928; Herbert Mitgang, "Again— Lincoln v. Douglas," *New York Times*, 19 October 1958. Plays: Arthur Gelb, "Rialto Gossip: Lincoln-Douglas Debates Being Adapted for Broadway and the Road," *New York Times*, 26 December 1954. Anniversary addresses: see, e.g., "Says Public Will Back Equal Rights," *Chicago Defender*, 18 October 1958. Television: John Carmody, "A 'Rivalry' with Flair," *Washington Post*, 12 December 1975. Most famous debates: Malvina Lindsay, "Hidden Persuader in 'Great Debates,'" *Washington Post*, 16 August 1958; "Anniversary and Analogy," *Washington Post*, 2 September 1858.

7. Herbert Mitgang, "Echoes of Mr. Lincoln and Mr. Douglas," *New York Times*, 9 February 1958.

8. Fixing on debates: "Thank You, Senator," *North American*, 8 September 1896; "Lincoln-Douglas Debates," *Morning Oregonian*, 4 October 1896; "With Respect to Various Office Seekers," *Milwaukee Sentinel*, 11 August 1899; Charles Willis Thompson, "Oratory Changes, but It Still Lives," *New York Times*, 23 August 1925. And coming of television: see, e.g., "Debating Tactics of Today Decried by Lewis Douglas," *Washington Post*, 19 May 1952; "For Old-Style Debate," *New York Times*, 29 August 1954; John Alsop, "Matter of Fact," *Washington Post*, 13 October 1958. Invoked in Kennedy/Nixon: see, e.g., "Topics," *New York Times*, 15 September 1960; "A Television Campaign," *Atlanta Daily World*, 2 September 1960. Moral seriousness: Marquis Childs, "The Viewers Gird for Great Debate," *Washington Post*, 28 August 1960. Philosophical depth: Arthur Miller, cited in W. J. Weatherby, "American Election on Television," *Guardian*, 15 October 1960. Rough directness: Arthur Crock,

"The Polite Debate," *New York Times*, 9 October 1960. Sufficient time: Emmet John Hughes, "52,000 TV Sets—How Many Votes?" *New York Times*, 25 September 1960. Genuine debate form: George E. Sokolsky, "These Days . . . Thought on Second Debate," *Washington Post*, 14 October 1960; *London Times*, cited in "Opinion of the Week: At Home and Abroad," *New York Times*, 2 October 1960.

9. Later politicians compare badly: see, e.g., "Debate Debased," *New York Times*, 7 March 1972. Cheap shots etc.: Herbert Mitgang, "The Air of Politics," *New York Times*, 7 September 1976. Fundamental disagreement: Arlen J. Large, "Lincoln-Douglas Debates: Deadly Television," *Wall Street Journal*, 10 September 1976. Unfettered: Haynes Johnson, "The 3 Candidates Should Set the Terms Themselves," *Washington Post*, 31 August 1980.

10. Politicians and alternative to contemporary electioneering, e.g., Bob Dole: "Dole Wants to Revive Lincoln-Douglas Style," *New York Times*, 2 December 1979; Mario Cuomo: "Cuomo Backs Idea of Campaign Debates," *New York Times*, 23 June 1984. Journalists: "Campaign Trail: ABC Wants Debate with a Difference," *New York Times*, 6 October 1988. Pundits: Howard Kurtz, "Campaign Debates: A Contest of Styles with Just a Few Defining Moments," *Washington Post*, 9 October 1992; John D. Tierney, "Back When Politicians Said What They Thought," *Wall Street Journal*, 4 March 1980. Political scientists: see, e.g., Lloyd Bitzer and Theodore Rueter, "The 1980 Debates," *New York Times*, 24 August 1980. Historians: Patrick Allitt, contribution to "The Presidential Debate of October 3, 2012, AHA Roundtable," available at www.historians.org/Perspectives/issues/2012/1210/2012-presidential-debate_patrick-allitt.cfm. Prestigious volumes on debates: see, e.g., Harry V. Jaffa, *Crisis of the House Divided: An Interpretation of the Issues in the Lincoln-Douglas Debates* (New York: Doubleday, 1959); Sigelschiffer, *The American Conscience*; Allen C. Guelzo, *Lincoln and Douglas: The Debates That Defined America* (New York: Simon and Schuster 2008). Mythic standard: "Campaign of Substance a Rarity Series: Campaign 92," *St. Petersburg Times*, 8 March 1992.

11. Mass franchise and changes speech: "Few Developments Are More Striking," *Argus*, 29 March 1890; Max Weber, *The Theory of Social and Economic Organization* (London: Oxford University Press, 1947), 386; Joseph S. Meisel, *Public Speech and the Culture of Public Life in the Age of Gladstone* (New York: Columbia University Press, 2001), 248–249. Midlothian voters: M. R. D. Foot, "Introduction," in W. E. Gladstone, *Midlothian Speeches* (New York: Humanities Press, 1971), 15.

12. Among the valuable works that have influenced my understanding of contemporary campaign speech and the electronic context are Kathleen Hall Jamieson, *Eloquence in an Electronic Age* (New York: Oxford University Press, 1988); Judith S. Trent, Robert V. Friedenberg, and Robert E. Denton Jr., *Political Campaign Communication: Principles and Practices* (Lanham, MD: Roman and Littlefield, 2016); Robert P. Hart, *Campaign Talk: Why Elections Are Good for Us* (Princeton, NJ: Princeton University Press, 2000); Joshua Meyrowitz, *No Sense of Place: The Impact of Electronic Media on Social Behavior* (New York: Oxford University Press, 1985); Paddy Scannell, *Radio, Television and Modern Life: A Phenomenological Approach* (Oxford, UK: Blackwell, 1996); Jon Lawrence, *Electing Our Masters: The Hustings in British Politics from Hogarth to Blair* (Oxford, UK: Oxford University Press, 2009).